RESEARCH HIGHLIGHTS IN SOCIAL WORK 33

Addictions and Problem Drug Use
Issues in Behaviour, Policy and Practice

Edited by Michael Bloor and Fiona Wood

Jessica Kingsley Publishers
London and Philadelphia

First published in the United Kingdom in 1998 by
Jessica Kingsley Publishers Ltd
116 Pentonville Road
London N1 9JB, England
and
325 Chestnut Street
Philaelphia PA 19106, USA

Copyright ©1998 Robert Gordon University, Research Highlights Advisory Group, School of Applied Social Studies
Second Impression 2002

Library of Congress Cataloging in Publication Data
A CIP catalogue record for this book is available from the Library of Congress

British Library Cataloguing in Publication Data
A CIP catalogue record for this book is available from the British Library

ISBN 1 85302 438 4

Printed and Bound in Great Britain by
Athenaeum Press, Gateshead, Tyne and Wear

DATE DUE FOR RETURN

RESEARCH HIGHLIGHTS IN SOCIAL WORK 33

Addictions and Problem Drug Use

This book may be recalled before the above date.

Research Highlights in Social Work series
This topical series examines areas of particular interest to those in social and community work and related fields. Each book draws together different aspects of the subject, highlighting relevant research and drawing out implications for policy and practice. The project is under the editorial direction of Professor Joyce Lishman, Head of the School of Applied Social Studies at the Robert Gordon University.

Reparation and Victim-focused Social Work

Edited by Brian Williams
ISBN 1 84310 023 1
Research Highlights in Social Work 42

Adult Day Services and Social Inclusion

Better Days
Edited by Chris Clark
ISBN 1 85302 887 8
Research Highlights in Social Work 39

The Changing Role of Social Care

Edited by Bob Hudson
ISBN 1 85302 752 9
Research Highlights in Social Work 37

Effective Ways of Working with Children and their Families

Edited by Malcolm Hill
ISBN 1 85302 619 0
Research Highlights in Social Work 35

Children and Young People in Conflict with the Law

Edited by Stewart Asquith
ISBN 1 85302 291 8
Research Highlights in Social Work 30

Working with Offenders

Edited by Gill McIvor
ISBN 1 85302 249 7
Research Highlights in Social Work 26

Contents

Part IV: The Impact of HIV

Part V: Providing and Assessing Services

List of tables

Introduction

Fiona Wood and Michael Bloor

Addictive behaviour is important to both social work practice and policy; it is inescapably part of the social context within which we live. Addictive behaviour is shaped by influences beyond the individual with the problem and most social workers will encounter substance misuse within the context of some other acute social problem such as financial crisis or homelessness.

Towards the close of the twentieth century substance misuse has taken on a new importance. This is seen most obviously in the concern surrounding drug use and HIV and hepatitis. Furthermore, with increasing emphasis on effective interventions and resource effectiveness within the public sector, policy makers are forced to consider the financial costs of addiction, prevention and treatment.

There are a number of varying definitions surrounding addictions and problem drug use. Many of these terms such as 'misuse' and 'abuse' have ideological overtones. Identifying use as a 'problem' is itself problematic: drug use is not always, even often, a problem. Defining drug use as a problem demands attention to the sociological question: a problem to or for whom? The term addiction relates to dependency and therefore implies compulsive use, impaired control over using the substance and a preoccupation with obtaining and using the drug. Problem drug use has enjoyed popularity as a descriptive label and implies recognition of the social consequences of addiction.

The intention of this book is to provide readers with an increased understanding of addiction and problem drug use. While social workers and students of social work constitute one important audience for this work, we hope that we have successfully attracted contributions which will be of interest to audiences - professional and lay - beyond the world of social work practice. We aim to cover addictions in a broad sense and include a number of different types of addiction from legal drugs such as tobacco, alcohol and prescribed drugs, to steroids and illicit drugs, to gambling. We have also covered a number of issues relating to drug use such as the historical dimension, effective interventions, epidemiological patterns and prevalence, users perspectives, risk behaviours and comparative drug policy. The contributions to this book therefore embrace both policy and practice issues and intend to provide the reader with a review of recent research and debate in the field. The chapters are arranged in five sections relating to prevalence, legal addictions, drug and alcohol policy, the impact of HIV and providing and assessing services for problem users.

Prevalence

In the first section, Gordon Hay's contribution summarises the available statistical information on the prevalence of substance misuse in the United Kingdom. He reviews a number of methods of estimating prevalence, both direct and indirect, and discusses recent research in this field.

Legal drugs

In her chapter on adolescent smoking Jane Frankland outlines the prevalence of smoking among young people within the UK and reviews research which has examined the reasons why adolescents start smoking. The chapter provides a review of previous smoking prevention initiatives and reviews best practice on smoking cessation methods. Mark Griffiths argues that gambling is an addictive behaviour. He reviews the literature on pathological gambling, concentrating on adolescent fruit machine gambling, an aspect which social workers are likely to encounter frequently in their work. Some forms of prescribed drugs have also been shown to cause addiction. In the last chapter of this section, a former benzodiazepine user carefully describes her experiences of the drug and of the responses of health care professionals to her addiction.

Drug and alcohol policy

Virginia Berridge's chapter (an update of her previous work published in V. Berridge and P. Strong (1993) *AIDS and Contemporary History*, Cambridge University

Press) provides an historical perspective on contemporary British drugs policy. She draws on the analogy of the impact of war on social policy to discuss the extent to which AIDS has been a catalyst for change through evoking a period of political emergency reaction. Dutch drug and alcohol policy has met with much international interest and Inge Spruit reviews major policy principles in The Netherlands. The main principles of Dutch drug and alcohol policy are focused first on a well organised network of prevention and care; and second, on the minimisation of risks to individual drug and alcohol users and to the rest of Dutch society.

The impact of HIV

Fiona Wood reviews recent research on the transmission of HIV and risk behaviour amongst injecting drug users. The chapter provides information on the size and nature of the HIV epidemic and likely future trends. Specific responses to the HIV epidemic in relating to injecting drug users are then discussed in more detail in following chapters. Lawrie Elliott examines the history and effectiveness of needle exchange provision in a thorough review of the literature. Tim Rhodes and Gerry Stimson outline the development of community HIV prevention responses among injecting drug users. They describe the role of outreach services in the context of the policy shift to an emphasis on harm reduction and identify principles that are relevant to community interventions.

Providing and assessing services

Andrew McBride and colleagues highlight the extent of androgenic anabolic steroid use, why and how these steroids are used and problems associated with their use. The authors go on to discuss what services are available for users of these drugs and how such services should be configured. Jan Keene's chapter on effective interventions for problem drinkers reviews the research evidence for matching clients to treatment interventions. She discusses why theoretical perspectives on intervention actually has little influence on practice and suggests that in practice method of intervention is more likely to be based on practical utility of particular methods with individual clients.

Our topic area is a large one and we have not been able to find room for coverage of all its aspects. But the topic area is also one that is rapidly changing and we are confident that the contents of this book will be judged to be of clear contemporary relevance.

PART I
The Size of the Problem

CHAPTER 1

Estimating the Prevalence of Substance Misuse[1]

Gordon Hay

Introduction

In this chapter I aim to summarise the available statistical information on the prevalence of substance misuse in the United Kingdom. I examine official data sources on illicit substance use, and look at surveys, in particular general population surveys, in which information on alcohol consumption and smoking has been gathered. I also give a brief review of the methods used in estimating the prevalence of substance use and summarise some of the more relevant research into substance misuse prevalence estimation.

I begin this chapter by examining why people wish to estimate the prevalence of substance misuse. I define prevalence in the second section before giving a broad overview of the techniques that are available in the third section. In the fourth section I focus on survey methods which are particularly useful in examining alcohol consumption. I change the focus to drug misuse by examining enumeration in the fifth section, moving on to techniques which estimate the size of hidden populations such as mark-recapture methods. I conclude with a comparison between the

1   The Centre for Drug Misuse Research is funded by the Chief Scientist Office of the Scottish Office Department of Health. The opinions expressed in this paper are not necessarily those of the Scottish Office Department of Health.

The author is grateful for the assistance and encouragement of Fiona Wood, Elise Birks and Prof Neil McKeganey in the preparation of this chapter.

different methods, giving a synthesis from different research on how big the problem is.

Why estimate prevalence?

It is clearly important to have accurate information on the nature and extent of drug misuse within an area so that possibly limited resources can be directed in the most efficient way. Information is required at many levels, from national information on the prevalence of the use of drugs such as ecstasy in order to evaluate the relative success or failure of education strategies, to local service providers requiring information on problematic drug misuse in their area. Such information is useful not only as a separate entity, but also in relation to needs assessment and service audit. There is a triangular nature concerning information on the nature and extent of drug misuse in a particular area; information is needed to examine how well existing agencies are providing services for their clients and how the needs of the unknown number of drug users can be met. For example, a recent Scottish Office Drugs Task Force Report (Scottish Office 1994, p.37) states that 'future service development must be based on a systematic and comprehensive assessment of the nature, extent and distribution of need.'

Without knowing how many drug users there are in an area, the relative success or failure of different policies will be hard to evaluate. The effectiveness of drug policies has been questioned by Sutton and Maynard (1993, p.455) who pose the question 'Are drug policies based on fake statistics?'. They note that the government spends millions on a problem that they cannot quantify with any certainty. While there is a general feeling that the use of drugs is becoming more common, without accurate figures describing the number of people using drugs over time, this will only be speculation.

What is prevalence?

Before going on to describe the different methods of obtaining information on the prevalence of substance misuse, it is worthwhile to discuss the various terminology and definitions.

The prevalence of a certain social attribute is defined as the proportion of people possessing that attribute. It is often expressed as a percentage, or sometimes as 'per thousand' or even 'per million' of the total population. The actual number of individuals is sometimes used instead of the prevalence, however without information on the baseline population, this number may be meaningless. If there are an estimated 1000 drug users in one city and 2000 in another city, without knowledge of the relative sizes of these two cities, the two figures cannot be directly compared.

When discussing percentages care must also be taken in the different interpretation of the baseline population. Drugs or alcohol are more commonly used by people in the 15 to 34 age group. That is not to say that children under 15 do not drink, or people aged 35 or over do not use drugs, but when calculating a percentage, the age range of the baseline population is often one which includes those that are more likely to use substances; using the total population as a baseline would therefore result in a lower prevalence value. This is often the case when a sample of people are asked about their substance use. If the sample are predominantly in the 15 to 34 age group, then the proportion currently using drugs would probably be greater than that in the 15 to 54 age group.

The concept of prevalence also requires some indication of the time period that is being examined. Alcohol use and especially drug misuse can be transient activities so that someone using drugs one month may not be using them the next; therefore the concept of current use may refer in different contexts to use within the past week, past month or past year. In addition, lifetime usage is often described, therefore care must be taken in comparing lifetime usage between different age groups, given that older people may have had a longer time to use drugs.

The incidence of a particular social attribute is defined as the proportion of people who have started to possess the particular attribute in a preceding time interval, that is, the number of new cases. This term is more commonly used when talking about diseases, however there is limited usage when examining substance misuse in schoolchildren where it is sometimes known as uptake. Care must also be taken in comparing various prevalence figures in relation to what this figure actually refers to. There is a defined difference between point prevalence which can be thought of as the number of people who are using substances at that particular time, and period prevalence, which may refer additionally to people who have used drugs within a longer time period, such as a month or a year. There may also be definitional problems relating to both drug use and alcohol use. Terms such as drug use, drug dependence, drug addiction may refer to different groups of people; similarly there may be difficulties in defining what a problem drinker actually is.

Techniques of estimating prevalence

There are various methods of estimating the prevalence of substance use, and there is usually no single method that can be thought of as the best. The prevalence of the use of licit drugs can be gathered from surveys, although it may be questionable how willing people are to admit excessive levels of consumption. Using surveys can be thought of as a direct method, however, as both alcohol and tobacco sales are subject to taxation, examining data from Customs and Excise can be used as an indirect method of obtaining estimates of the total population consumption (Brewers and Licensed Retailers Association 1995). In the case of alcohol consumption, estimates of total consumption gathered from surveys is usually less than that obtained from examining revenue from taxation (Goddard 1991). The prevalence of illicit drugs can also be gathered from surveys, but in the case of drugs such as heroin, alternative methods of estimation are required.

Enumeration is a direct method of estimating the prevalence of drug use, in which the number of known drug users is obtained by combining data from various sources and eliminating the double counting caused by overlaps between data sources. An indirect method known as mark-recapture can use this overlap data, along with the number of known drug users, to estimate the size of the unknown drug-using population. Other indirect methods which can be considered include network analysis techniques such as snowballing or multiplier techniques.

Surveys

Information on alcohol consumption can be gathered from the General Household Surveys undertaken by the Office of Population Censuses and Surveys (OPCS 1996a). Biennially since 1978, respondents have been asked questions about their alcohol intake. The responses are coded into alcohol consumption levels which make it possible to analyse the data with respect to the government's recommended sensible levels of alcohol consumption and levels which are considered dangerous as described in the Health of the Nation Report (Department of Health 1992). The format of the questions makes it improbable that the respondents' weekly alcohol intake is accurately recorded and there is an impression that the information obtained is an underestimate. This may, in part, be due to respondents' reluctance to report heavy drinking which may be seen as socially unacceptable but also because of the sampling strategy of the General Household Survey which omits people who may be more likely to drink excessively. This, however, is not seen to be too problematic as the results of the survey are used in comparison with previous years and to compare average alcohol consumption levels between different socioeconomic groupings of people. Other *ad hoc* surveys undertaken by the OPCS look further into drinking and in particular problem drinking, where the extra effort spent specifically on examining alcohol use permits more in-depth questioning and analysis, for example the surveys undertaken by Goddard (1986; 1991) to assess the impact of the changes in licensing laws.

In a similar fashion to the General Household Survey being used to set and monitor targets for alcohol and tobacco consumption, it has been suggested that the government's expenditure on drug misuse should warrant the funding of a similar survey which could 'simply and with moderate expenditure' measure the extent of drug misuse, (Maynard and Sutton 1993, p.456). Although there was a feasibility study undertaken by the Office of Population and Census Surveys by Goddard (1987), a specific national drug survey has not yet been undertaken. Questions concerning drug misuse have been included in both the 1993 Scottish Crime Survey (Hammersley and Anderson 1994) and the 1994 British Crime Survey (Ramsay and Percy 1996), but in a similar manner to the General Household Surveys which briefly explored alcohol and tobacco consumption, the format of the questions means that the results can only be taken as broad generalisations. Respondents were asked if they have ever taken certain drugs, including cannabis, amphetamine, LSD, ecstasy and heroin. Again in a similar fashion to the General Household Survey, just as the information gathered on what may be deemed as 'sensible' drinking can be thought more accurate than the information concerning heavy or problematic drinking, the British Crime Survey can be thought to be more accurate in reporting the levels of cannabis use than the levels of heroin or other opiate use due to the social acceptability of the former drug. There does remain the methodological problem that both the General Household Survey and the British Crime Survey are less likely to include harder-to-contact people who may be more likely to be heavy drinkers or problematic drug users, in particular sub-populations such as the homeless or those living in institutions.

This problem is recognised in a series of reports, resulting from the 1993 OPCS Survey of Psychiatric Morbidity, which include information on alcohol and drug dependence. The first reported on the prevalence of psychiatric morbidity among adults living in private households (OPCS 1995) using a sample of 10,000 adults and a supplementary sample of 350 adults with psychosis. This was followed by two samples of over 1000 adults each which looked at adults living in institutions specifically catering for people with mental illness (OPCS 1996b) and then people living in hostels for the homeless and people living in similar institutions (OPCS 1996c). By using a screening instrument in which respondents were asked if scenarios such as 'I have woken up the next day not being able to remember some of the things I have done the night before' had happened to them in the last 12 months, the prevalence of alcohol or drug dependence was found. Again care must be taken in the interpretation of such figures, in particular when comparing drug dependence with drug use.

There are, however, some difficulties in using surveys to estimate the prevalence of substance misuse. As noted above, people may be reluctant to divulge information on matters which are deemed to be socially unacceptable. In addition very few people use drugs such as heroin, therefore detecting the use of such drugs within a general population survey is quite difficult. There are, in addition, the problems resulting from people filling in the questionnaire wrongly; one or two incorrectly completed questionnaires may, in small surveys, exaggerate the use of certain drugs and in some cases the sample sizes needed to obtain worthwhile results often make the costs of sampling prohibitive.

There can be benefits in using surveys. For example, information on substance use in children, including solvent use and smoking, can be gathered by surveys of schoolchildren, in particular the repeated studies by the Schools Health Education Unit (Balding 1995) which report the prevalence of smoking, drinking and drug use in children aged between 11 and 15. This prevalence information can be complemented by research such as Barnard, Forsyth and McKeganey (1996) which examined the psychosocial factors surrounding young people's substance use.

Enumeration

There are a range of data sources which can be thought of as indicating the number of substance users in a particular locality. This indicator idea found favour in the 1980s where Hartnoll *et al.* (1985), in the Drug Indicators Project, examined how the data from various sources can be pieced together, like a jigsaw, to give a fuller picture of the nature and extent of drug misuse in an area of North East London.

Many of the data sources described are available throughout the United Kingdom, indeed some of them are collated at a national level.

The most established data source on drug misuse is the Home Office Index of Addicts (Home Office Research and Statistics Department 1996a). Although medical practitioners are legally required to notify the Home Office about anyone whom they know or suspect to be addicted to cocaine or one of a range of opiods, such as heroin, there are limits to how useful this index is for estimating the prevalence of drug misuse. Not everyone who is addicted to drugs will come into contact with medical practitioners, and not all practitioners pass on the details of addicted patients to the Home Office. More recently, Regional Drug Misuse Databases have been established throughout the Regional Health Authorities in England, as well as databases which cover Scotland and Wales (Department of Health 1996). (There is not, as yet, a Regional Drug Misuse Database in Northern Ireland.) These databases record information on people who contact a range of services, including non-statutory specialist drug services, but the information collated in these databases cannot be used to give a true picture of the prevalence of drug misuse. Information is only gathered on new clients at agencies or those that have returned to the agency after a period of six months or more; therefore the data may perhaps only be considered as a measure of the incidence of drug misuse in an area. The databases are useful as an epidemiological tool, recording information concerning the use of all drugs, including cannabis and ecstasy, as well as other sociodemographic characteristics of the individual drug user.

There are other information sources which can also be used as indicators, such as the number of people citing drug injecting as a reason for an HIV test; the number of people recorded as coming into contact with social work departments due to problems related to drug or alcohol use; the number of people attending hospital for alcohol or drug related problems (Scottish Health Service 1996); the number of people failing breath tests (Home Office Research and Statistics Department 1996b); the number of seizures of controlled substances and the number of people convicted under the Misuse of Drugs Act (Home Office Research and Statistics Department 1996c); or the number of people dying from drug overdoses or diseases characteristic of problematic alcohol use such as liver cirrhosis (Frischer *et al.* 1993a; Anderson 1988).

On their own, each of the sources of data listed above can only give a partial insight into the prevalence of substance misuse. It cannot always be assumed that there is a direct link between an increase in the number of people recorded in a particular data source and the number of people using drugs or alcohol. For example, the data concerning those that are convicted for either drug offences or drink-driving depend on the operational policies of the police. An initial method of collating such data would be to perform a multi-source enumeration. This is similar to what the Regional Drug Misuse Databases do with data from different statutory and non-statutory agencies but this process is not restricted to the data sources which report to the regional databases; it can also include the police, needle exchanges or other agencies in which drug users can be found by using a screening instrument. Indeed the process of multi-source enumeration can often be an encouragement for agencies to collate their existing information in a more systematic form. To avoid double counting, it is necessary to obtain enough information from each data source to identify each individual drug user; however, this requirement has to be weighed against the confidentiality requirements of each source. Hence initials, sex and date of birth are often used to sift out multiple occurrences. It should be noted that information collated from data sources using this unnamed identifier information can be imprecise, especially as the accurate collection of names and dates of birth may not be the highest priority for some agencies working with drug users. However, this exercise can be useful in describing the known drug-using population.

Information on the nature and extent of the unknown population of drug users is also required to give the complete picture of drug use, and in particular the size of the unknown population of drug users is needed to obtain an estimate of the total number of drug users. There are several different ways of doing this, as described below.

Mark-recapture and multiplier techniques

A methodology, commonly referred to as mark-recapture or capture-recapture, has increasingly been used to estimate the prevalence of drug misuse. As the name suggests, this methodology was originally developed by ecologists who were interested in estimating the size of animal populations. Two analogous examples are presented here, one from ecology, and one from an early application of mark-recapture in estimating the prevalence of drug misuse. An ecologist wants to estimate the number of fish there are in a lake: therefore a sample of fish are caught, counted, marked in some way and then released. At a later date, the ecologist returns to catch another sample and, by checking for marks, the number of fish seen in both samples is known and the ratio of previously caught to previously uncaught fish in the second sample can be found. As it can perhaps be assumed that the ratio of caught to uncaught in the first sample is the same as the ratio of previously caught to previously uncaught in the second sample, the total population size can be estimated by multiplying the number seen in the first sample by the inverse of the ratio. An example concerning drug misuse may illustrate the method more clearly.

Hartnoll *et al.* (1985), as part of the Drug Indicators Project, applied capture-recapture methodology when estimating the prevalence of opiod use in the Inner London boroughs of Camden and Islington. They collected data concerning opiod users who had attended a drug clinic and those that had been admitted to a hospital for infectious diseases because of their drug use. By comparing these sources of data they found that 20 per cent, or a fifth, of the hospital sample had also attended the drug clinic. Thus the total number of opiod users could then be estimated to be five times the number who attended the drug clinic. Thus the size of the hidden population of drug users was estimated by merging two existing sources of data and examining the overlap between them.

These two simple examples mask some of the problems of the mark-recapture methodology. In Hartnoll's case, if those who are attending the clinic were more likely to have been admitted to the hospital then the resultant figure would be an underestimate. Thus, if there is some kind of relationship between data sources the estimate will be biased. Unfortunately it is often unclear if such relationships, or interactions, are present and therefore the validity of estimates obtained when examining two data sources are often questionable.

In a similar manner to the two sample mark-recapture methods, the prevalence of drug misuse can be estimated by applying a multiplication factor to other indicators, in particular data on drug-related deaths or the Home Office Index of Addicts. In-depth studies of drug use and mortality suggest that 1–2 per cent of drug injectors die per annum (Ghodse *et al.* 1985). Thus, taking the upper level, an estimate of the number of drug injectors can be found by multiplying the number of deaths in the injecting population by 50. Research has also shown that the Home Office Index of Addicts contains between 10 and 20 per cent of addicts in various areas throughout the country, suggesting a multiplication factor of between 5 and 10 (Hartnoll *et al.* 1985).

The inaccuracy of these estimates reflects that the multiplication factors will vary between different areas and between different times, leading some to suggest that these factors are little more than a guess.

The capture-recapture methodology can compensate for this problem by employing three or more sources. The extra information present in the third sample can be used to examine whether or not dependencies are present between data sources, and if they are, the estimate of the total population size can be adjusted accordingly. Frischer (1992) used three sources of data which held information on drug injectors in the city of Glasgow in 1989. These were combined data from treatment agencies, an HIV test register and the police. In total, information was gathered on 1738 individuals, and the overlap between the data sources can be described by Table 1.1.

These data can be analysed using statistical packages which examine contingency tables. In short, the seven pieces of information in this table can be used to

Table 1.1: Summary of data collected, in a contingency table which denotes presence or absence from three data sources of 1738 drug injectors

		HIV	
Police	*Agencies*	Present	Absent
present	present	5	23
present	absent	15	366
absent	present	109	831
absent	absent	389	*

Source: Frischer 1992

predict the missing value, which would be an estimate of the number of drug users not present in any of the three data sources, or the unknown drug-using population. This is known as log-linear analysis. Different relationships between the data sources can be described using this analysis, for example if it was thought that those drug injectors attending treatment agencies were more likely to have been tested for HIV, then this relationship can be included. The decision to include dependencies can be taken by examining how similar the observed overlap pattern is to what would be expected if such dependencies were actually present. Thus different models can be fitted to the observed data and a preferred model would be one that closely fits the observed data.

There is currently some debate as to the validity of applying these methods, which were initially developed to estimate the size of animal populations, when estimating the prevalence of drug misuse. The methodology is, however, well established in disease registers, such as those concerning insulin dependent diabetes mellitus (Karvonen *et al.* 1993). It is recognised that registers which collate data from various sources have an inherent underascertainment, that is, there will be cases missing from the register. However, in these situations the underascertainment which is to be estimated is usually a much smaller proportion of the known population than the proportion of drug misusers that are not identified using mark-recapture.

There are several assumptions inherent when applying mark-recapture, and as yet the effect of any violations of such assumptions is often unknown. For example, it is assumed that the drug-using population is closed, or in other words that no drug users cease using drugs or new people start using drugs during the time period over which the data is collected. It is also assumed that all drug users behave in the same way with respect to their chances of being included in the sampled data sources. There may be some drugs users that have virtually no chance of being included in the data sources that are used in the analysis. For example, younger drug users may be less likely to have developed problems connected to their drug use and hence are less likely to be included in data collated from treatment agencies. Frischer (1996) discusses at greater length the methodological issues surrounding the use of mark-recapture and other prevalence estimation methods whereas Hay (1997) presents a warning that mark-recapture may sometimes offer unrealistic estimates.

Another technique which sometimes employs information on the ratio of known to unknown drugs users is network analysis. Parker and colleagues used this method in studying drug misuse in the Wirral area of Merseyside (Parker, Bakx and Newcombe 1988). In this process, a single drug user is identified by an interviewer, and this drug user then goes on to identify other drug users. The interviewer then interviews these drug users to identify other drugs users that they know. This process is repeated and a chain of contacted drug users is created. These contacts can therefore be collated in the same way as a multi-source enumeration, or the ratio of known to previously unknown drug users can be used to estimate the total prevalence of drug misuse, in a similar fashion to mark-recapture or multiplier methods. Again these methods rely on assumptions whose validity cannot readily be tested, and they may be more time-consuming and expensive to undertake than other forms of prevalence estimation.

Levels of substance misuse

Synthesis

In this section we aim to draw together some of the information obtained from research and official statistics on substance use. We begin by exploring estimates of serious drug misuse obtained from mark-recapture studies and compare this information to that extracted from surveys. We then present information on alcohol consumption and smoking.

Mark-recapture studies have been undertaken in a few areas of the United Kingdom, most recently the cities of Liverpool (Squires *et al.* 1995), Glasgow (Frischer *et al.* 1993b), Dundee (Hay and McKeganey 1996) and Wales (Bloor, Wood and Palmer 1997). Table 1.2 summarises the results from these four studies.

As can be seen from Table 1.2, the estimates from the area are varied; however, the hidden populations that are being estimated in each case differ. The more restrictive definition in the Glasgow study, which only examined injecting, contrasts with the estimates of both the Liverpool and Dundee research which examined a wider drug-using population. The Welsh estimates for serious drug use is the widest definition and is defined as drug use serious enough to warrant attention by the agencies that were included in the study (drug treatment agencies, probation, and police arrest). The estimate that almost 3 per cent of the population aged between 15 and 55 in Dundee use opiates or benzodiazepines contrasts with the results

Table 1.2: **Summary of results from recent mark-recapture studies** into drug
misuse prevalence in the United Kingdom

Area and Year	Drugs Referred to	Age	Prevalence
Glasgow, 1990	Drug Injecting	15–55	1.35
Liverpool, 1991	Heroin, Methadone, Cocaine	15–29	1.69
Dundee, 1995	Opiates or Benzodiazepines	15–55	2.88
Wales, 1994	Serious Drug Use	15–55	5.34

from the 1993 Scottish Crime Survey (Hammersley and Anderson 1995). It is estimated from this survey that only 0.4 per cent of the population aged 12–59 had
ever used heroin, and that only 1 per cent of the population had used misused temazepam, a commonly used benzodiazepine, within the preceding 12 months.
Comparable figures from the 1994 British Crime Survey (Ramsay and Percy 1996)
suggest that 1 per cent of males had used heroin in England and Wales.

The figures for drugs such as cannabis may be more realistic in this survey; 25
per cent of males and 17 per cent of females had reported ever using this drug,
whereas 6 per cent of males and 4 per cent of females had reported using it in the
preceding month. These prevalence figures would mean that over 1.5 million people aged between 16 and 59 in England and Wales can be thought of as cannabis
users, using data from the 1991 census and extrapolating from the 1994 British
Crime Survey results.

The figures concerning drug dependence from the OPCS psychiatric morbidity survey are, as expected, lower than those which refer to drug use, such that 2.2
per cent of people were judged to be dependent on drugs at some time within the
preceding 12 months. This compares to the 4.7 per cent of the population that the
same survey identified as being dependent on alcohol.

More general information on alcohol consumption, and excessive alcohol consumption can be obtained from the 1994 General Household Survey. Although on
average men drank 15.4 units a week and women 5.4 units, over 27 per cent of men
and 13 per cent of women drank more than the recommended sensible limits. The

General Household Survey also presented data on cigarette smoking. On average 28 per cent of men and 26 per cent of women were current smokers. These figures are less than those reported in the Health Education Authority's Health and Lifestyles Survey (HEA 1995) in which 33 per cent of men and 30 per cent of women were smokers, smoking on average 18 and 16 cigarettes respectively per day.

Conclusion

Various methods for estimating the prevalence of substance misuse have been described above. It is important to note that there is not one 'best' method for obtaining information on the extent of substance misuse. The preferred method will depend on the way the information will be used. For example, the British Crime Survey would not be useful in determining the prevalence of drug injecting within a city. This information will be required by service providers at a local level in determining the need for control strategies such as needle exchanges or the provision of substitute prescribing. In contrast, a national advertising campaign highlighting the problems of ecstasy use, or the problems related to alcohol use, such as drink-driving, will rely more heavily on information obtained from national surveys.

Information is also required at a local level in respect to which drugs are actually being taken in that locality. The data from the regional drug misuse databases suggest that the pattern of drug misuse varies throughout the country. However, since most of the data collated by these databases come from drug services they may reflect the types of drug use that services are already providing for and not what may be happening in the community at large. There is perhaps a vicious circle in that this data may then be used to plan further services catering for the same drug problems. This may be the case where methadone maintenance is now common for treating opiate users, whereas there is little service provision for amphetamine users, and indeed little contact by amphetamine users with these services.

It is clear that questions relating to the prevalence of substance misuse cannot simply be answered by examining one source of data or using a specific research method. Indeed, the Institute for the Study of Drugs and Drug Addiction compared information on drug misuse to that of a jigsaw with several pieces missing (ISDD 1994). I have, however, described the pieces of the jigsaw that are currently available and how these may be pieced together to provide the required information on the prevalence of substance use.

References

Anderson, P. (1988) 'Excess mortality associated with alcohol consumption.' *British Medical Journal 297*, 6652, 365–372.

Balding, J. (1995) *Young People in 1995*. Exeter: Schools Health Education Unit, University of Exeter.

Barnard, M., Forsyth, A. and McKeganey, N. (1996) 'Levels of drug use among a sample of Scottish schoolchildren.' *Drugs: Education, Prevention and Policy 3*, 1, 81–89.

Bloor, M., Wood, F. and Palmer, S. (1997) *Estimating the Prevalence of Injecting Drug Use and Serious Drug Use in Wales*. Cardiff: Social Research Unit, Cardiff University.

Brewers and Licensed Retailers Association (1995) *Statistical Handbook*. London: Brewers and Licensed Retailers Association.

Department of Health (1992) *The Health of the Nation: a Strategy for Health in England*. London: HMSO.

Department of Health (1996) *Drug Misuse Statistics - for the six months ending 31 March 1996: England*. London: Government Statistical Service.

Frischer, M. (1992) 'Estimated prevalence of injecting drug use in Glasgow.' *British Journal of Addiction 87*, 2, 57–66.

Frischer, M. (1996) *Estimating the Prevalence of Drug Misuse in Scotland: a Critical Review and Practical Guide*. Edinburgh: Scottish Office Central Research Unit.

Frischer, M., Leyland, A., Cormack, R., Goldberg, D.J., Bloor, M., Green, S.T., Taylor, A., Covell, R., McKeganey, N. and Platt, S. (1993a) 'Estimating the population prevalence of injection drug use and infection with Human Immunodeficiency Virus among injection drug users in Glasgow, Scotland.' *American Journal of Epidemiology 138*, 3, 170–181.

Frischer, M., Bloor, M., Goldberg, D., Clark, J., Green, S. and McKeganey, N. (1993b) 'Mortality among injecting drug users: a critical reappraisal.' *Journal of Epidemiology and Community Health 47*, 1, 59–63.

Ghodse, A.H., Sheehan, M., Taylor, C. and Edwards, G. (1985) 'Death of drug addicts in the United Kingdom, 1967–1981.' *British Medical Journal 290*, 6466, 425–428.

Goddard, E. (1986) *Drinking and Attitudes to Licensing in Scotland: The Report of Two Surveys Carried Out on Behalf of the Scottish Home and Health Department*. London: OPCS.

Goddard, E. (1987) *The Feasibility of a National Survey of Drug Use*. London: OPCS.

Goddard, E. (1991) *Drinking in England and Wales in the Late 1980s*. London: HMSO.

Hammersley, R. and Anderson, S. (1994) *Use of Controlled Drugs in Scotland: Findings from the 1993 Scottish Crime Survey*. Edinburgh: Scottish Office Central Research Unit.

Hartnoll, R., Daviaud, E., Lewis, R. and Mitcheson, M. (1985) *Drug Problems: Assessing Local Needs. A Practical Manual for Assessing the Nature and Extent of Problematic Drug Use in a Community*. London: Drug Indicators Project.

Hay, G. (1997) 'The selection from multiple data sources in epidemiological
    capture-recapture studies.' *The Statistician 46*, 4, 515-520.

Hay, G. and McKeganey, N. (1996) 'Estimating the prevalence of drug misuse in Dundee,
    Scotland: an application of capture-recapture methods.' *Journal of Epidemiology and
    Community Health 50*, 4, 69–472.

HEA (1995) *Health and Lifestyles, A Survey of the UK Population Part 1*. London: Health
    Education Authority.

Home Office Research and Statistics Department (1996a) *Statistics of Drug Addicts Notified
    to the Home Office, United Kingdom, 1995*. London: Government Statistical Service.

Home Office Research and Statistics Department (1996b) *Breath Test Statistics, England and
    Wales, 1995*. London: Government Statistical Service.

Home Office Research and Statistics Department (1996c) *Statistics of Drugs Seizures and
    Offenders dealt with, United Kingdom, 1995*. London: Government Statistical Service.

ISDD (1994) *Drug Misuse in Britain, 1994*. London: ISDD.

Karvonen, M., Tuomilehto, J.P., Libman, I. and LaPorte R.E. (1993) 'A review of the
    recent epidemiological data on the world-wide incidence of type 1
    (insulin-dependent) diabetes mellitus.' *Diabetologia 37*, 6, 883–892.

OPCS (1995) *The Prevalence of Psychiatric Morbidity Among Adults Living in Private
    Households*. London: OPCS.

OPCS (1996a) *General Household Survey 1994*. London: HMSO.

OPCS (1996b) *The Prevalence of Psychiatric Morbidity Among Adults Living in Institutions*.
    London: OPCS.

OPCS (1996c) *The Prevalence of Psychiatric Morbidity Among Homeless Adults*. London:
    OPCS.

Parker, H., Bakx, K. and Newcombe, R. (1988) *Living with Heroin*. Milton Keynes: Open
    University Press.

Ramsay, M. and Percy, A. (1996) *Drug Misuse Declared. Results from the 1994 British Crime
    Survey*. London: HMSO.

Scottish Health Service (1996) *Scottish Health Statistics*. Edinburgh: Scottish Health Service.

Scottish Office (1994) *Drugs in Scotland: Meeting the Challenge. Report of Ministerial Drugs
    Task Force*. Edinburgh: Scottish Office Home and Health Department.

Squires, N.F., Beeching, N.J., Schlecht, B.J.M. and Ruben, S.M. (1995) 'An estimate of the
    prevalence of drug misuse in Liverpool and a spatial-analysis of known addiction.'
    Journal of Public Health Medicine 17, 1, 103–109.

Sutton, M. and Maynard, A. (1993) 'Are drug policies based on "fake" statistics?' *Addiction
    88*, 4, 455–458.

PART II
Legal Addictions

CHAPTER 2

Tobacco Use Among Young People
A Review of Research and Recommendations

Jane Frankland

Introduction

This chapter summarises recent research evidence and recommendations in the area of adolescent tobacco smoking. The issue of young people's use of cigarettes is an important one for a number of reasons. First, the impact of tobacco smoking on health—with increased risk of diseases such as lung cancer and coronary heart disease—is well known. Young people who smoke are of particular significance from a health viewpoint, as it has been shown that early smokers are more likely to become adult smokers and to smoke more heavily, resulting in greater overall exposure to tobacco and thus greater risk of these diseases (Reid *et al.* 1992; US Department of Health and Human Services 1994). Additionally, young smokers suffer more minor health complications, such as respiratory infections, fairly quickly after adopting regular smoking (Gold *et al.* 1996; Prokhorov *et al.* 1996; Royal College of Physicians 1992). Second, tobacco use may also have a less direct effect on health. There is recent evidence that its use may be related to other health-compromising behaviours, in particular to use of alcohol and other drugs (US Department of Health and Human Services 1994). Third, surveys show that adolescent smoking levels have remained fairly stable over the last decade. This fact must be taken in the context of declining adult smoking rates, decades of health warnings and prevention initiatives and work to reduce smoking among young people to levels set in United Kingdom Government targets (Department of Health 1992; Health Promotion Authority for Wales 1990; Scottish Office Home and Health Department 1991).

With these facts in mind, this chapter outlines the prevalence of smoking among young people in the United Kingdom and considers some of the reasons why adolescents start to smoke. It then presents a review of past smoking prevention initiatives and highlights the current thinking on the way forward to slow present smoking trends.

Prevalence of smoking among young people

Regular surveys of smoking among secondary school pupils have been undertaken on behalf of the United Kingdom government since 1982. The latest of these (Diamond and Goddard 1995) carried out in 1994, found that 12 per cent of 11 to 15-year-olds in England and Scotland, and 9 per cent in Wales were regular smokers (defined as smoking at least one cigarette per week). In addition, 9 per cent of this age group in England and Scotland and 8 per cent in Wales were occasional smokers, smoking less than one cigarette per week. Levels of adolescent smoking have remained relatively stable in all three countries since 1986.

Smoking predictably increases with age. In England in 1994 for instance, only 2 per cent of girls and 1 per cent of boys reported smoking regularly in their first year of secondary school (age 11–12 years), rising to 30 per cent of girls and 28 per cent of boys by year 11 (age 14–15). The greatest increase in numbers of regular smokers in all three countries was between school years 10 and 11, at age 13 to 14 years. Additionally, smoking appears more and more to be a female activity. In England in 1994, 13 per cent of girls and 10 per cent of boys were regular smokers. Boys however, do tend to be heavier smokers, consuming a greater number of cigarettes per week than girls. These and other surveys in the UK (Smith *et al.* 1994a) thus highlight trends in adolescent smoking that are cause for concern.

Why young people smoke

In order to influence adolescent smoking levels, it is important to understand the factors which impact on smoking behaviour, and numerous studies over several decades have identified a wide range of risk factors associated with smoking uptake. These factors can be summarised as personal factors, such as knowledge and beliefs about smoking, sociocultural factors, including the influence of family, friends and peers, and environmental factors, such as the availability and price of tobacco (Stead, Hastings and Tudor-Smith 1996). The uptake of smoking has been divided into separate stages (Flay *et al.* 1983), broadly summarised as a pre-paratory stage, then moving through trying and experimentation to regular smoking and addiction. The factors that influence smoking behaviour differ depending on the stage of smoking. Among young people the process of becoming a smoker is a complex and erratic one which involves a whole range of interacting influences and motivations (Goddard 1992).

This section does not attempt to provide a comprehensive review of all risk factors for smoking contained in the literature, and refers the reader to other sources for this (Conrad, Flay and Hill 1992; Royal College of Physicians 1992; US Department of Health and Human Services 1994). Instead, the section highlights a number of important areas for special consideration, namely gender and smoking, the effect of educational disadvantage and alienation on smoking, the influence of 'significant others' on smoking habits, the relationship between smoking and social and economic disadvantage and the accessibility of cigarettes in terms of their sale to young people and their price.

Gender and smoking

As mentioned earlier in the chapter, more adolescent girls than boys now report being smokers. There is not as yet a full understanding of why this is, but what is clear is that young women who smoke are putting themselves at risk of additional health problems such as breast and cervical cancer. While boys and girls share many motivations for smoking, some predictive factors are gender-specific.

Changing patterns of adult smoking in the developed world help to shed some light on patterns of adolescent smoking. Smoking has been a predominantly male activity throughout most of the twentieth century but gender differences began to decrease around 1950, due to slower uptake and increased cessation among men. By the 1980s gender differences had virtually disappeared, this change being largely but not wholly explained by changing gender roles and the growing social acceptance of smoking among women (Waldron 1991). Additionally, during the latter half of the century, tobacco advertising and specific cigarette brands have been successfully targeted at women (Amos 1996; Pierce, Lee and Gilpin 1994; Waldron 1991) and young adolescent women may have been particularly drawn to them (Covell, Dion and Dion 1994).

Research has found certain risk factors which are specific to female smokers. An association has been found between female smoking and psychological factors such as stress (Charlton and Blair 1989; Oakley, Brannen and Dodd 1992; Waldron 1991) depression and anxiety (Patton *et al.* 1996). It has been suggested that the earlier maturation of girls leads them to experiment with smoking sooner than boys, and that their smoking behaviour compares to that of boys one or two years older (Swan *et al.* 1989). Girls are found to use smoking as a means of weight control (French *et al.* 1994) and as a means of resistance both to authority and to the dominant culture of femininity (Wearing, Wearing and Kelly 1994). Clayton (1991) suggests that female smoking is related to self-confidence, social experience and rebellion, while smoking among boys is associated with social insecurity.

Research has also suggested that there are gender-specific reasons for abstention from smoking. Men and boys may decide not to smoke due to a greater interest in sports fitness (Waldron 1991; Wearing *et al.* 1994), while smoking interventions may in the past have inadvertently been targeted at young men to the exclusion of young women (Waldron 1991).

School influences: educational disadvantage and alienation

Smoking has been connected to schooling in two ways. First, a number of studies have found a relationship between performance at school, measured by levels of academic achievement, and smoking (Oakley *et al.* 1992; Stanton and Silva 1991; US Department of Health and Human Services 1994), although other studies have failed to find such a relationship (Conrad *et al.* 1992). Smoking has also been found to be especially high amongst pupils with special educational needs, such as mild learning disorders, emotional and behavioural disorders (Fidler *et al.* 1992) and Attention-Deficit hyperactivity disorder (Milberger *et al.* 1997).

Second, studies have connected response to the school environment with increased smoking levels. Nutbeam *et al.* (1993) considered 15-year-olds' attitudes to school in relation to health behaviours in 11 countries involved in a cross-national study. The authors found a relationship between alienation from school and certain health-compromising behaviours, particularly smoking and alcohol use. Another study found smoking to be an important expression of opposition and source of self-esteem for pupils who were in conflict with the school (Nash 1987). In a review of 27 prospective studies, encompassing some 300 predictors of smoking onset, Conrad *et al.* found higher academic values and expectations, commitment and satisfaction, little problem behaviour or truancy, high academic aspirations and high levels of involvement in school activities all to be related to not smoking.

The influence of 'significant others'

The extent and nature of the influence of parents, siblings, friends and peers on smoking behaviour is well researched and all are found to be strong predictors of smoking among young people. The nature, relative importance of and interaction between these three sources of influence are complex. Many surveys have found that pupils who report having friends or peers who smoke are more likely to smoke themselves. Among secondary school pupils in England for example (Diamond and Goddard 1995), three-quarters of regular smokers but only one in twenty non-smokers reported that all or most of their friends smoke. A number of explanations have been suggested for this apparent relationship. Young people who smoke have been thought to exert a direct pressure, in the form of encouragement to smoke or of ridicule for not smoking, on their non-smoking peers (Royal College of Physicians 1992). An alternative explanation is that young people choose as their friends other young people with similar habits, of which smoking might be one (Eiser *et al.* 1991). Two studies, one in the United States (Ennett, Bauman and Koch 1994) and a more recent study undertaken in Scotland (Michell 1997), have shown that smoking is adopted by specific peer groups and that rather than experiencing pressure from peers to smoke, these groups choose to smoke for particular reasons. Michell for instance found that 'top girls' smoked because of images of sexiness and sophistication, 'low-status pupils' smoked to gain popularity, and 'trouble-makers' smoked as an act of rebellion, while smoking was of no relevance to other pupils. The latter study is part of recent work (Michell 1997; Michell and West 1996) which has questioned accepted thinking on the nature of the association between peers and smoking. In a study employing both qualitative and quantitative methods the authors found very few reports of coercive pressure to smoke, and instead they suggest that adolescents who want to smoke seek out smoking opportunities, while those who do not wish to smoke avoid situations in which smoking occurs. Other research has suggested that young people may in fact be as much involved in the promotion of non-smoking amongst their peers as they are active in encouraging them to smoke (Stanton and McGee 1996).

Many surveys have found that young people are more likely to smoke if they have parents and siblings who smoke. Again, the 1994 survey of secondary school children in England (Diamond and Goddard 1995) found that 7 per cent of pupils who lived with non-smoking parents were themselves regular smokers, compared to 10 per cent whose father smoked, 20 per cent whose mother smoked and 15 per cent where both parents smoked. This and other studies (Glendinning, Shucksmith and Hendry 1997; Goddard 1992) have found young people living with lone parents to be at increased risk of smoking. In fact Goddard (1992) found that the adolescents most likely to start smoking over the three-year study period were those living with a single parent, whether that parent smoked or not. Diamond and Goddard (1995) also found that, of those English pupils who reported being regular smokers, 30 per cent had a brother or sister who smoked while only 7 per cent did not.

Normative expectations of smoking and perceptions of family and friends' approval of smoking have been identified as risk factors for smoking uptake (Conrad *et al.* 1992). Recently, style of parenting, in terms of levels of communication, support and control, has also been related to children's smoking (Cohen, Richardson and Labree 1994; Glendinning, Shucksmith and Hendry 1997).

The relative importance of parental, sibling, friend and peer influence is largely unconfirmed. The source of influence appears to vary over time, with parental influence being important at a young age, to be succeeded by siblings, and finally by friends and peers in respect of older children. The 1994 survey of secondary school children (Diamond and Goddard 1995) found the relationship with siblings' smoking behaviour to be stronger than the relationship with parental smoking, but also found that the importance of siblings' smoking declined with age, possibly due to an increase in the influence of friends' smoking. Goddard (1992) found parents' smoking to be associated with their children's smoking habits only among adolescents who did not have siblings who smoked.

Social and economic disadvantage

In recent years, there has been criticism of the individualist nature of explanations of the causes of smoking, which fail to take account of the fact that a person's social and economic standing may influence their choice to smoke. The majority of this work to date has been in the field of adult smoking. In particular, Graham's study of low income women (Graham 1987) found smoking to be a means of coping with social and economic deprivation and with the caring role in which women were engaged. Smoking was, for instance, important as a means of remaining calm in times of stress and was one small luxury that the women could afford. Oakley, Brannen and Dodd (1992) follow Graham by examining the origins of young people's smoking in the material and social pressures that they face. They claim the main reasons for adolescent smoking to be a response to material circumstances, life satisfaction and stress, and peer sociability. They argue, in particular, that smoking is a response by young women to the stress they experience in their lives, which is mainly derived from their relationships with their parents.

Accessibility of cigarettes

Surveys (Diamond and Goddard 1995; Smith *et al.* 1994a) show that, despite the illegality of sale of cigarettes in the UK to under-16-year-olds, a large proportion of young people do purchase cigarettes from shops. In Wales in 1992 for instance (Smith *et al.* 1994a), 37 per cent of 11 to 12-year-old, three-quarters of 13 to 14-year-old, and 94 per cent of 15 to 16-year-old weekly smokers reported frequently obtaining cigarettes in this manner. Furthermore, price is a vitally important factor governing the use of tobacco (Royal College of Physicians 1992). Townsend, Roderick and Cooper (1994) conclude from analysis of data from the British General Household Survey that smokers, and in particular, those from lower socioeconomic groups and women of all ages, including teenagers, are responsive to cost changes.

Smoking prevention projects

The majority of smoking interventions with young people have to date taken place in schools, with the aim of prevention rather than cessation. Early interventions concentrated on the provision of knowledge about the health effects of smoking, in the belief that adolescents would not smoke when they understood the consequences (Thompson 1978). However, the interventions proved unsuccessful, and it became clear that young people who smoked were far from ignorant of the effects of cigarettes. As the risk factors for smoking were increasingly researched, efforts were made to design programmes that were directly related to these factors. Many subsequent interventions were based on the psychosocial processes involved in becoming a smoker. These have been divided into two broad categories (Flay 1985): the social influences approach highlights the social pressures to smoke from friends, family and the wider society, and teaches skills with which to resist these pressures; programs which teach broader, more general social competence skills are termed the life/social skills approach.

Since the late 1970s many interventions based on these principles have been evaluated. The interventions embodied one or other of these approaches, although they varied in the components that made up the intervention. For example interventions varied in length, number of sessions and the age of the target population. Sessions were led by project staff (Flay *et al.* 1989; Murray *et al.* 1989), teachers (Vartiainen *et al.* 1990) or peer leaders (Vartiainen *et al.* 1990). Some included booster sessions (Flay *et al.* 1989) use of video programmes (Murray *et al.* 1989), or use of the mass media (Flynn *et al.* 1992). Short-term evaluations of many initiatives appeared hopeful, with projects successfully delaying the onset of tobacco use for between one and four years (Bruvold 1993). The North Karelia Youth Project, for example, found one-third fewer smokers in intervention than in control schools immediately after the programme and six months and two years later (Vartiainen *et al.* 1990). The Waterloo School Smoking Prevention Trial (Flay *et al.* 1989) was successful in preventing the onset of smoking over a similar time period.

A number of key projects have more recently undergone a longer term evaluation of between five and ten years after the intervention (Flay *et al.* 1989; Klepp, Tell and Vellar 1993; Murray *et al.* 1989; Perry *et al.* 1992; Vartiainen *et al.* 1990). Results of these evaluations have proved less positive, with all but the Minnesota Heart Health Project (Perry *et al.* 1992) finding that effects measured at earlier evaluations had dissipated. The success of the Minnesota project warrants some description and explanation. The 'Class of 1989 Study' was a school-based smoking intervention which formed part of a community wide cardiovascular disease prevention project. While pupils received smoking education based on the social influences approach, the whole community participated in interventions that included risk factor screening and mass media education. The study found that both weekly smoking prevalence and intensity of smoking were lower in the intervention group than the control group throughout the seven-year follow-up period.

The authors propose that smoking education programmes in schools may need to be supported by booster sessions and by community-wide intervention in order to maintain short-term effects on smoking behaviour.

It is evident therefore that teaching about smoking can quickly be undermined by what happens outside the classroom (Michell 1994; Smith *et al.* 1992). Consequently, in recent years there has been a move in the UK and Europe to promote 'whole school' intervention which involves consideration of the school environment and school policies related to smoking as well as health education teaching (Parsons, Stears and Thomas 1996). School policies which address pupils' smoking behaviour have been shown to be related to a decrease in prevalence (Pentz *et al.* 1989) but surveys have shown that these are not yet universal (Smith *et al.* 1992; Smith *et al.* 1994b). While there are obvious reasons for smoking education to take place in schools, there is also a case for out of school activity. There are, however, few out-of-school projects that have been formally evaluated. A notable exception are Smoke Busters Clubs, which are growing in number in the UK, and which aim to promote a non-smoking norm in a positive and fun way to young people aged 11–14 years. The first published evaluation of Smoke Busters tentatively concludes that after 22 months of the club's existence, members were twice as likely to remain non-smokers as non-members. Because of the method of evaluation, this result cannot be definitely attributed to the club, and a longer term evaluation is required before more firm conclusions can be made (van Teijlingen and Friend 1993).

While there is an extensive amount of research into risk factors and prevention of smoking, there is a lack of research on cessation of smoking among adolescents. Adolescent smokers generally do appear to desire a non-smoking status. Around one-third of regular smokers surveyed at English secondary schools (Diamond and Goddard 1995) said that they would like to give up smoking, while more than half of the boys and almost three-quarters of the girls who smoked had made an attempt to give up. However, tobacco is an addictive substance and adult experience shows cessation to be difficult. Adolescent smokers have been found to become quickly addicted to nicotine and to suffer the same withdrawal symptoms as adults (US Department of Health and Human Services 1994). Cessation initiatives to date tend to be targeted at adults, and young people who wish to quit may have limited access to appropriate help (Holland, McGrellis and Arnold 1995).

Current recommendations

Several decades of smoking interventions directed at young people have failed to impact on smoking levels. In the light of this, a number of recent reviews (Elders *et al.* 1994; Mitchell 1994; Reid *et al.* 1992; Royal College of Physicians 1992; Stead *et al.* 1996) have supplied recommendations on the way to progress. These recommendations are summarised in the remainder of this chapter.

To date, schools have carried the major responsibility for adolescent smoking education. It has become obvious, however, from the study of smoking interventions and the factors associated with the uptake of smoking, that a singularly educational approach to smoking reduction is insufficient (Elders *et al.* 1994; Mitchell 1994; Reid *et al* 1992; Royal College of Physicians 1992; Stead *et al.* 1996). School-based interventions can at best delay uptake of smoking for a few years (Michell 1994). While this is not an unworthy outcome, and does not make school educational initiatives redundant, it alone will not result in desired reductions in smoking among young people (Reid *et al.* 1992). Additionally, education in schools is not making an impact on certain groups of pupils, such as females and those who are alienated by the school system, who are at high risk of smoking (Michell 1994; Stead *et al.* 1996).

What the above-mentioned authors (Royal College of Physicians 1992; Reid *et al.* 1992; Mitchell 1994; Stead *et al.* 1996; Elders *et al.* 1994) recommend is a multi-faceted and multi-disciplinary approach to smoking prevention and cessation for young people. Educational initiatives need to continue but must be supported by intervention on other levels. For instance, the Royal College of Physicians has concluded that impact will only be made on young people's smoking through a comprehensive strategy that reduces smoking in the general population (Royal College of Physicians 1992). The report suggests that this should involve the development of health-promoting communities in which young people live, both within and outside school, community-based campaigns and legislation and fiscal policy, for instance to curb sales of cigarettes to minors and to increase the price of tobacco. Interventions also need to be appropriately targeted at sub-groups of the adolescent population (Stead *et al.* 1996) such as are described earlier in this chapter.

Considering the major health consequences of smoking, there is both a prevention and cessation role for all professionals in contact with young people. While a small amount of work has been completed by health workers such as General Practitioners (Townsend *et al.* 1991), the potential for involvement by many other professionals has generally not been realised. Valentich (1994) for instance, writing in Canada, claims that social workers are failing to address the issue of smoking with their clients. She lists a number of opportunities for their involvement, including counselling and education, helping to cope with the stresses which might lead to smoking, developing no-smoking policies, and lobbying government and the tobacco industry for change. Professionals can also impact young people through their own example, and indirectly by tackling smoking with their adult clients, who are role models for their children.

Smoking remains the greatest cause of premature death and disease in the developed world. There is an urgent need for appropriate educational initiatives placed in the context of wider community, legislative and fiscal action, ensuring that young people are getting a consistent no-smoking message from all sectors of their lives.

References

Amos, A. (1996) 'Women and smoking.' In R. Doll and J. Crofton *Tobacco and Health.* London: Royal Society of Medicine Press Limited.

Bruvold, W.H. (1993) 'A meta-analysis of adolescent smoking prevention programs.' *American Journal of Public Health 83*, 6, 872–880.

Charlton, A. and Blair, V. (1989) 'Predicting the onset of smoking in boys and girls.' *Social Science and Medicine 29*, 813–818.

Clayton, S. (1991) 'Gender differences in psychosocial determinants of adolescent smoking.' *Journal of School Health 61*, 3, 115–120.

Cohen, D.A. Richardson, J. and Labree, L. (1994) 'Parenting behaviours and the onset of smoking and alcohol use: a longitudinal study.' *Paediatrics 94*, 3, 368–375.

Conrad, K.M., Flay, B.R. and Hill, D. (1992) 'Why children start smoking cigarettes: predictors of onset.' *British Journal of Addiction 87*, 1711–1724.

Covell, K., Dion, K.L. and Dion K.K. (1994) 'Gender differences in evaluations of tobacco and alcohol.' *Canadian Journal of Behavioural Science 26*, 3, 404–420.

Department of Health (1992) *Health of the Nation. A Strategy for Health in England.* London: HMSO.

Diamond, A. and Goddard, E. (1995) *Smoking Among Secondary School Children in 1994.* London: HMSO.

Eiser, J.R., Morgan, M., Gammage, P., Brooks, N. and Kirby R. (1991) 'Adolescent health behaviour and similarity-attraction: friends share smoking habits (really), but much else besides.' *British Journal of Social Psychology 30*, 339–348.

Elders, M.J., Perry C.L., Eriksen M.P. and Giovino, G.A. (1994) 'The report of the Surgeon General: preventing tobacco use among young people.' *American Journal of Public Health 84*, 543–547.

Ennett, S.T., Bauman, K.E. and Koch, G.G. (1994) 'Variability in cigarette smoking within and between adolescent friendship cliques.' *Addictive Behaviours 19*, 3, 295–305.

Fidler, W., Michell, L., Raab, G. and Charlton, A. (1992) 'Smoking: a special need?' *British Journal of Addiction 87*, 1583–1591.

Flay, B.R., D'Avernas, J.R., Best, J.A., Kersell, M.W. and Ryan K.B. (1983) 'Cigarette smoking; why young people do it and ways of preventing it.' In P.J. McGrath and P. Firestone (eds) *Paediatric and Adolescent Behavioural Medicine.* New York: Springer.

Flay, B.R. (1985) 'Psychosocial approaches to smoking prevention: a review of findings.' *Health Psychology 4*, 5, 449–488.

Flay, B.R., Koepke, D., Thomson, S.J., Santi, S., Best, A. and Brown, K.S. (1989) 'Six-year follow-up of the First Waterloo School Smoking Prevention Trial.' *American Journal of Public Health 79*, 10, 1371–1376.

Flynn, B.S., Worden, J.K., Secker-Walker, R.H., Pirie, P.L., Badger, G.J., Carpenter, J.H. and Geller, B.M. (1994) 'Mass media and school interventions for cigarette smoking prevention: effects 2 years after completion.' *American Journal of Public Health 84*, 7, 1148–1150.

French, S.A., Perry, C.L., Leon, G.R. and Fulkerson, J.A. (1994) 'Weight concerns, dieting behaviour, and smoking initiation among adolescents: a prospective study.' *American Journal of Public Health 84*, 11, 1818–1820.

Glendinning, A., Shucksmith, J. and Hendry, L. (1997) 'Family life and smoking in adolescence.' *Social Science and Medicine 44*, 1, 93–101.

Goddard, E. (1992) 'Why children start smoking.' *British Journal of Addiction 87*, 17–25.

Gold, D.R., Wang, X.B., Wypij, D., Speizer, F.E., Ware, J.H. and Dockery, D.W. (1996) 'Effects of cigarette smoking on lung function in adolescent boys and girls.' *New England Journal of Medicine 335*, 13, 931–937.

Graham, H. (1987) 'Women's smoking and family health.' *Social Science and Medicine 25*, 47–56.

Health Promotion Authority for Wales (1990) *Health for All in Wales. Strategic Directions for the Health Promotion Authority for Wales.* Cardiff: Health Promotion Authority for Wales.

Holland, J., McGrellis, S., and Arnold S. (1995) *Protective Factors in Adolescent Smoking: A Literature Review.* London: University of London.

Klepp, K.I., Tell, G.S. and Vellar, O.D. (1993) 'Ten-year follow-up of the Oslo Youth Study Smoking Prevention Program.' *Preventive Medicine 22*, 4, 453–462.

Michell, L. (1994) *Smoking Prevention Programmes for Adolescents: A Literature Review.* Oxford: Anglia and Oxford Regional Health Authority.

Michell, L. (1997) 'Loud, sad or bad: young people's perceptions of peer groups and smoking.' *Health Education Research 12*, 1, 1–14.

Michell, L. and West, P. (1996) 'Peer pressure to smoke: the meaning depends on the method.' *Health Education Research 11*, 39–50.

Milberger, S., Biederman, J., Faraone, S.V., Chen, L. and Jones, J. (1997) 'ADHD is associated with early initiation of cigarette smoking in children and adolescents.' *Journal of the American Academy of Child and Adolescent Psychiatry 36*, 1, 37–44.

Murray, D.M., Pirie, P., Luepker, R.V. and Pallonen, U. (1989) 'Five- and six-year follow-up results from four seventh-grade Smoking Prevention Strategies.' *Journal of Behavioural Medicine 12*, 2, 207–218.

Nash, J. (1987) 'Sparking up–smoking and style in school.' *Health Education Journal 46*, 4, 152–155.

Nutbeam, D., Smith, C., Moore, L. and Bauman, A. (1993) 'Warning! Schools can damage your health: alienation from school and its impact on health behaviour.' *Journal of Paediatric Child Health 29*, S25–S30.

Oakley, A., Brannen, J. and Dodd, K. (1992) 'Young people, gender and smoking in the United Kingdom.' *Health Promotion International 7*, 2, 75–88.

Parsons, C., Stears, D. and Thomas, C. (1996) 'The health promoting school in Europe: conceptualising and evaluating change.' *Health Education Journal 55*, 311–321.

Patton, G.C., Hibbert, M., Rosier, M.J., Carlin, J.B., Caust, J. and Bowes, G. (1996) 'Is smoking associated with depression and anxiety in teenagers?' *American Journal of Public Health 86*, 2, 225–230.

Pentz, M.A., Brannon, B.R., Charlin, V.L., Barrett, E.J., MacKinnon, D.P. and Flay, B.R. (1989) 'The power of policy: the relationship of smoking policy to adolescent smoking.' *American Journal of Public Health* 79, 7, 857–862.

Perry, C.L., Kelder, S.H., Murray, D.M. and Klepp , K.I. (1992) 'Community-wide smoking prevention: long-term outcomes of the Minnesota Heart Health-Program and the Class of 1989 Study.' *American Journal of Public Health 82*, 9, 1210–1216.

Pierce, J.P., Lee, L. and Gilpin, E.A. (1994) 'Smoking initiation by adolescent girls, 1944 through 1988: an association with targeted advertising.' *JAMA 271*, 8, 608–611.

Prokhorov, A.V., Emmons, K.M., Pallonen, U.E. and Tsoh J.Y. (1996) 'Respiratory response to cigarette smoking among adolescent smokers: a pilot study.' *Preventive Medicine 25*, 5, 633–640.

Reid, D.J., Killoran, A.J., McNeill, A.D. and Chambers, J.S. (1992) 'Choosing the most effective health promotion options for reducing a nation's smoking prevalence.' *Tobacco Control 1*, 185–197.

Royal College of Physicians (1992) *Smoking and the Young.* London: RCP.

Scottish Office Home and Health Department (1991) *Health Education in Scotland: A National Statement*. Edinburgh: HMSO.

Smith, C. Nutbeam, D. Moore, L. Roberts, C. and Catford, J. (1994a) 'Current changes in smoking attitudes and behaviours among adolescents in Wales 1986–1992.' *Journal of Public Health Medicine 16*, 2, 165–171.

Smith, C., Frankland, J., Playle, R. and Moore, L. (1994b) 'A survey of health promotion in Welsh primary schools, 1993.' *Health Education Journal 53*, 237–248.

Smith, C., Roberts, C., Nutbeam, D. and MacDonald, G. (1992) 'The health promoting school: progress and future challenges in Welsh secondary schools.' *Health Promotion International 7*, 3, 171–179.

Stanton, W.R. and McGee, R. (1996) 'Adolescent's promotion of non-smoking and smoking.' *Addictive Behaviours 21*, 1, 47–56.

Stanton, W.R. and Silva, P.A. (1991) 'School achievement as an independent predictor of smoking in childhood and early adolescence.' *Health Education Journal 50*, 2, 84–88.

Stead, M., Hastings, G.B. and Tudor-Smith, C. (1996) 'Preventing adolescent smoking: a review of options.' *Health Education Journal 55*, 31–54.

Swan, A.V., Melia, R.J.W., Fitzsimons, B., Breeze E. and Murray, M. (1989) 'Why do more girls than boys smoke cigarettes?' *Health Education Journal 48*, 2, 59–64.

Thompson, E.L. (1978) 'Smoking education programs 1960–1976.' *American Journal of Public Health 63*, 3, 250–257.

Townsend, J., Roderick, P., and Cooper, J. (1994) 'Cigarette smoking by socio-economic group, sex, and age: effects of price, income, and health publicity.' *British Medical Journal 309*, 923–927.

Townsend, J., Wilkes, H., Haines, A. and Jarvis, M. (1991) 'Adolescent smokers seen in general practice: health, lifestyle, physical measurements, and response to anti-smoking advice.' *British Medical Journal 303*, 947–950.

US Department of Health and Human Services (1994) *Preventing Tobacco Use Among Young People. A Report of the Surgeon General*. Atlanta, Georgia: US Department of Health and Human Services, Public Health Service, Centers for Disease Control and Prevention, National Center for Chronic Disease Prevention and Health Promotion, Office on Smoking and Health.

van Teijlingen, E.R. and Friend, J.A.R. (1993) 'Smoking habits of Grampian school children and an evaluation of the Grampian Smoke Busters campaign.' *Health Education Research 8*, 1, 97–108.

Valentich, M. (1994) 'Social work and the development of a smoke-free society.' *Social Work 39*, 4, 439–450.

Vartiainen, E., Fallonen, U., McAlister A.L. and Puska, P. (1990) 'Eight-year follow-up results of an adolescent smoking prevention program: the North Karelia Youth Project.' *American Journal of Public Health 80*, 1, 78–79.

Waldron, I. (1991) 'Patterns and causes of gender difference in smoking.' *Social Science and Medicine 32*, 989–1005.

Wearing, B., Wearing, S., and Kelly, K. (1994) 'Adolescent women, identity and smoking: leisure experience as resistance.' *Sociology of Health and Illness 16*, 5, 626–643.

CHAPTER 3

Against the Odds
An Overview of Gambling Addiction

Mark Griffiths

Gambling is one of the few activities that cuts across all barriers of race, class and culture. Although almost all national surveys into gambling have concluded that there are more gamblers than non-gamblers (e.g. Cornish 1978), most of those participating are what might be termed 'normal' or 'social' gamblers who occasionally bet on a horse race, play bingo or buy lottery tickets. Estimates based on survey data indicate that 80 per cent to 94 per cent of British (Cornish 1978), 24 per cent to 68 per cent of American (Culleton 1985; Culleton and Lang 1985) and 81 per cent to 92 per cent of Australian (Grichting 1986; McMillan 1985) adults have gambled at some time in their lives. Of these, approximately a quarter to a third gamble on a regular basis (Culleton 1985; Culleton and Lang 1985; Royal Commission on Gambling 1978). The UK has now witnessed the introduction of the National Lottery and scratchcards and by the end of the first year lottery ticket sales had reached £4.4 billion (£3.3 billion from the National Lottery and £1.1 billion from scratchcards) with over 60 per cent of the adult population gambling every week (Kellner 1995).

It would appear that 'normal' or 'social' gambling is of no moral danger to most individuals in society because controlling the impulse to gamble is within their personal limits, i.e. money used for gambling is produced from their own disposable income on the basis of what they can afford to lose. However, for a small minority, gambling can become a way of life and lead to severe negative consequences. This chapter will briefly review the literature on pathological gambling and then concentrate on adolescent fruit machine gambling, particularly because (i) most of the recent research in the United Kingdom has been into this type of gambling addiction and (ii) it is this type of gambling addiction that social workers are most likely to come across in their work (Griffiths and Sparrow 1996).

Pathological gambling as an addiction

Pathological gambling refers to a state where an individual is chronically and progressively unable to resist impulses to gamble. This inevitably leads to a situation where gambling compromises, disrupts and/or damages family, personal and vocational pursuits. To most people this appears to be like any other form of addictive behaviour. However, as Dickerson (1989) points out, it is not hard to understand the initial resistance to classifying pathological gambling as an addiction. Many people's conceptions of what constitutes an addiction comes from the term 'drug addiction' (Walker 1989). However many leading authorities now view non-drug habitual behaviours as *bona fide* addictions (e.g. Miller 1980; Orford 1985). While pathological gambling does not involve the ingestion of a substance, numerous researchers have noted its similarity to other addictive behaviour including withdrawal symptoms on the cessation of gambling (Wray and Dickerson 1981), dependence (Moran 1970) and tolerance (Dickerson 1984; Griffiths 1993a). Custer (1975) has gone as far as calling pathological gambling the 'purest addiction' because no external drug is administered to the biological system.

Pathological gambling: prevalence and history

Estimates of the number of probable adult pathological gamblers vary from 0.2 per cent to 1 per cent in the UK (Dickerson 1974; Royal Commission 1978), 0.77 per cent to 3.4 per cent in the U.S. (Kallick *et al.* 1979; Culleton 1985; Sommers 1988; Volberg and Steadman 1988; 1989) and 0.25 per cent to 1.73 per cent in Australia (Dickerson and Hinchy 1988). These surveys have also indicated that pathological gambling is twice as common among males as it is among females, that non-whites have higher rates than whites, and that those with poor education are more likely to be pathological gamblers (Lesieur and Rosenthal 1991). In 1980, pathological gambling was recognised as a mental disorder in the third edition of the Diagnostic and Statistical Manual (American Psychiatric Association 1980) under the section 'Disorders of Impulse Control' along with other illnesses such as kleptomania and pyromania. The more contemporary view is that excessive gambling is an addiction and this has been reflected in the fact that the latest DSM criteria (DSM-IV) are based on the criteria for psychoactive substance abuse (see Table 3.1). It can also be found in the latest version of the International Classification of Diseases (ICD-10).

Adolescent fruit machine gambling

Fruit machines are an extremely profitable source of income for their owners and from the early 1980s onwards, there was a steady and significant increase in their numbers in the UK. Such an escalation has been mirrored by an increase in the number of problem gamblers seeking help. For instance, Gamblers Anonymous reported that in the latter half of the 1980s, 50 per cent of all new members were fruit machine gamblers with about half of those being children and the remainder young people in their late teens and early twenties (Moody 1987). Further to this, the actual number of children, adolescents and adults who experience problems as a result of their gambling activities almost certainly significantly exceeds the numbers requesting professional assistance. At its simplest level, fruit machine addiction is a form of pathological gambling and can be described as a chronic (and often uncontrollable) urge to gamble which disrupts the individual's whole life. Contrary to popular myth, there is no consistent evidence to suggest there is an addictive personality or that any particular social class is more susceptible to fruit machine addiction than any other.

The UK is the only country in the world where children and adolescents can legally gamble on fruit machines. It is perhaps unsurprising therefore that there has been a major upsurge of interest in this particular form of gambling in recent years. It has been argued by a number of people that the attraction to such an activity lies in the fact that fruit machines (a) require a low initial stake, well within the means of most people, (b) provide a particularly inconspicuous form of gambling and (c) represent the most easily accessible form of gambling generally and for young people in particular in the UK.

Adolescent fruit machine gambling is a widespread phenomenon yet we still know little about it in comparison with other addictive behaviours. To date there have been about 20 studies examining adolescent fruit machine playing. Although all of them have examined the behaviour in different ways, it is possible to give some approximate indicative rates of fruit machine play in adolescence (see Table

3.2). All studies have reported that boys play on fruit machines more than girls and that as fruit machine playing becomes more regular it is more likely to be a predominantly male activity. Very few female adolescent fruit machine addicts have been identified by researchers.

So why do adolescents play fruit machines?

This question is not easy to answer as there are many reasons. However, research does suggest that irregular ('social') gamblers play for different reasons than the excessive ('pathological') gamblers. Social gamblers usually play for fun, because their friends or parents do, to win money and/or for excitement. Pathological gamblers appear to play for very different reasons. Among the excessive players there appear to be at least two subtypes (Griffiths 1995). The first type of pathological gambler appears to be addicted to the fruit machines themselves and play to test their skill, to gain social rewards, and most of all for excitement (i.e. they get a 'high' or 'buzz' from playing the machines). This is called a 'primary addiction'. The second type of pathological gambler appears to play fruit machines as a form of escapism, where the machine is an 'electronic friend'. The players are usually depressed, socially isolated and are those who fit the media's stereotypical 'lone addict' image. This is called a 'secondary addiction' in that the player uses the fruit machine to escape a primary problem. If the primary problem is resolved (e.g. relationship problem, broken home etc.), the excessive fruit machine playing disappears. Such a distinction has obvious clinical usefulness and may also explain conflicting research, some of which states pathological fruit machine playing is a social activity and some which states it is a solitary activity.

The way of determining whether fruit machine addiction is addictive in a non-metaphorical sense is to compare it against clinical criteria for other established addictions. Brown (1993) has postulated that addictions consist of a number of common components. It is an adaptation of these components (Griffiths 1996) that will be used as the basis for determining whether fruit machine addiction is a *bona fide* addiction. These components are outlined below:

- *Salience:* This is when the particular activity becomes the most important activity in the person's life and dominates their thoughts, feelings and behaviour. For instance, even if the person is not actually engaged in the behaviour they will be thinking about the next time they will be.

- *Mood modification:* This is the subjective experience that people report as a consequence of engaging in the particular activity (i.e. they experience a 'buzz' or a 'high').

- *Tolerance:* This is a process whereby increasing amounts of the particular activity are required to achieve the former effects. For instance, a gambler may have to gradually increase the size of the bet to experience a euphoric effect that was initially obtained by a much smaller bet.

- *Withdrawal symptoms:* These are unpleasant feeling states and/or physical effects which occur when the particular activity is discontinued or suddenly reduced, e.g. the shakes, moodiness, irritability etc.

- *Conflict:* This refers to conflicts between the addict and those around them (interpersonal conflict) or from within the individual themselves (intrapsychic conflict) which are concerned with the particular activity.

- *Relapse:* This is the tendency for repeated reversions to earlier patterns of the particular activity to recur and for even the most extreme patterns typical of the height of the addiction to be quickly restored after many years of abstinence or control.

The problem with the identification of fruit machine addiction is that there is no observable sign or symptom like other addictions (e.g. alcoholism, heroin addiction etc.). Although there have been some reports of a personality change in fruit machine addicts (e.g. Moody 1987; Griffiths 1990), many parents may attribute the change to adolescence itself. It is quite often the case that many parents do not even realise that their son or daughter has a problem until they have been in trouble with the police. Despite the problems of identification and diagnosis of fruit machine addiction there is now an abundant literature which indicates that fruit machines are addictive. Using empirical evidence in addition to case study material it is argued that there is sufficient evidence that fruit machines are addictive, fulfilling each of the addiction component characteristics outlined above:

Salience

There is no doubt that for some individuals fruit machine playing is the most important thing in that person's life. There are many studies which highlight that for a small minority of individuals, fruit machine playing is a high frequency activity (i.e. played at least once a day) and that even when they are not actually playing them they are thinking about the next time they do (Griffiths 1990; Huxley and Carroll 1992; Fisher 1993). Quotes from ex-fruit machine addicts (Griffiths 1993) highlight the case:

> If I wasn't actually gambling I was spending the rest of my time working out clever little schemes to obtain money to feed my habit. These two activities literally took up all my time.

> Gamble, gamble, gamble your life away...you might as well have put it down the drain. You've got to face the truth that you're having a love affair, and it's with a machine whose lights flash, takes your money and kills your soul.

> During four or five years of compulsive gambling I think I missed about six or seven days of playing fruit machines – keeping in mind that about four or five of those days were Christmas days where it was impossible to gain access to a gambling machine... As you have probably gathered, I ate, slept and breathed gambling machines... I couldn't even find time to spend with the people I loved. The machines were more important than anything or anyone else. All I can remember is living in a trance for four years...as if I'd been drunk the whole time.

Mood modification

There are now many studies which have reported that fruit machine playing is an exciting and arousing activity. These have included both subjective self reports from interviews and questionnaires (Dickerson and Adcock 1987; Griffiths 1990) and objective experimental studies which have measured heart rate as an indicator of arousal (Leary and Dickerson 1985; Griffiths 1993a). A typical retrospective self report (Griffiths 1993b) highlights the case:

> I would always be looking forward tremendously to playing machines and I couldn't get them fast enough. During play I always got this kind of feeling – being 'high' or 'stoned' would be the best way of describing it. I was very often uncontrollable in my excitable actions, like a five-year-old at Christmas-time.

There are also self reports of excitement from gamblers while playing on the machine. For instance, in one study (Griffiths 1994) in which players thought aloud continuously while playing, they reported things like:

> 60p! I'm in the money! I'll take it, I'll take it...That was quite exciting.

> Tremendous...it's getting quite exciting now, isn't it?...I'm getting quite excited by this 'Fruitskill' − don't know what the hell it's doing though!

Tolerance

Again, there are now a number of studies reporting cases of fruit machine players who have to gamble more and more and with increasing amounts of money to get the desired arousal level that they once got gambling with lesser amounts of money.

> The cheap stake machines become boring so you play another big (expensive stake) one this time, after all, you've just seen somebody win off the next machine next to it and they won four pounds.

Most of the evidence is of a self report nature as demonstrated in the quote above (from Griffiths 1993b). However, in one study (Griffiths 1993a) it was reported that both regular and non-regular fruit machine players' heart rates increased significantly during the playing period by approximately 22 beats per minute. However, the interesting finding was that after playing fruit machines, regular players' heart rates started to decrease at once, whereas non-regular players' heart rates did not change significantly. In terms of an addictive model of fruit machine playing, both regular and non-regular players get a 'high' physiologically when playing, but the non-regular players stay 'higher' for longer, meaning they do not have to play as fast or as often to induce the arousal peaks. Regular players, in contrast, could be seen as becoming more tolerant to the playing 'highs', meaning they have to play either faster or more often to experience the initially desired effect. It was argued that the study could be viewed as the first study to show an objective measure of tolerance in fruit machine playing.

Withdrawal

A number of studies have indicated that fruit machine addicts who cease playing on the machines experience 'withdrawal' effects such as irritability and moodiness (e.g. Griffiths 1990). However, all of the evidence is self report only and consequences such as 'irritabilty' and 'moodiness' may not in themselves be considered *bona fide* withdrawal effects by some people. This is perhaps one addictive component where more research is needed to confirm the existence of an identifiable withdrawal syndrome in fruit machine addicts.

Conflict

There is much evidence in the literature that fruit machine addiction causes interpersonal conflict although there is perhaps less evidence for intrapsychic conflict. (This is perhaps because many fruit machine addicts do not admit they have a problem – even to themselves). In addition to case studies showing parent–child conflict (Griffiths 1991; 1993c), there is evidence showing teacher–pupil conflict (Moran 1987; Griffiths 1990). The following quote portrays a typical parent–child conflict situation (Griffiths 1993c) concerning 'David' (a fruit machine addict) and his parents:

> David's parents were considering divorce because they had so many arguments. David's mother felt the rows were upsetting David and driving him out of the house into the arcades to play on the machines. It was a vicious circle. David was driving his parents into arguments which led them to be worried and unhappy which drove David into the arcades which led to more arguments and so on. (p.392)

Relapse

Relapse is a common occurrence among fruit machine addicts. There are now numerous reports in the literature demonstrating that fruit machine addicts often return to their addictive pattern of playing after controlled periods of abstinence. Typical case study example quotes are again outlined below (taken from Griffiths 1993c):

> I normally started playing when I was depressed. The first time I gave up [fruit machines], I was doing well until I split up with my girlfriend which triggered me off again. ...then came a series of family rows... I returned to the machines full time. Whenever I felt depressed or maybe rejected, the urge to play the machines became even bigger... I needed to counteract it by gambling.

Miscellaneous negative consequences

Like other addictive behaviours, fruit machine addiction causes the individual to engage in negative behaviours such as truanting in order to play the machines (e.g. Huff and Collinson 1987; Moran 1987; NHTPC 1988; Griffiths 1990), stealing to fund machine playing (e.g. Barham and Cormell 1987; Moran 1987; Spectrum Childrens Trust 1988; Griffiths 1990), getting into trouble with teachers and/or parents over their machine playing (Moran 1987; Griffiths 1990), borrowing or the using of lunch money to play the machines (e.g. NHTPC 1988; Griffiths 1990), poor schoolwork and in some cases aggressive behaviour (Moran 1987; Griffiths 1990). From the brief preceding outline it would appear that fruit machine addiction is a *bona fide* addiction – although evidence for genuine withdrawal symptoms may be considered lacking.

Towards a risk factor model of fruit machine addiction

One consequence of the recent upsurge in research into adolescent fruit machine gambling is that we can now start to put together a 'risk factor model' of those individuals who might be at the most risk of developing pathological fruit machine playing tendencies. Below is a list of 'risk' factors. Each one in itself does not indicate that a person will have problems with slot machines but those individuals who experience a cluster of these factors will be more likely to experience slot machine addiction (see Table 3.3). This list is probably not exhaustive but it does incorporate what is known empirically and anecdotally about excessive fruit machine playing. As research into the area grows new items to such a list will be added while factors, signs and symptoms already on these lists will be adapted and modified.

Although (as mentioned earlier) there is a problem with the identification of fruit machine addiction in that there is no observable sign or symptom like other addictions, there are a number of possible warning signs (see Table 3.4) to look for although individually many of these signs could be put down to adolescence. However, if several of them apply to a child or adolescent it could be that they have a gambling problem.

Implications for social work

Hopefully it has been demonstrated that there is now considerable evidence that fruit machine gambling is a significant problem for a minority of adolescents. There is a growing body of research which suggests that those adolescents, and indeed adults, who gamble excessively on these machines engage themselves in a range of usually acquisitive-type offending in order to fund an increasingly costly habit. Addictive behaviour and its relative link with criminal activity has long been an area of research interest (e.g. alcohol, and to a lesser extent narcotic drug use). As a consequence, such activities have increasingly come to occupy a position of significance on the agendas of both welfare and legal professions.

Addiction, whether to gaming machines or to any other substance or activity, ought to be a major concern to both probation and juvenile justice practitioners. For a minority of addicted individuals the means by which such habits are supported inevitably brings them in to conflict with the law and subsequently before the criminal courts. The government have made no secret of their intention to place persistent offenders at the top of their political agenda. For example, low-level criminality associated with drug use has been defined as a serious threat to community safety and hence the legitimate object of increased judicial attention (Home Office 1995).

There seems little reason to assume that the acquisitive-type offending in respect of addictive gambling will receive a different penal response from criminality associated with any other form of addiction, drug use included. The latter now formally categorised as a major contributory factor threatening community safety may well be set to become the object of increasingly harsh penal sanction. Moreover, the secrecy which commonly surrounds addictive behaviour often resists enquiry and thus denies the court access to crucial mitigating material. To all intents and purpose, such individuals appear before the courts as persistent offenders with little or no regard for the victims who suffer their behaviour.

What constitutes the right information to collect about an offender and the subsequent format for its presentation has long been, and continues to be, an area of debate for criminal justice practitioners. Offenders remain uncertain about how information, particularly relating to drug use or gambling will be received. Thus, certainly in relation to the issue raised by this chapter, the motivation for offending may well remain undiscovered throughout both pre-court enquiries and in any subsequent sentence supervision.

Recent trends in penal policy, particularly those espousing the relative crime reductive merits of selective incapacitation have the potential to impact disproportionately on those whose offending has become entrenched in some form of addictive behaviour. The presently popular strategy of targeting, and temporarily removing from circulation persistent offenders, is a debate beyond the confines of this discussion (see Home Office 1996). However, considering the evidence which links, at least at some level, addiction to gaming machines and acquisitive offending, such behaviour – particularly if undisclosed – has the capacity to characterise such individuals as both persistent and menacing. In the absence of evidence to the contrary, such individuals may well be destined to suffer the worst excesses of the justice system.

The main intention of this chapter is to raise a relatively new issue within a practice arena. The essentially covert nature of fruit machine addiction allows parallels to be drawn with a range of other addictive behaviours which may have links with offending behaviour and hence many of the issues raised throughout may be familiar to a range of criminal justice professionals. Particularly under partnership arrangements, both drugs and alcohol have found increased prominence as practice issues. However, in many respects, gambling generally – and fruit machines in particular – have remained peripheral to this debate. Whilst accepting that the numbers concerned may be small, the actual scale of the problem is yet to be established. The findings presented throughout this chapter are far from anecdotal. They represent significant advancements in understanding the scale and complexity of a hitherto unexplored problem. However, what remains apparent is the limitations of such information, particularly as it applies to practitioners, whose day-to-day business is to engage with and explore the offending behaviour of their clients. To such ends it is hoped that fruit machine addiction, like other addictions, will become an issue worthy of serious consideration.

References

American Psychiatric Association (1980) *Diagnostic and Statistical Manual of Mental Disorders (3rd Edition)*. Washington D.C.: American Psychiatric Association.

American Psychiatric Association (1987) *Diagnostic and Statistical Manual of Mental Disorders (3rd EditionRevised)*. Washington D.C.: American Psychiatric Association.

American Psychiatric Association (1994) *Diagnostic and Statistical Manual of Mental Disorders (4th Edition, Revised)* . Washington D.C.: American Psychiatric Association.

Barham, B. and Cormell, M. (1987) *Teenage Use of Amusement Arcades in Bognor Regis.* Bognor Regis: WSIHE.

Brown, R.I.F. (1993) 'Some contributions of the study of gambling to the study of other addictions.' In W.R. Eadington and J.A. Cornelius (eds) *Gambling Behavior and Problem Gambling.* pp. 241–272. Reno: University of Nevada Press.

Cornish, D.B. (1978) *Gambling: A Review of the Literature and its Implications for Policy and Research.* London: HMSO.

Culleton, R.P. (1985) *A Survey of Pathological Gamblers in the State of Ohio.* Philadelphia: Transition Planning Associates.

Culleton, R.P. and Lang, R.P. (1985) *The Prevalence Rate of Pathological Gambling in the Delaware Valley in 1984.* Forum for Policy Research and Public Service, New Jersey: Rutgers University.

Custer, R.L. (1975) 'Characteristics of compulsive gamblers.' Paper presented at the second Annual Conference on Gambling, June, Lake Tahoe, Nevada.

Dickerson, M.G. (1974) 'The effect of betting shop experience on gambling behaviour.' Unpublished PhD dissertation, University of Birmingham.

Dickerson, M.G. (1984) *Compulsive Gamblers.* Longman: London.

Dickerson, M.G. (1989) 'Gambling: a dependence without a drug.' *International Review of Psychiatry 1*, 157–172.

Dickerson, M. and Adcock, S. (1987) 'Mood, arousal and cognitions in persistent gambling: preliminary investigation of a theoretical model.' *Journal of Gambling Behavior 3*, 3–15.

Dickerson, M. and Hinchy, J. (1988) 'The prevalence of excessive and pathological gambling in Australia.' *Journal of Gambling Behavior 4*, 135–151.

Grichting, W.L. (1986) 'The impact of religion on gambling in Australia.' *Australian Journal of Psychology 38*, 45–58.

Griffiths, M.D. (1990) 'The acquisition, development and maintenance of fruit machine gambling in adolescents.' *Journal of Gambling Studies 6*, 193–204.

Griffiths, M.D. (1991) 'Fruit machine addiction: two brief case studies.' *British Journal of Addiction 86*, 465.

Griffiths, M.D. (1993a) 'Tolerance in gambling: an objective measure using the psychophysiological analysis of male fruit machine gamblers.' *Addictive Behaviors 18*, 365–372.

Griffiths, M.D. (1993b) 'Factors in problem adolescent fruit machine gambling: results of a small postal survey.' *Journal of Gambling Studies 9*, 31–35.

Griffiths, M.D. (1993c) 'Fruit machine addiction in adolescence: A case study.' *Journal of Gambling Studies 9*, 387–399.

Griffiths, M.D. (1995) *Adolescent Gambling.* London: Routledge.

Griffiths, M.D. (1996) *Nicotine, tobacco and addiction,* 384,18.

Griffiths, M.D. and Sparrow, P. (1996) 'Funding fruit machine addiction: the hidden crime.' *Probation Journal 43,* 211–213.

Home Office (1995) *Tackling Drugs Together: A Strategy for England and Wales 1995–1996.* London: HMSO.

Home Office (1996) *Protecting the Public: The Government's Strategy on Crime in England and Wales.* London: HMSO.

Huff, G. and Collinson, F. (1987) 'Young offenders, gambling and video game playing.' *British Journal of Criminology 27,* 401–410.

Huxley, J. and Carroll, D. (1992) 'A survey of fruit machine gambling in adolescents.' *Journal of Gambling Studies 8,* 161–180.

Kallick, M. Suits, D. Dielman, T. and Hybels, J. (1979). *A Survey of American Gambling Attitudes and Behaviour.* Ann Acbor, M.I: Institute for Social Research, University of Michigan.

Kellner, P. (1995) 'Game for anything (NOP Poll).' *The Sunday Times Magazine,* November 12, p.23.

Leary, K. and Dickerson, M.G. (1985) 'Levels of arousal in high and low frequency gamblers.' *Behaviour Research and Therapy 23,* 635–640.

Lesieur, H.R. and Rosenthal, R.J. (1991) 'Pathological gambling: a review of the literature.' *Journal of Gambling Studies 7,* 5–39.

McMillan, G.E. (1985) 'People and gambling.' In G. Caldwell, B. Haig, M. Dickerson and L. Sylvan (eds) *Gambling in Australia.* Sydney: Croom Helm.

Miller, W.R. (1980) *The Addictive Behaviors.* Oxford: Pergamon Press.

Moody, G. (1987) 'Parents of young gamblers.' Paper presented at the seventh International Conference (June 1997) on Gambling and Risk Taking, Reno, Nevada.

Moran, E. (1970) 'Varieties of pathological gambling.' *British Journal of Psychiatry 116,* 593–597.

Moran, E. (1987) 'Gambling among schoolchildren: the impact of the fruit machine.' London: National Council on Gambling.

NHTPC (1988) 'Gambling machines and young people.' London: National Housing and Town Planning Council.

Orford, J. (1985) *Excessive Appetites: A Psychological View of the Addictions.* Chichester: Wiley.

Sommers, I. (1988) 'Pathological gambling: estimating prevalence and group characteristics.' *International Journal of the Addictions 23,* 477–490.

Royal Commission on Gambling (1978) *Report of the Royal Commission on Gambling 1976-1978.* London: HMSO

Spectrum Childrens Trust (1988) 'Slot machine playing by children: results of a survey in Taunton and Minehead.' London: Spectrum Childrens Trust.

Volberg, R.A. and Steadman, H.J. (1988) 'Refining prevalence estimates of pathological gambling.' *American Journal of Psychiatry 145*, 502–505.

Volberg, R.A. and Steadman, H.J. (1989) 'Prevalence estimates of pathological gambling in New Jersey and Maryland.' *American Journal of Psychiatry 146*, 1618–1619.

Walker, M.B. (1989) 'Some problems with the concept of "gambling addiction": should theories of addiction be generalized to include excessive gambling?' *Journal of Gambling Behavior 5*, 179–200.

Winters, K.C., Stinchfield, R. and Fulkerson, J. (1993) 'Patterns and characteristics of adolescent gambling.' *Journal of Gambling Studies 9*, 371–386.

Wray, I. and Dickerson, M.G. (1981) 'Cessation of high frequency gambling and "withdrawal" symptoms'. *British Journal of Addiction 76*, 401–405.

Further reading

Anderson, G. and Brown, R.I.F. (1984) 'Real and laboratory gambling, sensation seeking and arousal.' *British Journal of Psychology 75*, 401–410.

Fisher, S. (1993) 'Gambling and pathological gambling in adolescents.' *Journal of Gambling Studies 9*, 277–288.

Griffiths, M.D. (1994) 'The role of cognitive bias and skill in fruit machine gambling.' *British Journal of Psychology 85*, 351–369.

Ide-Smith, S. and Lea, S.E.G. (1988) 'Gambling in young adolescents.' *Journal of Gambling Behavior 4*, 110–118.

Lesieur, H.R., Cross, J., Frank, M., Welch, C., Rubenstein, G., Moseley, K. and Mark, M. (1991) 'Gambling and pathological gambling among college students.' *Addictive Behaviors 16*, 517–527.

Rachlin, H. (1990) 'Why do people gamble and keep gambling despite heavy losses?' *Psychological Science 1*, 294–297.

Table 3.1: DSM IV criteria for pathological gambling

The revised criteria now state that pathological gambling is indicated by at least four of the following (Lesieur and Rosenthal 1991):

(1) as gambling progressed, became more and more preoccupied with reliving past gambling experiences, studying a gambling system, planning the next gambling venture, or thinking of ways to get money

(2) needed to gamble with more and more money in order to achieve the desired excitement

(3) became restless or irritable when attempting to cut down or stop gambling

(4) gambled as a way of escaping from problems or intolerable feeling states

(5) after losing money gambling, would often return another day in order to get even ('chasing' one's losses)

(6) lied to family, employer, or therapist to protect and conceal the extent of involvement with gambling

(7) committed illegal acts such as forgery, fraud, theft, or embezzlement, in order to finance gambling

(8) jeopardized or lost a significant relationship, marriage, education, job, or career because of gambling

(9) needed another individual to provide money to relieve a desperate financial situation produced by gambling (a 'bailout')

('Dimensions' for each of these criteria are: (1) progression and preoccupation, (2) tolerance, (3) withdrawal and loss of control, (4) escape, (5) chasing, (6) lies/deception, (7) illegal acts, (8) family/job disruption and (9) financial bailout.)

Table 3.2: Prevalence of adolescent fruit machine gambling
in the United Kingdom (from Griffiths 1995)

- Two thirds of adolescents play fruit machines at some point in their adolescent lives
- One third of adolescents will have played in the last month
- 5–10 per cent of adolescents are regular fruit machine players who play at least once a week
- 0.5–6 per cent of adolescents are probable pathological gamblers or have severe gambling difficulties.

Table 3.3: List of risk factors in fruit machine addiction (from Griffiths 1995)

- More likely to be male (16–25 yrs)
- Begin playing fruit machines at an early age (at around 8 years)
- Less likely to play fruit machines to win money
- More likely to have had big win on fruit machines earlier in their playing careers
- More likely to have begun playing fruit machines with their parents or alone
- More likely to be depressed before playing fruit machines
- More likely to be excited during playing fruit machines
- More irrational during the playing of fruit machines
- More attracted to the 'aura' of the fruit machine
- View fruit machine playing as a skilful activity
- More likely to have bad grades at school
- More likely engage in other addictive behaviours (smoking, drinking alcohol, illegal drug use)
- Slightly more likely to come from the lower social classes
- More likely to have parents who have a gambling (or other addiction) problem

- More likely to have a history of delinquency
- More likely to engage in stealing money and truanting from school to play the machines

Table 3.4: Possible warning signs of fruit machine addiction in adolescents (from Griffiths 1995)

- a sudden drop in the standard of schoolwork
- going out each evening and being evasive about where they have been
- personality changes such as becoming sullen, moody, or constantly on the defensive
- money missing from home
- selling expensive possessions and not being able to account for the money
- loss of interest in activities they used to enjoy
- lack of concentration
- a 'couldn't care less' attitude
- not taking care of their appearance or hygiene. (This is a common symptom, perhaps due to lack of respect or because they are so preoccupied with their addiction that they simply forget their normal routine.)

CHAPTER 4

Prescribed Addiction

Kate Fay

Introduction

To understand the efficacy of the benzodiazepine drugs as tranquillisers and sleeping pills it is necessary to know how these drugs work on the brain. And to understand benzodiazepine addiction and withdrawal, it is necessary to understand the body's compensatory reaction to that action.

Throughout the brain and spinal cord there are GABA receptors which both inhibit neural activity and, indirectly, alter the production of neurotransmitters, such as noradrenaline, serotonin, dopamine and acetylcholine. The benzodiazepines act on these receptors to increase their inhibitory activity and reduce the flow of some of these neurotransmitters and so induce, among other things, calm, sleep, lack of emotion, and relaxed muscles; and they begin to act in minutes.

After about two weeks of the continuous presence of these chemicals, the brain begins to compensate for this increased inhibition by reducing the intrinsic inhibitory action of the GABA receptors, and increasing the production of some neurotransmitters, thereby producing the state of neuroadaption known as tolerance; and this state of tolerance takes at least one year and often two or three, in the absence of the drug, to revert to normality.

So what does tolerance mean for everyday behaviour and experience? It means that the only way the person involved can limit their excitability and alertness – their readiness for 'flight or fight', the fundamental survival mechanism – is by taking the drug. Between doses, as the level of the chemical in the brain decreases, they have only their weakened GABA receptors to modify their experience, and, at the same time, an increased flow of noradrenaline etc. This is an intolerable state to be in, and the only solution is to take more of the drug, because the person's natural ability to modify neural activity has been weakened and there is nothing else which will do that job. That is the basis of the chemical addiction to a benzodiazepine.

Under these circumstances the benzodiazepine addicts know they cannot manage without the drug, and they are right. They are as right as diabetics who know they cannot manage without insulin. However, benzodiazepine addicts do not know why. They usually assume, with the support of most professionals involved, that this is a weakness of character, if not full-blown mental illness. This is the nature of psychological dependence.

At the same time it seems that there is no compensatory reaction in the areas mediating emotion, memory or sensory experience; they remain anaesthetised as long as the drug is present, and for some time after it is stopped. It is also necessary to understand that after the drug is stopped the initial detoxification period takes between six to eight weeks compared to five to ten days for heroin or alcohol, and neurophysiological recovery takes years.

Recovery is interspersed with periods of intense withdrawal symptoms. This is not fully understood but is probably connected with the fat-soluble nature of the drug, its long-term storage in the body's fat cells and its cyclical release into the bloodstream over many years.

How it began

It all started in 1980 when standing in my kitchen I had what is commonly called a panic attack. I didn't know that was what it was; I only knew that I couldn't breathe, life itself seemed to be draining from my limbs, my heart was pounding, and suddenly I was full of dread and 'running for my life'. I didn't know that the dread and the running were part of the attack, I thought they were a reasonable response to what I could only think was a heart attack. The doctor, when I went to him, told me there was nothing wrong with my heart and to go home.

I didn't think of myself as an anxious person then, though I was under pressure, living in a squat with three small children and no money, but a year later I certainly was. The attacks came unpredictably, leaving me quite helpless – I could only think it must surely be a serious physical illness. And so I became more and more anxious, with all the symptoms – depersonalisation, derealisation and fear. The doctor diagnosed 'stress' but I didn't know what that meant. Then he prescribed Valium, and it worked like a dream.

I had heard of Valium. I knew some people disapproved of it and regarded taking it as a weakness. I knew it was called a tranquilliser. But now it seemed it could also control these strange, frightening episodes. And if it could do that, then I could and did stop being anxious: it all added up. It also made me feel a bit cut off and sleepy, but if those were the only side effects, I could live with them.

A year went by and I heard, by chance, a Woman's Hour programme with a psychologist describing what he called a 'panic attack'. He explained what it was, how it happened and how to deal with it. I bought his book and practised his breathing exercises; it was such a relief to understand it at last. But even so I didn't stop the Valium; I now felt shaky and nervous every morning when I woke, and dizzy, and anyway I still might have a panic attack and one 2mg tablet three times a day cured all that, more or less, and I could always take some more if I still felt bad.

And so the years went by, and now I always seemed to be unwell with nausea and stomach pain, diagnosed as diverticulitis, dizziness, blurred vision. I always felt low and depressed. I never wanted to go anywhere or do anything. Then I started getting intense stomach pain: an ulcer perhaps, but a diagnostic test showed nothing. And then I lost the sight in one eye and again extensive test showed nothing and after a month it cleared.

There was never a problem in getting a repeat prescription, I simply phoned the surgery and asked for one, and picked it up the next day. After about five years, however, I would sometimes take more tablets then were prescribed for the month and then the doctor would call me in to tell me I must stick to my 6mgs a day. On the last occasion he explained that his practice had a policy of not increasing the dose for younger people, although it wouldn't matter for older people. He didn't explain why and I didn't ask. From what I now know, it means a policy of keeping one age group in chronic withdrawal, and the other increasingly drugged. Either way it was a policy of keeping everyone concerned in a state of continuous ill-health. Whether he understood the nature of addiction and tolerance and its symptomatic equivalence to withdrawal I don't know.

None of the four doctors I saw in that practice ever connected my perpetual ill-health with their prescription of Valium, although all my symptoms have been recorded as common 'side-effects' in research reports since the early 1960s and in self-help books. None of them ever told me the drug was addictive and when I said on different occasions to each of them that as soon as my youngest child was settled in school I would stop taking it, none of them warned against stopping suddenly. Now in the tenth year of taking Valium, I decided to start psychotherapy. I thought if I resolved my emotional problems, the fear and depression, then I would regain my health, stop having panic attacks and give up the Valium. When I told the therapist I was taking it, he simply said that I should stop. But I did not; I thought I would wait until I was a bit better and stronger.

The Nightmare Year

Now it was 1991 and that Christmas I went down with 'flu, or did I? Anyway, I thought I had, and that it would be a good moment to give up smoking and stop the Valium. Well, the Valium was easy, I just didn't take any more, no craving. No 'perhaps I'll have a bit' – nothing. But smoking: that was too difficult, perhaps I'd just cut down.

I have no idea how long I stayed sane: one night and a day? two? three? What I remember is waking in the early hours, from a deep sleep to complete alertness in an instant, and flinging myself out of bed in utter terror. I hung over the banister waiting for the cataclysm which would end all existence. One day when I can read 'The Second Coming' and 'Things fall apart the centre cannot hold' with manageable emotion, I will know I am completely well. But not yet, the memories are still too vivid.

I must have slept again. But the next morning I was storming round the house shaking, shouting, unable to keep still, and over and over again asking the question 'what is this? what's happening? Is this the breakdown the psychotherapist says must happen before I can build a new healthy life? What forgotten horrors lie in my past that will manifest themselves like this?' A few hours passed before I wondered if, maybe, not taking any Valium might have something to do with it. I found the number for the nearest drugs project, phoned them, described how I was and that a few days previously I'd stopped taking Valium – could that have anything to do with it?

'Yes, of course,' was the answer, 'that is exactly what happens.' 'What should I do?' I asked, 'shall I start taking it again?' 'That would be a shame,' they said, 'now you've got this far why not carry on and see it through?'. This might be appropriate advice to someone coming off heroin when the acute withdrawal lasts only 5–10 days, and is expected and understood, but I had a family and a job and I didn't know I was an addict, or what the consequences of addiction were. I started the tablets again, but took less, until after a few days as the fear built up I'd take another 2 mgs for a few days and then back to 6mgs or 4, and so I went on varying the dose: trying to come off, failing, trying again. Clearly I was very sick emotionally; clearly the drug suppressed that sickness and the only way to get well was to stop taking it and face whatever emerged. The psychotherapist said so and I thought he was right. That was going to be difficult because apart from the fear I was physically ill. The 'flu kept recurring with mild delirium, aches and weakness, although, strangely, a normal temperature.

By the end of February I'd become very weak down my left side. I kept knocking things over and stumbling when I walked. I had pins and needles down my leg and arm and the left side of my face was numb. Sheer terror – had I had a stroke? Was I dying? What now? Off to the doctor again and this time 'neuritis' was the diagnosis, which I immediately connected with the temporary loss of sight the year before. This was the second time: so could it be multiple sclerosis? 'Well, yes it could, but it probably wasn't,' was the answer, but he said he would send me for tests.

The specialist asked about my symptoms – the loss of sight, the weakness, and the pins and needles. 'Well, yes,' he said considering, 'different times, different parts of your body; that is certainly characteristic of multiple sclerosis'. And so he tested my reflexes and finally drew something across the sole of my foot. I knew this was the deciding moment, would my toes go up or down? Up for multiple sclerosis, down for normality – I'd read it in my neighbour's Reader's Digest family health book. Down they went, curled in against the tickle, and in came the consultant to confirm that, whatever else was wrong with me, I didn't have multiple sclerosis. And in my flat distant way I was relieved – of course I was, anyone would be. So why did I feel so little, except the usual thick-headedness and incipient panic? And so I played the part: 'Isn't it wonderful? What a relief,' but all I really wanted was to be left alone.

I was still ill and so I tried the doctor one last time and he took blood tests, 'for everything testable,' he said. Please, please find something treatable, I thought. But there wasn't anything at all to find, no bugs, no anaemia, no cancer. My sister-in-law had suggested Lymes disease from sheep ticks, which would have been better than nothing, but nothing it was – nothing at all. I was completely well – except for blurred thinking, blurred vision, dizziness, unreality and perpetual fear. And if that had no physical basis, then obviously I was emotionally ill; so back to therapy.

The problem was that I was now so terrified of the therapist, I could hardly speak to him. When I said I was so afraid, he'd ask what of, and when I said I didn't know, he'd say I was afraid of myself and I was right to be. I was an emotional anorexic, dead from the neck down, no feelings. And in a year nothing about me had changed. Why, he wanted to know, did I not tell him what I'd done? What had happened each week before I saw him? I didn't do that because there was nothing to tell. Twice a week I went to work, and it was always the same. And on the other days I did the chores and then sat around waiting for the time to pass, and the night to come. Apart from fear and boredom, feeling nothing. Apart from keeping as still as possible, doing nothing. How could I tell him that?

The autumn came and I was still no better although I was back at work. I gave up the psychotherapy and accepted a doctor friend's suggestion that this was a post-viral syndrome and that in time I would probably get better. From my point of view I could still only function adequately when I'd taken enough Valium. It was clear I was dependent and I understood the addiction as an emotional weakness and felt that I must resolve my fears and depression before I could overcome it.

The drugs project had sent me details of a tranquilliser support group and in November, on a dark Wednesday evening, I went along. I had to do something. Group therapy might not be that threatening and if it was, I need not go back. There was a group of people sitting in a rather drab dark room, chatting. After a while one of them asked me to tell her, but only if I wanted to, what I was taking and how I was. I said I usually took about 9mgs of Valium, but that I'd been ill all year and I wasn't sure if I was well enough to come off it yet.

She asked about my illness. And so I went through it all from the diverticulitis on. And with each symptom there was almost a chorus of responses. 'Oh yes, I've got that. I had that. Do you remember so and so? He had that. Did you only lose the sight in one eye? I lost it in both, but only for two days. Did they call it diverticulitis? It's usually irritable bowel for a woman. Dizzy? That is your blood sugar – eat little and often. Multiple sclerosis? You're the first one for a long time but do you remember...? And 'flu – oh we've all thought we've had 'flu. It's the drugs, dear, just the drugs. Have you been upping and downing? Well, there you are then, no wonder you've been so ill.' 'And I'm so afraid all the time.' 'Of course you are dear –

these drugs make you afraid, that is the one thing everybody gets, even if they were only given them in the first place for muscle pain.'

I was astonished and then utterly relieved: years of misery and illness made sense of in one conversation. The following week we planned my withdrawal; first to level out on a fixed amount until I felt better; then when I felt ready, to reduce the amount by 1/2mg; then wait and see how it went, and when I felt ready again, another 1/2mg. 'The discipline is in curbing your impatience and coming off slowly. If you can do it slowly you'll only have to do it once!'

The next day I went to the doctor to explain what I was doing and to ask for his support. He asked how long I thought it would take me to stop taking the Valium, and I said, guessing, that perhaps it would take a year. He looked doubtful and told me I could do it in three weeks, but if I wanted to take my time he would not stop me. The group met every week and in between I could phone Esther or Joan for reassurance. Esther had founded the group ten years before. She had visited a doctor just to talk years ago following a harrowing family event, had been prescribed Tranxene followed by Ativan and rapidly gone into chronic withdrawal ending up in a psychiatric hospital for six years and diagnosed schizophrenic. When I met her she'd been off the drugs, and well, and back in her very demanding job, for ten years.

Over the following years I met all sorts of people; they all had the same story to tell of fear and illness – with variations: the ones who had spent years in psychiatric hospitals diagnosed as schizophrenic, manic depressive or having a personality disorder; and the ones who'd been so ill and afraid, not knowing what was wrong with them.

Once we were joined by a professional, a psychiatric social worker. He listened to us describing our experiences to each other, the fear, the pain, the agoraphobia, the problems breathing, and all the rest, both being on and coming off the drugs, and then as he left he announced that what we really needed was to find within ourselves what we had got from the drugs. Clearly he had not understood what we had been saying, that what we had been talking about was what we had got from the drugs, and his response just confirmed everyone's experience of professional help. Over the next month I stuck to 10 mgs a day and sure enough the influenza symptoms disappeared as well as the neck pain. I felt better than I had for a year.

Then I reduced the dose by 2 mgs and a few days later I went into a week of feeling very afraid, dizzy and unreal. Then I settled back into feeling less unwell. So it went on. I could phone Esther, James, Harriet or Joan for reassurance every day if I needed to. And every week I went to the meeting. I thought I was going slowly, reducing the dose every two or three weeks. I was still going to work two days a week and keeping house, so I did not take any notice when people suggested that I was reducing too quickly.

Now it was May again and I'd been reducing the dose for 16 months and I was down to 3.5mgs. After that last cut I finally had to take time off work, because the muscles around my eyes simply stopped functioning. I could focus as long as I kept quite still, but each time I moved my head it took a minute or so to re-focus. And as far as driving or even walking went I simply could not even get to work. This was the first time withdrawal became so disabling.

Of course I phoned Esther and she said (as she always did) that if I was worried I should see the doctor, but they were quite sure it was the last cut I had made. Well, I was worried, but not that worried. The doctor had never understood all my other problems as being tranquilliser-induced and the last thing I needed was to have my little bit of certainty undermined. I'd already lost the sight in one eye and had years of blurred vision, and he had not connected that with Valium. Why would he be able to help with this?

After a week or so my sight was back to normal, so I did another 1/4 mg cut and went back to work. I did, however, suggest to the people I worked with that I might go into the local psychiatric hospital to come off the last few milligrams, and get it over with. I still believed in spite of everything I had heard, that I could stop the last bit, go through perhaps a slightly worse withdrawal, get over it in a week or two and that would be that.

A few days later, three days after the last cut, I went to work and was outside, topping up the soil for some container-grown trees, when the sense of dread became suddenly unbearable. I could only say that I was going home and went, driving fast and erratically. Arriving home I fled to the bedroom.

The next day, light-headed and afraid, I did the chores and lay down to sleep. Waking at lunch time, I came downstairs and turned the radio on to hear the announcement that John Smith had died. It felt as though I had been hit by an enormous solid wall of stone, or a huge wave of sound, loud and deep – a reaction way beyond any personal feeling I'd expect to have. And then the next morning the world I knew disintegrated.

I spent most of the following month in bed, paralysed with dread. As it abated, I knew I could not face this reaction every time I reduced the drug and so I asked the doctor to admit me to the local psychiatric hospital to come off the rest.

Hospital

We arrived at the hospital about mid-morning and were greeted by Eddie, the nurse who would be my main contact. There were forms to fill in and questions to answer and then an interview with the ward psychiatrist. The only thing I really remember was her saying how wrong it was of my GP to issue repeat prescriptions all those years, and my feeling reassured that she understood my situation. We must have talked about panic attacks, but I doubt if I tempted fate by explaining that I no longer got them. However, I did explain that I'd been reducing the Valium over the last 16 months and was now down to 3.75mgs, that I had gone too quickly and it had made me very ill, and that I wanted to come off the last bit in hospital. And she suggested that the most important thing was to deal with my panic attacks. I said that could wait until I was well; the most important thing, to me, was to get off the drug. And so the scene was set.

My husband left soon after this exchange. I was trembling inside, thick-headed, and cut off. I started to cry. This psychiatrist must have seen my tears, because she announced that I was depressed and she would help me to take anti-depressants. I said I was sad, not depressed, and I did not want to take anything. She also offered sleeping pills. I didn't think to ask if they would be Temazepam, another Benzodiazepene drug, or chloral hydrate which isn't. I assumed the worst and said I would let her know. But this still was not the end. She now told me that I would need to take Stellazine, a major tranquilliser normally prescribed for psychosis. I was prepared for this one (although I had not expected it); I really thought my wish – simply to come off the last of the Valium – was accepted.

People in the group had said so often that you go into hospital to come off one thing and come out on half a dozen other pills and the worst were the major tranquillisers because they suppressed withdrawal and so one either never recovered and took them for life, or eventually stopped them, and went through it all again.

So 'No thank you' I said. She explained she wanted me to take it because she was a compassionate doctor and couldn't bear to see me in such distress. 'Well, you take the tablet,' I thought, 'and I'll get on with getting well'. But I was too scared to say it, I explained again that as far as I knew it was the Diazepam (valium) which was making me ill and that after the last bout of withdrawal I just wanted to be somewhere 'safe' and undemanding to come off the rest. So that was it until the afternoon, when Eddie suggested we have a chat about my panic attacks.

I told the story again, how I had been chatting to the man next door in my kitchen and cooking. And since reading 'For people who panic', and learning to breathe properly, I vary rarely got them; they were not the issue, the issue was coming off Diazepam. 'Will you stand by me in withdrawal?' I asked for the first of many times to come. 'Yes, of course, but we must deal with your anxiety,' was the answer.

The day was nearly over. One last 'therapy' session to go: the psychiatrist drew me to one side, after tea – 'you never told me there was a man in your kitchen when you had your panic attack' – I only wish I'd been well enough to enjoy the comedy.

If you ever want to study the character of denial, there's nothing like listening to a professional dealing with tranquilliser addiction.

The next morning the psychiatrist spoke to me again. She explained that they had a drug, chlordiazepoxide, which was not a major tranquilliser which would ease the withdrawal effects of coming off Diazepam (valium) and I believed her. I think I believed her because I so wanted it to be true and because for the first time she seemed to have acknowledged that tranquilliser withdrawal was in itself a terrible experience. I was to start on 20mgs, 5mgs four times a day and cut the Diazepam down to nothing over the following week. And so I took the first dose. Of course it wasn't long before I realised it was Librium, another Benzodiazapine drug.

The next morning the consultant psychiatrist arrived for her ward round and suggested she and the clinical psychologist should talk to me in the garden. I asked why I should be given Librium to come off Valium. She explained it was because I had refused Stellazine. Did I realise that I could bring on a fit coming off 3.25 mgs of Valium in a week? 'Nasty things, fits,' she added, 'and you'd lose your driving licence, wouldn't that be a nuisance?' The Stellazine would prevent that. But if I would not take it, Librium was the next best thing.

She looked to the psychologist for confirmation. He nodded thoughtfully: yes, indeed that was the best solution. I tried once more to say that it just didn't make sense, but 'Trust me, I'm a professional,' she said. A little while later the ward psychiatrist came out to tell me that I should explain to my husband that the equivalent between Librium and Valium was 1gm to 1mg. It is hard now to remember how afraid I was and how foggy my head felt so I accepted this nonsense. But I do remember thinking that, since I at least knew how to get off a Benzodiazepine drug (like Librium), and that I knew nothing about major tranquillisers (like Stellazine), I might as well give in. I did at least say clearly that I was not leaving the hospital while I was still taking anything at all.

That evening Esther came to pick me up and take me to the group meeting. I described what had happened and how I'd given in to it. There was no judgement; it was accepted without question that I was in no state to fight this kind of pressure. But there was the reassuring confirmation that chlordiazepoxide was indeed also known as Librium and that 20mgs was equivalent to 10mgs of Diazepam and that the worst that could happen was that it could just add time to my withdrawal.

After taking all that Librium and the last of the Valium over the following week, I felt a bit better. More in touch, rather less woolly-headed and I could easily go to the physiotherapy department each morning for Keep Fit. The physiotherapists were very helpful, giving me time on my own to practice breathing correctly, and relaxation classes. In the afternoon I walked round the grounds – beautifully planted – or I went to Occupational Therapy for painting and pottery.

People who visited would say how much better I looked and I could only say 'yes, but I'm drugged'. And although I was no longer desperately afraid, I knew I would never choose this kind of mental health: it was not my real self and it felt far too precarious. The terror was only a little further away and as soon as tolerance to the drug dose set in it would be back. In fact taking more Benzodiazapine drugs than I ever had before didn't even restore me to the state I was in before coming off. And so there was absolutely no temptation to opt for staying on the drug.

I wrote a statement at that point to say that even if when off the drug I was anxious or depressed, I would rather be that and drug-free than 'well' and drug-dependent.

Over the next two weeks the Valium was stopped and the Librium decreased and during those weeks I was functioning – I could share meals and did not need to eat in solitude. I could go for walks and talk to the other people on the ward. I felt shaky, dizzy, cut-off and anxious, but it was bearable. People from the support group came to visit. Esther picked me up each Wednesday evening and took me to the group meeting.

When I was down to 5mgs of Librium I thought the psychiatrist would want me to come off it more slowly and I asked the ward sister how that would happen. She said that I could work it out myself: 'It's empowering'. So off I went and wrote out a plan for reducing by ¼ mg every three days, coming off on the twelfth day, and I left it for her in the office. The next morning, duly empowered, I joined the queue at the drugs trolley and explained what to give me to the nurse there. He looked doubtful and then checked my notes and said that I wasn't written up for any more chlordiazepoxide at all.

Now as the days passed the withdrawal symptoms intensified. I felt I was going to explode inside. I could not keep still. I couldn't be near other people, or inside the building. At the same time, I couldn't bring myself to go any distance outside; I just walked round and round the ward in the garden. And now I couldn't chew or swallow ordinary food, while at the same time I would get pangs of hunger every hour or so which in themselves brought on intense terror; so I ate bowls of 'Ready-Brek' or Weetabix with milk and if the milk ran out, with water.

Now, two years later, in the group we laugh at the memory of me and my bowl of Redibrek – I couldn't go anywhere without it. At mealtimes I would collect my food and take it out to the garden right under the hedge, but usually I couldn't eat it anyway.

The ward sister seemed to understand this one, she said it was the same for some people coming off heroin. I learned later it would have lasted only five days or so for them, whereas for me it was five months.

I could no longer walk to the physiotherapy department or go to Occupational Therapy and the psychiatrist called over one morning to say that if I would not take part in what was offered there was no point in my being in hospital; what was the matter with me? I tried to tell her how it felt, that the withdrawal was now really bad. 'It cannot be withdrawal,' she said, 'you came off the Valium two weeks ago and you were all right.' I tried to explain that that was because I was still taking Librium, and now that had stopped the Benzodiazapine withdrawal was in full flood. But she was not having it. Coming off the Valium had not been a problem and I could not have become addicted to the Librium in just two weeks, she knew, because it was often given to alcoholics for that length of time while they stopped drinking and they did not get addicted.

What could I do? Where could I go? Suppose she was right and all the books I had read and the people I had spoken to were wrong. And even if she was not right, how could I cope? Well, I did what I always did: phoned Esther or Harriet or James (I cannot remember who). They talked me through the terror.

There was not much more to go. The next day, sweating and shaking and wringing my hands, I went to the staff nurse for comfort, reassurance, anything, but she explained that my symptoms were not so much physical withdrawal as grief for the loss of the drugs I had depended on for so long. Then the charge nurse (my next hope) told me that the drugs had masked my true state of mind all these years and if I would not take them any more then of course it would be revealed and I would have to live with it. That sent me scurrying to the phone again, where James's response came close to melting the wires. Now it was the weekend and my husband was visiting. Speaking to the duty psychiatrist, it was clear she had no understanding of addiction to, or withdrawal from 'the most commonly prescribed drug in the Western world.' So we packed my things and he took me home.

I arrived home and while there was no question in my mind that it was the house that I had lived in for the last 16 years (the garden was full of flowers, the trees still in the summer air), it was so unfamiliar, all so far away as if I were encased in a glass shell. The dread was crawling through my skin and I knew that at any moment I could explode in terror, endlessly.

The only thing that I could do was to lie on my bed, very still, alone, and that is what I did for most of the next four months. By now I had been off the drugs for ten days and the withdrawal symptoms were in full flood: my chest was so tight that I felt that I was not really breathing, my head thick and humming, my stomach churning and clenching; I kept falling asleep and a few seconds later I would wake with a shock. This would go on all through the night. I still had to eat every hour. Weetabix and a half pint of milk washed down with decaffeinated tea.

My thoughts were all of the futility of life, of the waste and hopelessness and all around the dark echoing emptiness. And then I would telephone Esther, or Jenny, or James so that they could tell me yet again that they had had those thoughts, those feelings, that desperation. And that it was the pills. And that I would get well.

Sometimes, when it was hard to breathe, Gladys would go through the instructions for relaxation and then count as I breathed in and out.

Part of the despair was the inability to do anything normal. Still, at least I could go to the loo alone. Gladys, when recovering, had had to telephone someone to talk to her as she crawled upstairs into the bathroom and back to her sitting room floor. And I was not as bad as Penny, who was so terrified at the sight of her sitting room walls caving in on her that her husband put up a tent in the room for her to be in. 'And look at us now,' they would say, 'we are working, travelling, bringing up our children; look at Sarah, she didn't go out of the house for 20 years and now she's a nurse.'

'Yes, but how long? When will I be better?' No one would say definitely. And they were right not to – partly because recovery is unpredictable, and also because to know the likelihood of an insane three months, a horrible nine months, and then another difficult year, would, at that point, have been unendurable. I suppose it was the hope I could get from other people's experiences that made it bearable. And lying very still. But when I got up and felt the trembling inside, and the depths of my disassociation from my world, my body, my mind, then what made it bearable was to smash my head against the kitchen wall until the pain and numbness blotted it out for a few moments. And I could stumble back to bed.

More than a year later, when I described this at a group meeting, Esther rolled up her sleeve to show the scars from the cuts she had made with a stanley knife, trying to overwhelm with pain her desperation in acute withdrawal.

As the months went, by I realised that there were more and more things that I could do: I could sometimes sit at the kitchen table and share a meal with my family; I could go outside for a while; sometimes, cook and do the washing up, sometimes. But as often as I took a step forward it would collapse again and I would be back, hiding in the bedroom. I was utterly frustrated: I wanted to get on with my life, it was frightening watching the months and years slipping away. I wanted to try, to be brave. But how can you, when the mental mechanisms you would use no longer work?

Now, in November, came the first precious moment of recovery. I was in bed and my daughter came and cuddled beside me and I put my arm round her – well, that is what mothers do, isn't it? And welling up inside me came a wonderful, glowing, peaceful feeling belonging to our closeness. And then I wondered why – had I eaten something? was there something in the supper? wine perhaps? And then: is this what love feels like? Is this affection? And suddenly I knew that, for the first time in her ten years, I was feeling love for this child of mine.

Over the following months the fear subsided and my feelings slowly emerged. Music could be unbearably beautiful and colours extraordinarily intense. And with the subtle emotions of pleasure, gratitude and disappointment, each time I would have to stop and identify what it was. Because after 15 years of feeling nothing, I did not know.

Now, two years and four months later, I am back at work and have visited friends in Israel. I have even swum in the Cornish sea, something I used to love and thought I would never do again; and best of all there is the joy of rediscovering my family. I still have a long way to go; my head is still thick and muzzy, my memory is unreliable, I easily get exhausted and then I feel remote and cut off, and I still hyperventilate for no apparent reason. But the support group is always there. I have spoken to David who is running his business and driving food out to Bosnia every few months, and to Steph, who, after 20 years in hospital diagnosed as manic-depressive, has taken 'A' levels in maths and economics, and has just started a degree course. 'How long were you off before you could start all that?' 'About three years' was their answer. 'Be patient, you'll make it.'

The last word must go to James who had come off Ativan, recovered, and was planning to work abroad. He phoned a while ago to say he had had bone cancer diagnosed and was in the middle of a course of chemotherapy. I could only say how terrible it was. 'Well, yes, it's terrible,' he replied, 'but it's not as terrible as being on and coming off benzos.'

In conclusion

Benzodiazepine addiction is an illness in itself, caused by this chemical alone. Non-professional support groups know this and know that the only cure is slow withdrawal and then healing over time. They simply offer the reassurance, support and encouragement that makes this possible.

Medical professionals rarely understand that this is the case (although the information has been available to them and the public for decades), and their ignorance has merely served to perpetuate and complicate the addicts' distress. In the end it is as simple as that.

Bibliography

Ashton, H. (1984) 'Benzodiazepine withdrawal; an unfinished story.' *British Medical Journal 288,* 12–28.

Ashton, H. (1986) 'Adverse effects of prolonged benzodiazepine use.' *Adverse Drug Reaction Bulletin* 118, 440-442.

Ashton, H. (1989) 'Anything for a quiet life.' *New Scientist,* May 1989, 52-55.

Ashton, H. (1991) 'Protracted withdrawal syndrome from benzodiazepines.' *Journal of Substance Abuse Treatment 8,* 12–28.

Hallstrum, H. (1993) *Benzodiazepine Dependence.* London: Oxford University Press.

Ritson, P. (1989) *Alive and Kicking.* Liverpool: Casa Publications.

Roche Products Ltd (1990) *Benzodiazepines and Your Patients; A Management Programme.* Available on request from Roche by prescribers.

Victims of Tranquillisers Newsletter (1995) Issue 1 V.O.T. Dr. R.F. Peart, 9 Vale Lodge, Vale Road, Bournemouth BH1 3SY.

PART III

Drug and Alcohol Policy

CHAPTER 5

AIDS and British Drug Policy
A Post-War Situation?

Virginia Berridge[1]

There appear to have been some radical changes in British drug policy since the advent of AIDS. After the discovery of the HIV virus among British drug users at the end of 1985, the pace of policy change was rapid. Major reports on AIDS and Drug Misuse followed, together with £17 million for the development of drug services. At least a hundred needle exchanges offering new for used syringes were the most tangible public expression of new developments, underlining the view that the danger of the spread of AIDS from drug users into the general population was a greater threat to the nation's health than the dangers of drug misuse itself. British drug policy and in particular the visible manifestation of a harm-minimisation approach in the form of needle exchanges, attracted world-wide attention. Some commentators as a result argued that AIDS had changed the direction of British drug policy, although others were more cautious (Fox, Day and Klein 1989; MacGregor 1989; Stimson 1990).

This paper was originally written in the early 1990s to look, from an historian's perspective, at the question of the 'newness' of British drug policy post AIDS. How far had drug policy been radically changed under the impact of AIDS? How far had AIDS been simply a vehicle whereby developments inherent in existing policy

1   This paper is based on earlier work which was published in V. Berridge and P. Strong (1993) *AIDS and Contemporary History*, Cambridge: Cambridge University Press. I am grateful to research contacts and other colleagues whose comments helped me to revise the original version of this paper.

had been achieved more quickly than might otherwise have been possible? From a longer-term perspective, how much was really new at all? How far did recent changes merely exemplify some very long-standing themes and tensions in British drug policy? One historical analogy was with the debates around the impact of war on social policy. Historians have in recent years begun to look more closely at the impact of World Wars I and II on social and health policy in particular. They have questioned the view that war was the only catalyst for radical change. In World War II, for example, the 'national consensus for social change' appears to have been less than unanimous, and the particular alliance of labour activism and senior civil servants of significance (Webster 1990). The roots of the National Health Service, established in 1948, can also be found not just in wartime change, but in pre-war debates and blueprints for health care. What war did was to enable this to happen more quickly and in rather a different fashion (the nationalisation of the hospitals, for example, rather than local authority control) than might otherwise have been the case. War served, too, to lay bare the deficiencies of the existing system. The chaotic overlap of hospital services and structures pre-war was quickly rationalised in the Emergency Medical Service in the war; war served to overcome vested interests and opposition to change, but essential continuities with the pre-war service remained (Fox 1986; Webster 1988).

AIDS, too, fits into this paradigm. Like war, it evoked a period of political emergency reaction which was at its peak from 1986 to 1987, but which, in the case of drugs, spilled over into 1988 with the government reaction to the Advisory Council on the Misuse of Drugs Part I report on AIDS and Drug Misuse. Many of the actions of central government in this period had a wartime flavour—the creation of an inter-departmental Cabinet committee chaired by William Whitelaw, Deputy Prime Minister, the 'AIDS week' on television in February 1987, when both television companies joined together on a wartime model; and the Commons emergency debate in November 1986 (Berridge 1996a).

This version of the paper, written in 1996, takes the analysis a stage further to take account of more recent policy documents. History is not a predictive discipline, but I have noticed how my earlier conclusions have stood the test of a small amount of passing time; the drug policy situation in 1996 does indeed resemble a post war situation.

Drug policy in the 1980s: before AIDS

How far did the emergency reaction of the 1980s stimulate genuine new departures? Let us briefly sketch developments in the preceding years. Drug policy in Britain has been characterised historically in terms of four distinct phases. The first, in the nineteenth century, saw gradually increasing professional controls inserted into a system of open availability of opiate drugs (Berridge and Edwards 1987). A more stringent reaction established during the 'cocaine epidemic' of World War heralded a new phase of policy (Berridge 1978). The 1920 Dangerous Drugs Act marked a penal reaction to drug use; but the Rolleston Report of 1926 reasserted what became known as the 'British System' of medical prescribing of opiates, a system of medical control operating within a more penal framework of national and international controls (Berridge 1984). It was not until the late 1960s that a new and third phase began. The development of a drugs subculture, over prescribing by a number of London doctors, were among the factors leading to a change in policy. The second Brain Committee report in 1965 led to changes in drug policy, in particular the limitation of the prescribing of heroin and cocaine to doctors licensed to do so by the Home Office; treatment of addiction was relocated in the 'clinics', hospital-based drug dependency units. These initially operated as prescribing centres, in the belief that 'competitive prescribing' would undercut and curtail the development of a black market in drugs. Changes in clinic policies in the 1970s, however, brought a decline in opiate prescribing and a rise in more active treatment methods, based on short-term methadone prescribing or on no prescribing at all (Edwards 1978; MacGregor 1974; Spear 1969).

The 'new drug problem'

In the early 1980s, drug policy again entered a new phase. A 'new' drug problem began to emerge. At the beginning of the 1980s, the numbers of addicts notified to the Home Office underwent a sharp increase although the numbers had in fact been rising more slowly since the mid 1970s. The 3425 addicts notified in 1975 had risen to over 12,000 by 1984. At the same time the amount of heroin seized by Customs rocketed. The real price of heroin in London is estimated to have fallen by 20 per cent between 1980 and 1983. The number of people involved in drug-related offences also rose steeply. Beneath this worrying surface rise in drug-related indicators there was also a realisation that the numbers of addicts or drug users was in reality far higher than the number notified to the Home Office–a multiplier of between five and ten was suggested. Customs and police between them probably at best seized only a tenth of the drugs coming into the country; a significant black market in drugs had developed. After some years of calm, Britain was clearly in the throes of a 'new drug problem' (Stimson 1987). That problem was dealt with, as this section of the paper will indicate, by changes in policy which nevertheless continued the twin track focus established in the 1920s. British drug policy remained, for all its surface change, a system of medical control operating within a framework of penal national and international policy.

This coincided with the emergence of drugs as a concern for politicians. Crucially however, they became not a political issue, but one of political consensus. From about 1984, the Conservative government took a direct interest in the formation of drug policy. In 1984 an interdepartmental working group of ministers and officials, the Ministerial Group on the Misuse of Drugs, was established, for the first time bringing together the 13 departments, from the Home Office and Department of Health to the Welsh Office and Overseas Development Administration, with an interest in the subject (Home Affairs Committee 1986; Home Office 1986; Social Services Committee 1985). The Group was chaired by a Home Office Minister. There were some signs that drugs might even emerge as an issue for political division between the parties (Owen 1985). But the incipient debate did not develop (Election '87). Some commentators have seen the 1980s as characterised by the politicisation of drug policy (Stimson 1987). But drugs in fact never became a party political issue, an issue for division between the parties. Drug control became an issue particularly associated with the Conservative government. But policy was essentially consensual and the main opposition parties did not significantly differ in their approach. In this, drug policy was a model for later AIDS policy-making, where issues of political difference between the parties were equally blurred.

The public face of Conservative political interest was a policy focused on a strong penal response to drugs, on both domestic and international fronts. In 1985, the government published the first version of its strategy document for drugs, *Tackling Drug Misuse* (Home Office 1986). The strategy had five main aspects, three of which were penal in orientation. The Commons Home Affairs Committee also called for heightened penal action (Home Affairs Committee 1985). Much of this was put into effect. Drug policy assumed new visibility at the level of international control. Increasingly, too, it acquired a European dimension, especially in the criminal justice arena.

Health policy on drugs: a time of change

The decline of a primarily medical response to drugs accompanied these other changes. British drug policy, as established in the 1920s, had a twin-track approach of penal control, symbolised by the lead role in policy taken by the Home Office, and of a medical reaction, underpinned by the departmental interest of the Ministry of Health. Since the 1926 Rolleston Report British drug policy had been based on a medical response to drug addiction, symbolised in that report by its re-affirmation of the disease model of addiction and by a doctor's clinical freedom to provide maintenance doses of opiate drugs as a form of treatment. The Rolleston Committee, although arising out of Home Office concern, was established as a Health Ministry Committee, and serviced by the Ministry, in particular by its doctor-civil servant secretary, E. W. Adams. But the resultant 'British system' of medical control operated as part of a legal system based on penal sanctions and international controls as laid down in the 1912 Hague Convention and the 1919 Versailles settlement (Berridge 1996b). How the balance operated could vary over time.

In the 1980s, that balance did begin to shift towards a penal response. But the 'British system' had in fact been in decline well before the Conservative government introduced its package of penal measures in 1984–86. The shift in the health side of drug policy had begun in the mid-1970s. It was marked by a number of factors: a decline in medical prescribing of opiate drugs and of the clinics as centres for the treatment of drug addiction; a change in the characterisation of drug addiction; and the rise of the voluntary sector and of drug treatment as part of primary health care. Perhaps most important of all, it had seen the consolidation of a new 'policy community' round drugs and the emergence (or re-emergence) of the concept of harm-minimisation as an objective of policy. It is worth looking briefly at all of these developments.

The specialist model for the treatment of drug addiction within the National Health Service as exemplified by the clinic system did not long adhere to the original blueprint. Between 1971 and 1978, the amount of heroin prescribed fell by 40 per cent (Lewis *et al.* 1985). Increasingly injectable and oral methadone were used, following American example; short-term treatment contracts based on withdrawal replaced longer-term prescribing. The clinics were effectively treating only addicts who were highly motivated to come off drugs. The reasons behind this change in treatment policy were complex and focused on clinic doctors' need to provide 'real treatment', rather than simply acting as glorified shopkeepers by handing out injectable heroin. The conflicts between the professional perceptions and needs of doctors working in the clinic system and the non-medical paradigm of junkies who simply wanted an available source of heroin recur in the medical literature of the time. This change in clinic policy was legitimated by research. A controlled trial of oral methadone prescribing versus injectable heroin conducted by researchers at University College Drug Dependence Unit provided the rationale for seeing the change of approach as a scientific issue rather than as one driven by professional needs (Hartnoll *et al.* 1980; for discussion of the impact of this trial on policy, see Berridge and Thom 1996). These developments, together with cuts in funding and resources, ensured that the clinics, by the early 1980s, had become what Mike Ashton called 'a backwater of our social response to drug abuse' (Ashton 1980). Withdrawal from prescribing was a central feature of the medical response. This change of tactic was enshrined in the guidelines of good clinical practice distributed to all doctors in 1984, which emphasised the limited role prescribing had to play (DHSS 1984). The weight of professional opinion against prescribing was demonstrated by the case of Dr Ann Dally, brought before the General Medical Council in 1987 for technical offences involved in prescribing in her private practice.

The 'medical model' of addiction as a disease requiring specialist treatment was disappearing in practice–and in theory as well. The older concept of addiction had given place, in official language at least, in the late 1960s, to the concept of dependence, enshrined in an official World Health Organisation definition. But in the 1980s, this changed to the concept of the problem drug taker, paralleling similar developments in the alcohol field. The change in definitions received official sanction in the 1982 Advisory Council on the Misuse of Drugs Report on Treatment and Rehabilitation (DHSS 1982). The 'normality' of the drug taker, an essential component of the sociology of deviance since the 1960s along with the sociological critique of disease and deviance, thereby received legitimation at an official policy level.

Accompanying this change in definitions was an emphasis on a multi-disciplinary approach, based on regional and district drug problem teams and local drug advisory committees. Although medical personnel would continue to take the lead, the involvement of other agencies, local authority, police and voluntary agencies was actively sought. The voluntary agencies in particular had already been playing a more prominent role in the provision of services since the late 1970s. The Treatment and Rehabilitation report encouraged a partnership between them and the statutory services. In 1983, the Department of Health mounted a Central Funding Initiative for the development of drug services on a national basis. Between 1983 and 1987, 17.5 million pounds was made available for the development of new community based services. Fifty-six per cent of grants were administered through health authorities; 42 per cent through the voluntary sector (MacGregor *et al.* 1991). The aim was to displace the old hospital-based London-focused specialist treatment system. A senior Department of Health civil servant recalled:

> ...Brain had bunged clinics into London...The most important thing was to try and get a few more services up and running... We had to get the voluntary and hospital services working together. We had to say to generalists and generic workers that the problems of drug users are the same as others – get on and deal with this homeless person and forget he's a drug user... (Black 1989)

This approach met resistance from a variety of quarters, from some of the London clinic establishment and from some voluntary agencies, suspicious of incorporation.

But the first half of the 1980s was marked also by the formation of a new 'policy community' around drugs. Richardson and Jordan have used this concept to delineate the way in which the central policy-making machinery is divided into sub-systems in departments (organised round areas such as alcohol or drugs). Close relationships can develop between these sub-systems and outside pressure groups, involving shared policy objectives and priorities (Jordan and Richardson 1987). For drugs, the 1980s saw a shift from a primarily medical policy community to one which was more broadly-based, involving revisionist doctors, the voluntary agencies, researchers, and, most crucially, like-minded civil servants within the Department of Health. The change can be characterised through the changed membership of the Advisory Council on the Misuse of Drugs, the main expert advisory body on drug policy. In the 1980s, it recruited to an originally mainly medical membership, representatives of the voluntary agencies, of health education, social science research, the probation service and of general practice.[2] Developments such as these were actively encouraged by civil servants in the Department of Health. The aim was to encourage a more bottom-up approach, to try and bring the voluntary agencies, drug and ex-drug users into a more active relationship with services.

This new policy community took the conclusions of the Treatment and Rehabilitation report as its bible. There were differences over questions of implementation and practice. But one policy objective, that of the minimisation of harm from drug use, found general support. This was an aim which had long received support from within the voluntary sector of drug services and also from doctors critical of the clinic's non-prescribing policies and their consequent effect on the black market. But it also became an official policy objective in the 1980s. In 1984, the ACMD's report on Prevention abandoned earlier divisions into primary, secondary and tertiary prevention in favour of two basic criteria, one of which was reducing the harm associated with drug misuse (Home Office 1984). But such objectives remained difficult to enunciate publicly in relation to drug use. They certainly lacked political acceptability. There was still a yawning gap between the 'political' and 'policy community' view of drugs. This gap was epitomised in the furore surrounding the government's decision to mount a mass media anti-heroin campaign in 1985–86. This essentially political decision ran counter to received research and internal policy advice which concluded that such campaigns should not be attempted and were potentially counter-productive (Dorn 1986). Here again, drug policy provided a model for later developments over AIDS. The model of a mass media campaign proved uncontroversial once the anti-heroin campaign had preceded it.

---

2   The membership of the ACMD is listed at the front of the reports on Treatment and Rehabilitation and Prevention (1984). Membership of the Working Group on AIDS and Drug Misuse is listed in the two ACMD AIDS reports, AIDS and Drug Misuse, Parts 1 and 2 (London, 1988 and 1989).

To sum up, 1980s drug policy pre AIDS had a dual face – a 'political' penal policy with a high public and mass media profile; and an 'in-house' health policy based on a rhetoric of de-medicalisation and the development of community services and harm-minimisation. Changes in the health aspects of policy were still largely dependent on the power of medical expertise in policy formation. Medicine might, as Jerry Jaffe commented in his 1986 Okey lecture, no longer sit at the top of the table, but the new system could not have moved forward if doctors and doctor civil servants had not wanted it (Jaffe 1987).

The impact of AIDS: the crisis response

What was the impact of AIDS upon an area of policy already in a state of flux? The nature of the problem presented by drug use changed. Late in 1985 reports from Edinburgh revealed a prevalence of HIV antibody seropositivity among injecting drug misusers which was considerably higher than in the rest of the United Kingdom and also higher than in parts of Europe and the United States (Peutherer *et al.* 1985; Robertson *et al.* 1986). The issue of potential heterosexual spread was not new. The blood transfusion question and the spread of the virus among haemophiliacs had in 1983–4, raised the question of the spread of the virus into the general population (Berridge 1996a). This was already part of the emergent AIDS 'policy community's' position. But drugs made the issue of spread into the general population more urgent. A Scottish Committee chaired by Dr D. McClelland, Director of the South East Scotland Regional Blood Transfusion Service, was set up to review the Scottish situation and to report on how to contain the spread of HIV infection and allay public concern. The report of this committee, published in September 1986, foreshadowed many of the more publicised statements of the later ACMD reports (SHHD 1986). It enunciated harm-minimisation as a primary objective. The threat of the spread of HIV into the general population justified a response based on the minimisation of harm from drug use and on attracting drug users into contact with services.

> There is…a serious risk that infected drug misusers will spread HIV beyond the presently recognised high risk groups and into the sexually active general population. Very extensive spread by heterosexual contacts has already occurred in a number of African countries… There is…an urgent need to contain the spread of HIV infection among drug misusers not only to limit the

harm caused to drug misusers themselves but also to protect the health of the general public. The gravity of the problem is such that on balance the containment of the spread of the virus is a higher priority in management than the prevention of drug misuse... (SHHD 1986,p.5)

Substitute prescribing and the provision of sterile injecting equipment to addicts were two major means by which these ends were to be achieved.

Members of the new policy community began to voice these objectives more openly. Reports of Dutch harm-reduction strategies and needle exchange projects became more frequent. These objectives were, as before AIDS, shared by civil servants in the Department of Health. 'We're going to get harm minimisation much more quickly,' commented one senior non-medical civil servant (to the author) in the autumn of 1986. Another saw it as the opportunity

> to go out and push out a bit further. Almost fortuitously the fact we'd already shifted our policy...was...a fertile seed bed from which we've been able to develop...We'd be weeping in our tea now...The pre-existing development of community servics enabled us to get harm-minimisation approaches off the ground more rapidly than if we'd been rooted in the old hospital based approach to drug misuse. (Black 1989)

The urgency of the situation enabled what had been a stumbling block to the unspoken objectives of drug policy pre-AIDS–political and media opposition to any suspicion of 'softness' on drugs–to be quietly overcome. Research was an important legitimating factor. In December 1986, Norman Fowler, Secretary of State for Social Services, announced the intention to set up a number of pilot needle-exchange schemes (building on some already in operation, in Liverpool and Swindon, for example). Assessment of effectiveness in preventing the spread of the virus was an important consideration. There were doubts in the Cabinet Committee on AIDS (set up in October 1986) about the provision of syringes; and early in 1987 a project to monitor and evaluate the pilot schemes was established at Goldsmith's College. In May 1987, the ACMD set up its own working group on AIDS and drug misuse, chaired by Ruth Runciman, a non-medical member of the Council. Of the working group's 13 members, six were non-medical. Part of the ACMD's report, ready in the Autumn of 1987, was not published by the government until March 1988, causing disquiet among some members of the working party. The Report, like the McClelland committee before it, declared the danger of the heterosexual spread of the virus to be a greater menace than the danger of drug use itself. It called for a range of harm-minimisation strategies, most notably needle-exchange and over-the-counter sales of syringes by pharmacists. Prescribing, too, was seen as an option to attract drug users into services (DHSS 1988). But the initial political reaction was lukewarm.

Although the goal of harm-reduction was accepted by Tony Newton, Minister of Health, in his statement to the Commons on 29 March 1988, only one million pounds was provided for the development of services, and the further results of evaluation were awaited. The response from Michael Forsyth, Scottish Health Minister, saw central funding of the two pilot schemes still in operation at an end–and a generally negative response to the particular criticisms of the Scottish situation in the ACMD Report. It seemed as though policy would founder on the rocks of political opposition. The summer of 1988 saw intense pressure from civil servants for a more positive response from ministers which brought a turnaround in the autumn, aided by research results from the Goldsmith's group which showed that users did change to lower-risk behaviours (although a disappointingly small proportion of attenders stayed on to achieve them). David Mellor, the new Health Minister, announced an extra three million pounds for the provision of services in England. The money was specifically to enable services to expand and dev lop in such a way as to make contact with more drug misusers in order to offer help and advice on reducing the risk of HIV infection. Only three hundred thousand pounds was allocated to Scottish services, despite the disparity in numbers of HIV positive drug users there in comparison with England. Further money followed for 1989/90 with an extra five million pounds available for the development of drug services. Coming on top of pre-existing AIDS allocations, the extra funding since 1986 gave health authorities at least 17 million to spend on drug services; money was being provided, too, on a recurrent basis. In Scotland the 1989/90 figure of 2.1 million pounds for drug services was less significant than the doubling of the general AIDS allocation to 12 million pounds. For some English projects funded by the earlier CFI, the money came just in time.

What, then had AIDS initially meant for drug policy? At the level of policy formulation it clearly, on the wartime model, meant the public establishment of the previous largely unspoken aims of policy. A senior medical officer commented,

'AIDS may be the trigger that brings care for drug users into the mainstream for the first time over...The drug world can come "in from the cold" through AIDS...it's a golden opportunity to get it right for the first time' (Black 1989). Drugs, so it was argued, had become a problem of public health rather than a question of individual pathology. Declaring prescribing to be a legitimate option appeared to deal with the prescribing question which had bedeviled drug policy in the 1970s and 1980s. The new 1980s policy community around drugs was strengthened by the support of some key politicians. References to normalisation and attracting drug users to services began to appear in Hansard as well as the pages of the in-house drug journals (Butler 1989). For some members of the policy community AIDS opened up the wider agenda of the liberalisation of drug policy (Wolf 1989).

A new departure for drug policy?

Policy in the UK is clearly in a state of flux and any historian would be unwise to attempt to lay down definitive statements about either present or future directions. The rest of this paper will simply raise a number of questions about the 'new drug policy' in the light of an historical perspective. It will argue that in general the changes, although real enough, exemplify and expand on long-standing themes and tensions within British drug policy. It will look specifically at four areas; at questions of the implementation of policy and whether this represents de- or re-medicalisation; at the 'newness' of the 'new public health approach' to drugs; at tensions between penal and medical approaches; and finally, at the long-term history of harm-minimisation as a policy objective.

The implementation of policy: demedicalisation or remedicalisation?

The nature of the implementation of policy is important for the rhetoric of policy and its practice can differ significantly. Undoubtedly local 'policy traditions' have been important as, for example, in Scotland, where psychiatrists had traditionally had little to do with drug users and where infectious disease specialists and GPs initially took on the increased medical involvement in drug use which resulted from the spread of HIV. AIDS, while nominally 'normalising' drug use, in some respects brought a revival of medical involvement both in practical terms and in conceptualisation of the issue. It brought doctors back more centrally into drugs through the emphasis on prescribing as an option and the focus on the role of the general practitioner. There was also a new emphasis on the general health of drug users. Clinic doctors began to be interested in hepatitis B and the general health of drug users, whereas previously these had hardly figured as part of clinic work. Such views were echoed at an official level. The need, underlined by the McClelland and the two ACMD Reports, of contacting drug users not normally in contact with services served to elevate the notion of treatment which initially resumed its place as an unchallengeable good. In another respect, too, AIDS served to revive earlier 'medical' arguments and themes in drug policy. The arguments for prescribing methadone as a 'bait' to attract people into services and hence away from syringe-sharing practices reproduced arguments in favour of the medical approach originally advanced in the 1960s and 1970s. Then, too, prescribing was an option which, so it was considered, would attract addicts to services and undercut the black market. The 'competitive prescribing' argument, criticised at the time, has revived via AIDS.

The role of the voluntary sector in drug services and its relationship to medical practice were also affected. The voluntary sector, in drug services as in AIDS more generally, was drawing closer to the statutory sector, and was often funded by it. The 'contract culture' brought about by NHS funding changes made this tendency clearer. Even within the voluntary sector, drug use, because of HIV, had become associated with illness. 'They champion the drug users' rights to treatment and to use drugs if they want because they have an illness and need a script...The voluntary sector ends up holding a disease model..' (Unpublished interview, drug consultant, January 1989). Increasingly, voluntary (non-medical) and statutory (medical) services were being brought into a closer relationship and the differences between them blurred. This was a process which pre-dated AIDS and owed much to more general trends in health policy.

Whether this can be seen as de- or re-medicalisation largely depends on individual perspective. But so far as the power relationships in policy-making went, the situation exemplified the long-standing policy influence of the medical profession. Without the support of influential and centrally placed doctors, the 'new departures' in policy could not have been sustained. Drug policy-making after, as before AIDS, has exemplified the influence of doctor civil servants as important in policy-making, a tradition going back to Dr E.W. Adams, a Ministry of Health civil servant and secretary of the Rolleston Committee in 1924–26 (Berridge 1984, 1996b; MacLeod 1967). The role of Dr Dorothy Black, senior medical civil servant in the Department of Health, was an important one. Social science expertise was brought into a policy advisory role; but medical expertise in defining policy, as for example through the role of the medical expert adviser to the Department of Health, remained central. To sum up, then, the 'non-medical' rhetoric of policy post AIDS disguised some clear tendencies towards sustained or even increased medical input in terms of treatment and services and revived some old medical-focused arguments of the 1960s. The nature of the symbiosis between medical and non-medical at the practical level is unclear and varied locally. Quite who was incorporating whom depends on perspective. At a national policy level, however, the centrality of medical influence remained.

The 'new public health' approach?

One aspect of this symbiotic inter-relationship between medical and non-medical has been the incorporation of drug use into a public health model of response. Two issues are central here; first, that a 'public health' response to drug use is nothing new. Historically, such responses have often been triggered in times of perceived crisis. And second, definitions of public health are themselves historically specific; the image of nineteenth-century environmentalist public health which this language conveys is far from the individual-focused public health of the 1980s and 1990s. To take crisis and the public health response first—one observer commented in 1988 on the parallels between the Advisory Councils Part 1 report on AIDS and Drug Misuse and the Brain Committee's report on drug addiction in 1965 (Druglink 1988). Like the ACMD, Brain also justified change in drug policy on public health grounds—addiction was a 'socially infectious condition', a disease which 'if allowed to spread unchecked, will become a menace to the community'. The remedies suggested by Brain—including notification and compulsory treatment—were classic public health responses. The balance required in drug policy in the 1980s between minimising the harm from drug use but not thereby promoting drug use is paralleled by Brain's attempt to graft the public health objective of preventing infection onto a system geared to individual treatment. There have always been tensions in drug policy, not simply between penal and medical forms of control, but between different forms of medical input either focused on the community or on the individual. In the nineteenth century, a 'public health' focus on opium adulteration, on child-doping or working-class-industrial opiate use was stimulated by the urban crisis of industrialisation. This gave place to individually focused medical theories of addiction and disease. Roy MacLeod has pointed to the focus on individual pathology rather than an environmentalist approach in late-nineteenth-century discussions of inebriety (MacLeod 1967). Likewise Brain's public health focus in 1965 was modified in practice to a focus on active medical treatment. There has always been an implicit tension between preventive and curative approaches, in this as in other areas of health policy.

The 'public health' paradigm itself, too, is worth closer examination–for 'public health' has not been an unchanging absolute. Its definition and remit has changed in the twentieth century, as the nature of state intervention in social issues has itself shifted (Lewis 1986). The environmentalist public health of the mid-nineteenth century narrowed under the impact of the bacteriological revolution. Social hygiene with its emphasis on individual responsibility for health was the reformulated public health of the 1900s; the 1970s and 1980s public health has, in its emphasis on individual lifestyle and on prevention, revived these earlier social hygienist concerns. Drug policy, both pre and post AIDS, with its emphasis on health education, on the role of the voluntary sector, on the drug user as a 'normal' individual responsible for his or her own actions and health, has epitomised some key elements of the redefinition. Certainly the 'public health paradigm' of post-AIDS policy is nothing new. As with past 'public health' responses the potential for a shift to an individualistic medical response is present. The conceptual distance is, on current definitions, not a large one.

Tensions between penal and medical approaches in policy

It is a commonplace to analyse drug policy in terms of competing penal and medical forms of control. Here AIDS has brought change–but the continuities with historical themes are also strong. Most obviously the twin-track nature of British drug policy remains in existence post AIDS. Penal policy still remains, albeit modified at the local level. Britain still adheres to a system of international control of drugs and there has been little modification of this at the international or European levels. In 1989, one senior Conservative politician succinctly summed up his view of drug control as 'increased controlled availability at home and stronger prohibition round the edges' (Senior Conservative politician. Comment at private meeting, 1989). How far the 'normalisation' of the drug user has penetrated beyond specialist drug and political circles is also debatable. At the local level in Britain there have been changes in the balance between penal and medical with police co-operation in the establishment of needle exchanges, policy participation in local drug advisory committees and links between police and services. The prisons issue has in particular symbolised the shifting balance between penal and medical. At one level, British prison policy has not changed to accommodate the demands for syringe and condom provision to prison populations enshrined in a 1986 WHO document. But the balance between penal and medical is changing. The potential impact of HIV among overcrowded prison populations has been one impetus among many behind the government's *Crime, Justice and Protecting the Public* White Paper (1990) which introduces the option of diversion of drug users into treatment rather than imprisonment. An historically minded observer could point to a long tradition of compulsory treatment in the drug and alcohol area with its roots in the inebriates legislation of the late nineteenth century. As Timothy Harding has commented, HIV 'has emphasised the health aspects of the penal response' (Harding 1990). As with the medical/non-medical alliance, the balance of power within the relationship is currently unclear.

The history of harm minimisation

This chapter has suggested that, despite the apparent revolution in the public rhetoric of drug policy achieved by AIDS, many aspects of post-AIDS policy were already inherent in drug policy in the 1980s. Harm minimisation is one obvious example which has already been discussed. But harm minimisation itself also has its history before the 1980s. It is only a re-statement in different circumstances of the principles enumerated in the Rolleston Report of 1926:

> When, therefore, every effort possible in the circumstances has been made, and made unsuccessfully, to bring the patient to a condition in which he is independent of the drug, it may...become justifiable in certain cases to order regularly the minimum dose which has been found necessary, either in order to avoid serious withdrawal symptoms, or to keep the patient in a condition in which he can lead a useful life. (Rolleston Report 1926)

Harm minimisation, although not categorised in those terms, received a clear expression in the 1920s; and it has been the basis of the British approach to drug control for much of the twentieth century. If one looks back even further, in the nineteenth century one focus of the professional self-regulation approach (apart from the establishment of professional status) was also the minimisation of harm to the customer (Berridge and Edwards 1987). The focus throughout was the reduction of harm to the individual user.

The long-term impact of policy change

The question of the long-term impact of policy change should also be considered. How long will the revived 'public health paradigm' persist? It would be an unwise historian or policy scientist who attempted to predict what the long-term balance of policy might be. The analogy of war and policy-change with which this article began does offer some suggestive indications. The 'public health' response to alcohol in World War I with state control of the alcohol industry and limited pub opening hours only partially survived the war (Rose 1973). The 'hard-line' emergency response to drugs at the same period was moderated in the 1920s (Berridge 1996b). War does lead to change—but long-standing themes and tendencies also express and reassert themselves. As this article has argued, the overall balance of power within policy is too complex and historically specific to be adequately subsumed under rhetorical barriers such as the 'public health' approach or the 'normalisation' of drug policy. Indeed the overall impression is of some long-standing tendencies—the role of medicine, the penal approach, even the revival of the nineteenth century role of the pharmacist—which have not been undermined and may even have been enhanced by the impact of AIDS. Whatever the future of drug policy in its post AIDS years, it will not escape from its history.

Postscript 1996: a post-war situation?

Writing from the vantage point of 1996, the suggestions in the earlier paper of a 'post-war' situation and the continuing renegotiation of the balance between penal/public health and medical approaches seem justified. What has happened in the interim? Tensions between the Home Office and the Department of Health over the creation of a national drugs office, a strategy advocated by the former, led to the creation of a Central Drugs Coordination Unit under the office of the Lord

President of the Council. Here was an interesting historic reversion to the departmental location of drug policy during its original period of pharmaceutical regulation in the late nineteenth century. Tony Newton, as Lord President, has chaired the Ministerial committee on drugs.

Two policy documents deserve attention: the government's White Paper *Tackling Drugs Together* of May 1995 and the earlier Scottish document, *Drugs in Scotland: Meeting the Challenge*, of 1994 (Scottish Office Ministerial Drugs Task Force 1994). For Scotland, AIDS among drug users was still a policy and practical reality and the Scottish document continued the focus on harm minimisation, with concern for the welfare of the individual drug user; explicit endorsement of safe drug use for young people; and a focus on harm reduction in prisons. Scotland, initially suspicious of harm minimisation in the 1980s, appeared to have embraced it more enthusiastically in the 1990s because of the continuing impact of AIDS among drug users.

In England, however, AIDS and drug use was no longer perceived as a crisis. The English policy document expanded the 'general population' focus of the earlier policy reports of the 1980s and refined it in different ways. The emphasis was on 'community safety' from drug use, with co-ordinated action at the local level through multi-agency and disciplinary Drug Action Teams and Drug Reference Groups. This prevention/public health paradigm animated much of the document, with its revival of drug education in schools as part of the focus on young people and prevention. The emphasis was on the protection of the public at large and the prevention of initiation, rather than the welfare of the individual drug user. Harm minimisation was more clearly the minimisation of harm to the community, rather than to the individual user. This again built on changes in emphasis within policy which had a long history.

The tensions and negotiations with penal and more directly medical approaches continued. The overall control framework at international and European levels of course still impacted on policy. Recent changes in Dutch drug policy resulted from that country's adherence to the Europe-based Schengen Treaty. At the national and local level, the tensions were exemplified in prison policy, where the White Paper legitimised drug testing in prison alongside the 'reform' of the Prison Medical Service and attempts to provide drug treatment in prisons. The tension between treatment and control continued. Arrest referral continued to recall the long history of compulsion in treatment; and the Home Secretary's call for mandatory minimum sentences for some drug offences re-emphasised the continuance of the penal tradition. Treatment itself survived the iconoclastic attempts of Brian Maw-hinney, as Minister of Health, to call its efficacy into question. The report of the Treatment Effectiveness Review, published in May 1996, quietly undermined that politician's position (Department of Health 1996). Widely seen as part of the medical 'old guard' defending its position on drug policy, the report was neverthe-less greeted with a 'sigh of relief' by the drug 'policy community'. It was in no one's interests to argue that treatment was ineffective (Comments from drug researcher to author, October 1996).

The backdrop to all this continued to be wider changes in government health policy, in particular the introduction of community care and its funding impact on the residential drug treatment sector, which one commentator saw as being 'fina-ncially squeezed to death' (Comment from drug researcher, November 1996). Lit-tle research was carried out to see how balances were operating at the local level. This might, according to one observer, identify 'too many problems and not enough solutions.' The situation in the mid-1990s was indeed the post-war one which the history of drug policy foretold. The moment of crisis had passed and the renegotiation of balances between penal/medical and penal/public health ap-proaches continued its long history.

References

Ashton, M. (1980) 'Controlling addiction: the role of the clinics.' *Druglink 13*, 1–6.

Berridge, V. (1978) 'War conditions and narcotics control: the passing of Defence of the Reealm Act 40B.' *Journal of Social Policy I*, 285–304.

Berridge, V. (1984) 'Drugs and social policy: the establishment of drug control in Britain, 1900–1930.' *British Journal of Addiction 79*, 17–29.

Berridge, V. (1996a) *AIDS in the UK: The Making of Policy, 1981–1984*. Oxford: Oxford University Press.

Berridge, V. (1996b) 'Stamping out addiction: the work of the Rolleston Committee 1924–1926.' In H. Freeman and German E. Berrios (eds) *150 Years of British Psychiatry. Volume II: The Aftermath*. London.

Berridge, V. and Edwards, G. (1987) *Opium and the People: Opiate Use in Nineteenth Century England*. London.

Berridge, V. and Thom, B. (1996) 'Research and policy; what determines the relationship?' *Policy Studies 17*, 1, 23–24.

Black, D. (1989) Hatfield Polytechnic conference, June 1989.

Butler, C. (1989) Speech in House of Commons Debate on Drug Abuse. *Hansard,* 9 June, cols. 470–74.

Department of Health (1996) *Report of an Independent Review of Drug Treatment Services in England.* London: HMSO.

Department of Health (1989) *AIDS and Drug Misuse, Part 2. Report by the Advisory Council on the Misuse of Drugs.* London: HMSO

DHSS (1982) *Treatment and Rehabilitation. Report of the Advisory Council on the Misuse of Drugs.* London: HMSO.

DHSS (1984) *Guidelines of Good Clinical Practice in the Treatment of Drug Misuse. Report of the Medical Working Group on Drug Dependence.* London: HMSO.

DHSS (1988) *AIDS and Drug Misuse Part 1.* London: HMSO.

Dorn, N. (1986) 'Media campaigns.' *Druglink 1*, 2, 8–9.

Druglink (1988) 'HIV top priority, says official report.' *Druglink 3*, 3,6.

Edwards, G. (1978) 'Some years on: evolutions in the "British System".' In D.H. West (ed) *Problems of Drug Abuse in Britain.* Cambridge.

Election '87 (1987) 'What the parties said about drugs.' *Druglink 2*, 5, 7.

Fox, D.M. (1986) 'The National Health Service and the Second World War: the elaboration of Consensus.' In H.L. Smith (ed) *War and Social Change. British Society in the Second World War.* Manchester.

Fox, D.M., Day, P. and Klein, R. (1989) 'The power of professionalism: AIDS in Britain, Sweden and the United States.' *Daedalus 118*, 93–112.

Harding, T. (1990) 'HIV infection and AIDS in the Prison Environment: a test case for the respect of human rights.' In J. Strang and G. Stimson (eds) *AIDS and Drug Misuse. The Challenge for Policy and Practice in the 1990s.* London.

Hartnoll, R.L., Mitcheson, M.C., Battersby, A., Brown, G., Ellis, M., Fleming, P. and Hedley, N. (1980) 'Evaluation of heroin maintenance in controlled trial.' *Archives of General Psychiatry 37*, 877.

Home Affairs Committee (1985) *Interim Report. Misuse of Hard Drugs.* London.

Home Affairs Committee (1986) *First Report from the Home Affairs Committee, Session 1985–86: Misuse of Hard Drugs.* London.

Home Office (1984) *Prevention. Report of the Advisory Council on the Misuse of Drugs.* London.

Home Office (1986) *Tackling Drug Misuse: A Summary of the Government's Strategy.* London.

Jaffe, J. (1987) 'Footnotes in the Evolution of the American National Response: some little known aspects of the first American Strategy for Drug Abuse and Drug Traffic

Prevention. The inaugural Thomas Okey Memorial Lecture. *British Journal of Addiction, 82(6)*, 587–99.

Jordan, A.G. and Richardson, J.J. (1987) *British Politics and the Policy Process.* London.

Lewis, J. (1986) *What Price Community Medicine? The Philosophy, Practice and Politics of Public Health Since 1919.* Brighton: Wheatsheaf.

Lewis, R., Hartnoll, R., Bryer, S., Daviaud, E. and Mitcheson, M. (1985) 'Scoring Smack: the illicit heroin market in London, 1980–83.' *British Journal of Addiction 80,* 281–290.

MacGregor, S. (1974) 'Choices for policy and practice.' In P. Bean (ed) *The Social Control of Drugs.* London.

MacGregor, S. (1989) 'Choices for policy and practice.' In S. MacGregor (ed) *Drugs and British Society. Responses to a Social Problem in the 1980s.* London.

MacGregor, S., Ettore, B., Coomber, R. and Crosier, A. (1991) *The Impact on Drug Services in England of the Central Funding Initiative.* London.

MacLeod, R.M. (1967) 'The edge of hope: social policy and chronic alcoholism, 1970–1900.' *Journal of the History of Medicine and Allied Sciences 22,* 215–45.

Owen, D. (1985) 'Need for a scientific strategy to curb the epidemic of drug abuse in the United Kingdom.' *Lancet,* 26 October, 958.

Peutherer, J.F., Edmonds, E., Simmonds, P. Dickson, J.D. *et al.* (1985) 'HTLV-III antibody in Edinburgh drug addicts.' *Lancet 2,* 1129.

Robertson, J.R., Bucknall, A.B.V., Welsby, P.D. *et al.* (1986) 'Epidemic of AIDS related virus (HTLV-III/LAV) infection among intravenous drug abusers.' *British Medical Journal 292,* 527.

Rolleston Report (1926) *Report of the Departmental Committee on Morphine and Heroin Addiction.* London.

Rose, M. (1973) 'The success of social reform? The Central Control Board (Liquor Traffic) 1915–21.' In M.R.D. Foot (ed) *War and Society.* London: Joseph Elek.

Scottish Office Ministerial Drugs Task Force (1994) *Drugs in Scotland: Meeting the Challenge.* Edinburgh: Scottish Home and Health Department.

SHHD (1986) *HIV Infection in Scotland. Report of the Scottish Committee on HIV Infection and Intravenous Drug Misuse.* Edinburgh: Scottish Home and Health Department.

Social Services Committee (1985) *Fourth Report of the Social Services Committee: Misuse of Drugs with Special Reference to the Treatment and Rehabilitation of Misusers of Hard Drugs.* London.

Spear, H.B. (1969) 'The growth of heroin addiction in the United Kingdom.' *British Journal of Addiction 64,* 245–255.

Stimson, G. (1978) 'The war on heroin: British policy and the international trade in illicit drugs.' In N. Dorn and N. South (eds) *A Land Fit for Heroin? Drug Policies, Prevention and Practice.* London: MacMillan.

Stimson, G. (1987) 'British drug policies in the 1980s: a preliminary analysis and suggestions for research.' *British Journal of Addiction 82,* 477–488.

Stimson, G. (1990) 'AIDS and HIV: the challenge for British drug services.' *British Journal of Addiction 85,* 329–339.

Webster, C. (1988) *The Health Services since the War. Volume 1. Problems of Health Care. The National Health Service before 1957.* London.

Webster, C. (1990) 'Conflict and consensus: Explaining the British Health Service.' *Twentieth Century British History 1,* 2, 115–151.

Wolf, M. (1989) 'Thinking about drug legalisation.' *Financial Times,* September 4.

CHAPTER 6

Deviant or Just Different?
Dutch Alcohol and Drug Policy

Inge Spruit

Introduction

A small country littered with coffee shops, where drug users in clogs aimlessly wander, a paradise for junkies all over the world – or an example of reprobation to the righteous? Dutch drug policy is subjected to a lot of international attention and political discussion and it is not always easy to discriminate between myths and facts. More attention is focused on the Netherland's drugs policy than its alcohol policy, although, like many other countries, alcohol problems are more prevalent.

The Netherlands is one of the most densely populated and urbanised countries in the world. The population of 15.5 million occupies an area of 41,526 square kilometers. Such population density puts pressure on the balance between individual freedom and social control. The Netherlands has an extensive social security system and everyone has access to health care and education.

The increase in research activity on the prevalence of alcohol and drugs has resulted in many facts and well-founded estimates. Twenty per cent of the population aged over 15 years do not drink alcohol. The per capita consumption in 1995 was 8.0 litres (Zwart and Mensink 1996) and comparison with other European Union countries shows the Netherlands in eleventh place behind (in order of consumption) Luxembourg, France, Portugal, Germany, Denmark, Spain, Belgium, Greece, Ireland and Italy, with only Great Britain having a smaller consumption per capita. Heroin use is the major illegal drug problem, affecting 25,000–27,000 'addicts', a figure approximately in line with France, Western Germany and Sweden (EMCDDA 1996). The number of cannabis users is crudely estimated to be

675,000 ranging from rare to regular users but only 0.2–0.5 per cent of those users become problem drug users in need of assistance (Spruit and Zwart 1997).

The main aim of the Dutch alcohol and drugs policy is to minimise the risks involved in the use of these substances to the users, to their social environment and to society as a whole (Ministry of Health, Welfare and Sport 1997). Protection of society includes issues such as public order and demand and supply reduction for illegal drugs. Individual health protection, harm reduction and improvement in the social environment of drug users are important aspects of policy.

Preliminary overview: a well-organised network of prevention and care
Prevention

Prevention plays an important role in Dutch alcohol and drug policies. Prevention activities are not aimed solely at preventing use, but also at preventing problems prior to use or as a consequence of use. The government oversees the development, implementation and evaluation of prevention, information and education. The implementation is largely in the hands of intermediary organisations in the fields of education, recreation addiction, youth work and social work and organisations working with ethnic minority groups (Spruit and Laar 1996).

The Dutch government sets a high value upon primary prevention within schools, the main aim being to steer the inevitable adolescent experimental behaviour in the right direction by means of credible information and facts and avoiding exaggeration of the risks. Alcohol and drug use have been stripped of their taboos and sensational images that previously acted as an attraction. In addition to offering factual information, national school prevention programmes also promote behaviourial skills such as teaching young people to deal with peer pressure and improving independent decision-making.

In relation to alcohol, the emphasis is on primary prevention. The aim is to prevent damage to health and society by promoting moderate drinking in general and total abstinence in high-risk situations. Mass-media campaigns, like the Alcohol Education Plan with a budget of 3 million guilders in 1995, were under the direct supervision of the government for nearly 10 years before being placed within a professional organisation in 1996. Since mass-media campaigns are not considered to be sufficiently effective alone, the Alcohol Education Plan is supported by small-scale information and education schemes at the local level, for instance in schools and youth centres.

For a long time there was reluctance to embark on large-scale anti-drugs campaigns, in order to avoid blowing the problem out of proportion and achieving the opposite effect. This approach was reviewed, very probably under pressure of the growing international and national interest in the results of Dutch addiction policy, following the express request from politicians to boost information in the field of drugs. The autumn of 1996 saw the launch of a mass-media campaign about cannabis which is due to be followed in the spring of 1997 by a campaign related to Ecstasy. In order to avoid the well-known (but not well-recognised!) adverse effects of 'just say no'-like campaigns, the main aim of these campaigns is to encourage people (especially parents) to base judgements on accurate information.

Secondary prevention, or harm reduction, takes place via the health care sector and social care sector and is aimed at preventing further deterioration in health. Alcohol-related information is aimed primarily at those who work in the health care sector. This includes doctors, social workers and nursing staff. The key issue in this context is to increase expertise in recognising problems and detecting problem drinking at an early stage.

The Facilities for Addiction Care have a role in prevention and play a key role in the promotion and implementation of drug prevention activities at local and regional levels. In some municipalities, the Municipal Health Service also plays a major role. Umbrella organisations, such as the Trimbos Institute and the Netherlands Association of Facilities for Addiction Care (NeVIV) are contracted by the government for the development of preventive methods and the co-ordination of local and regional efforts. There are also a number of spontaneous prevention activities with examples ranging from the prevention of developmental problems in the children of drug addicts to local initiatives from police or local authorities to prevent crime and neighbourhood decay.

Care

Dutch health policy encourages a variety of care, attuned to a wide range of need. The 1995 budget for 'addiction care' was more than 300 million guilders (100 million pounds sterling), about half of which went to inpatient and half to outpatient care. In 1995 there were 12 clinics for inpatient treatment of addiction with

961 beds and nearly 7000 registered patients. In addition eight general psychiatric hospitals made 3163 admissions to inpatient addiction care (Zwart and Mensink 1995). Addiction-related diseases, such as alcoholic liver cirrhosis or AIDS, are treated in general hospitals.

Outpatient care is provided by 16 government-funded Consultancies for Alcohol and Drugs, with a total of 130 branches across the country (Laar, Zwart and Mensink 1996). Their main tasks are prevention and assistance, including rehabilitation. Most of the larger facilities are part of an Addiction Care Centre with clinical and social shelter facilities. There are also 15 establishments for social care. Specialist projects (for example for homeless addicts, women, ethnic minorities, petty or first offenders, job-seekers, patients with Korsakov's syndrome due to excessive alcohol use) are geared to particular target groups. Detox and a subsequently drug-free existence are important, but not the only aim of care and assistance. There are also programmes for addicts who are unable to 'kick the habit' and may become otherwise isolated and deteriorate further, both physically and psychologically. In such cases care is aimed primarily at limiting damage to health and improving living conditions. Such harm-reduction activities include methadone programmes, distribution of clean needles, food and shelter, often in outreach and easy access programmes.

A new aim of care is that it is integrated and devotes attention to the overall living conditions of the clients: health, housing, finances, social skills, legal advice, work and education. This requires co-operation both between the various agencies in the addiction care sector and with agencies in other sectors such as general health care and the police and judicial authorities.

In 1995 the various outpatient facilities had 47,617 clients, of whom roughly half were alcohol clients and half drug clients. Of the drug clients presenting at outpatient facilities, 81 per cent presented with a heroin problem, 16 per cent with a cocaine problem, 11 per cent with a cannabis problem, 0.03 per cent with an amphetamine problem and 0.01 per cent with an Ecstasy (MDMA, MDEA, MDA or other substances of which pills sold as Ecstasy may consist) problem.

Finally there is also provision from non-statutory care organisations, for example from religious organisations or churches such as the Salvation Army. These voluntary organisations are often aimed at the homeless or special target groups (e.g., prostitutes, or isolated AIDS patients without a 'buddy'). They are not included in the government budget, but several of them are consultative partners at the local government level, although not to the same extent as statutory organisations.

Major policy principles

The Dutch government acts on the principle that effective strategies to combat (ab)use require a combination of voluntary restraint on the part of the users themselves and restrictions imposed by the authorities in the form of legislation and regulations. The strategy to reach this goal consists of three policy tools, with the interrelation of these being of particular importance. Education and prevention actions influence the demand side of the market at the community level, while the prevention work by health care and social services personnel tackle problems at the individual level. In addition, there are rules for the distribution of beer, wine and liquor to protect public order and to prevent alcohol abuse and crime. Although a great deal of attention is devoted to the Dutch government's relatively lenient attitude to drugs compared with other countries, the supply of drugs is in fact much more stringently regulated, both legally and in practice. Supplying drugs is completely banned (Opium Act), while supplying alcohol is regulated by various laws. Cohesion within the policy as a whole is also important, with safety and public order goals coinciding with credible and accessible care and prevention (Stam, Spruit and Laar 1997). Whether such a policy would always work, or whether it takes the Dutch to make it work within their society, is a question beyond the scope of this chapter. However, the majority of the professionals do agree with the principle of the policy whilst they may criticise it on detail.

Alcohol

Legislation and regulation

The Alcohol and Catering Act stipulates that running a bar, restaurant, café or club and selling alcohol requires a licence from the city council. It is forbidden to sell spirits to persons under 18 years of age and beer and wine to those under 16 years of age. In 1996 the government proposed to make this 18 years for all sales. Supermarkets are allowed to sell drinks with an alcohol content of under 20 per cent. Public drunkenness is banned under articles in the Dutch penal code, together with disturbing the peace and threatening personal, road and shipping safety under the influence of alcohol. The Road Safety Act prohibits a person driving a car, motorbike, moped or bicycle with an alcohol blood count of more than 0.5. For shipping the upper limit is 0.8. It is also forbidden to sell intoxicating drinks to people who are already drunk. Although not banned, advertising is subject to restrictions, but nevertheless advertising expenditure has increased enormously over the last five years (Spruit and Zwart 1997).

Policy

The Dutch alcohol policy since the 1985 Government Paper 'Alcohol and Society' is characterised by efforts to *moderate* alcohol use (Ministerie van WVC 1985). The government followed current scientific opinion and expected that a reduction in total alcohol consumption would result in a fall in the number of excessive drinkers, as well as reducing the negative social effects of problem drinking. Following the recommendations of the World Health Organisation, the 'Note 2000' aimed to reduce alcohol consumption levels to 25 per cent below the 1985 consumption by the year 2000 (Ministerie van WVC 1986). Achievement of this goal is improbable. Like so many countries, alcohol use in the Netherlands increased steeply during the 1960s and 1970s and started to decrease in the early 1980s. However, WHO concluded in 1993 that in 10 of the 26 European member states alcohol use had increased again by the end of the 1980s (WHO 1993). In the Netherlands alcohol use has decreased by 14 per cent since 1980 and is still decreasing, but very slowly. In 1993 WHO made a new European Action Plan, which did not attract as much attention as the 1986 plan. However, the Dutch alcohol policy was and still is in line with this plan: an important premise being the interaction between laws and regulations on the one hand and prevention on the other. For example, early detection is an important aspect among preventive strategy, health education is well developed following recent scientific research, self-regulatory activities of the alcohol industry are successfully implemented and there are restrictions in the field of advertising. The alcohol industry assists the development of corporate programmes on alcohol at work, aimed at early recognition and a safe climate to discuss alcohol problems (STIVA 1996). However, there is scope in the Netherlands for further implementation of WHO policy suggestions on the legal regulation of alcohol consumption, for example concerning violence, injuries and criminal damage.

Recent developments

The policy on all addictions is the primary responsibility of the Minister for Health. Since the 1987 paper on *Alcohol and Society* (Ministerie van WVC 1985) the government intended to revise the Alcohol and Catering Act, especially since regulations regarding distribution were considered to be outdated: alcohol sales, for example, cannot be banned in canteens of sport clubs. Prevention of crime and protection of the public order were important aspects of the new law of 1993 (Ministerie van WVC 1993).

The Netherlands have a relatively low rate of offences related to violence. However, the government noted that 40 per cent of those offences are alcohol-related (Ministerie van WVC 1995). Yet no measures have been taken to tackle this, contrasting sharply with the pace with which measures have developed regarding illegal drugs.

In 1996 regulations concerning permits to distribute alcohol were tightened, and there were some new measures, like further limiting alcohol distribution and improving road and shipping safety. However, the new alcohol law is yet to be implemented and consequently development of more institutional changes is hampered. There has been some uncertainty about European developments, such as the harmonisation of taxes, as well as conflicting economic and public health interests. It is possible that the attention paid to drug policy has resulted in a consequent neglect of alcohol policy.

In the context of penal law, the outpatient Facilities for Addiction Care have developed a project on Alcohol-related Offences and also provide 'Alcohol Traffic Courses' for convicted drunk-drivers. A new prevention impetus was introduced in June 1996, called The Educational Measure on Alcohol (Spruit and Laar 1996). This is a more intensive form of the Alcohol Traffic Course for people who are ordered by the Central Bureau of Driving Proficiency to take the course to ensure that they are still fit to drive.

Illegal drugs

Legislation and regulations

The possession, trade, sale, transport, production, import and export of all drugs listed in the Opium Act is punishable by law. The cultivation of hemp is banned except for cultivation for certain agricultural purposes. The use of narcotics is not prohibited. The highest priority in investigation and prosecution is given to the import and export of drugs and carries the most serious offences under the provisions of the Opium Act, while the possession of up to five grammes of cannabis is low priority. New legislation is being drafted to raise the maximum penalty for commercial hemp production (Spruit and Laar 1997). Penalties for offences against the Opium Act are high.

There are many laws which hit hard those active on the supply side such as drug-traffickers and manufacturers. Legislation has been developed to hit organised crime and to financially 'pluck out' money launderers and others earning money from crime. New legislation, enabling the local government to close down dealer houses and coffee shops, has now been passed.

Policy

The Minister of Justice is responsible for the enforcement of the Opium Act, and the Home Affairs Minister for the administration of prevention. The Minister of Health is responsible for the co-ordination of the drug policy and for the policies aimed at prevention and care. The ministries, especially those of Health and Justice, do actively work together explicitly striving for an integral policy instead of working against each other. At the local level the 'tripartite deliberation', between the mayor, the chief of police and the public prosecutor, is important. The payment of the government funds for outpatient facilities for addiction care is the responsibility of regions, which are aggregated from municipalities.

Soft drugs, hard drugs and the expediency principle

As in other European countries, drug use was introduced in the 1960s and became a problem in the 1970s. In 1970 the 'Baan committee' (named after its chairman) was formed to advise the government on narcotic drugs. They reported in 1972, discriminating drugs according to their health hazards (Baan report 1972). The government accepted the advice and in 1976 this resulted in the second amendment of the Opium Act (which dates back to 1919) and the discrimination between 'hard' and 'soft' drugs. Drugs carrying an unacceptable hazard to health ('hard drugs', such as heroin, cocaine, LSD and amphetamines) were listed on schedule I and hemp products ('soft drugs' such as hashish and marijuana) were listed on schedule II of the Opium Act. Since 1993 barbiturates and tranquillizers have been listed on schedule II due to the fact that the Netherlands ratified the Psychotropic Substances Treaty. In 1985 the Opium Act was amended again, now including special measures against drug trafficking, in order to ease the prosecution of the 'big fish' instead of just the smaller dealers. Schedules I and II have been adjusted several times as new substances entered the market such as MDMA and MDEA.

The recognition of the expediency principle is a more recent development. As in many countries, the expediency principle is applied on investigations and prosecution whereby the public prosecutor may decide not to initiate prosecution proceedings if it is in the public interest. Amsterdam was always the first area to encounter new drug problems and had some experience with new ways to deal with coffee shops: the 'AHOJ-G' criteria, demanding no Advertising (commercials), no Hard drug sale, no Nuisance, no selling to Young people and no Great quantities. Using the expediency principle, coffee shops obeying these criteria would not be prosecuted. In 1991 the Public Prosecution Department proclaimed support for this policy nationwide. The criteria became better defined once agreed that young people were those under 18, and that 'no great quantities' meant not selling more than 5 grammes (before 1996 an amount of 30 grammes was the limit) per buyer, and not having more than a trading stock of 500 grammes (Spruit and Laar 1997). In popular terms it became called the lenient or tolerant drug policy.

Application of the expediency principle is considered beneficial within the Dutch drug policy, because active prosecution of visible soft drugs for petty use is considered to do more harm to cannabis users (who would otherwise go 'underground') than to the dealers and traffickers, and therefore does not really contribute to demand and supply reduction. Investigation and prosecution is directed towards the more important priorities. Both the discrimination between soft and hard drugs and the policy of the expediency principle are considered to contribute substantially to harm reduction: there is no 'stepping stone' process (switching to hard drugs, especially heroin) visible in the cannabis using population. The very small proportion of addicted or problematic cannabis use is believed to be due to its 'de-criminalisation'. In general, by making a distinction between drug users and dealers, the government attempts as much as possible to prevent drug users from entering an illegal environment, where they are difficult to reach for prevention and intervention.

Balancing between care, prevention and the public order

Until the mid-1980s developments in care and prevention in the larger cities (especially Amsterdam) shaped national policy. An example is the acceptance of methadone treatment, not only to kick the habit, but also in maintenance programmes. The first government Note following the Opium Act was developed at the Ministry of Health and was titled 'Care and assistance, including prevention, in the area of addiction' (Ministerie van WVC 1985a). The main conclusion was that more effort had to go towards improving the effectiveness of care and prevention. In 1988 the Ministry of Justice took the initiative and wrote a Paper on 'pressure and compulsion', initiating a 'pressure and compulsion policy', followed in 1993 by the Paper 'Concerning the policy aimed at decreasing the public nuisance by addicts' on behalf of both the Ministries of Health and Justice (Ministerie van WVC 1993). Drug addicts who are repeatedly arrested may choose either to serve their entire sentence, or opt for treatment. If they choose the latter there are two options. One is treatment by suspension of preventive custody provided they enter clinical treatment and complete the programme; the other measure (article 47) permits drug addicts to subsitute their imprisonment by clinical treatment for imprisonment in the last term of their sentence. In the future there will be 150–200 beds reserved in addiction clinics for such treatment under pressure. At the other end, drug-free units were also created in prisons with the intention that detainees would be able to get care and assistance at the end of their sentence, in order to prevent them falling back into the habit on release. Other important issues were the development of outreach programmes (streetcorner work) and social integration (housing, employment, education and leasure time) (Zwart 1997).

Continuity and change announced in 1995: the integral policy as a principle

A growing proportion of heroin users are becoming older, making new demands on addiction care because of increasing vulnerability and co-morbidity. Meanwhile cocaine, and to a lesser extent crack, has taken a place in the market. Such users are more difficult to reach and to establish within addiction care. The rave scene (and associated Ecstasy use) developed relatively late compared with other

European countries, but subsequent explosive increases have compensated for the late start. Outpatient care was provided for 228 ecstasy users in 1995. The number of fatal accidents is unknown, because it is difficult to establish whether ecstasy was really used, but the number of accidents is suspected to be very low.

Worried about pills as a new drug trend, the Minister of Health stated in 1995 that despite every government effort 'there still are young people using these substances'. Traditional institutions had little contact with these new user groups, so the minister chose a new approach for harm reduction. In co-operation with the Association of Dutch Municipalities she developed recommendations for local governments to develop rules for house parties. Central to the memorandum were regulations relating to circumstances where the use of banned pills of unknown and known composition lead to increased risks (Ministerie van VWS 1995). In addition, targeted prevention was developed towards users and increased efforts of investigation and prosecution were directed at trafficking.

In the 1995 Government Paper which reviewed Dutch drug policy important points were considered to be: the public nuisance caused by a relatively small number of criminal and highly problematic hard drug users; organised crime; and foreign criticism on myths and facts (Ministry of Health and Welfare and Sports, a.o.1995). Three ministries – Health, Justice and Internal Affairs (which directs the police) – worked together formulating an 'integral approach' for ongoing and new problems and developments.

Integral approach to tackling public nuisance

It is not possible to discuss all the activities following the 1995 policy in this chapter. Subjects which attract a lot of public attention include funding issues, 'taskforce-forming' and activities at the policy level. Drug tourists and coffee shops are important policy items at the municipal level and a 'nuisance policy' has became a major topic, stimulated by a rapidly growing interest in developing drug policy by local governments. Nuisance exists in many forms: crime (theft, robbery), aggression and violence, deviant public behaviour and disturbance of the public order, filthiness and negligence in streets and drug houses, gathering of customers at dealer locations, decrease of value of houses and in sales of local shops, feelings of lack of safety in the neighbourhood and children growing up in an unhealthy environment. Such nuisance not only comes from drug addicts, but also from alcoholics, the homeless, psychiatric patients and other categories. Hard drug nuisance may involve very deviant and violent behaviour. Research from 1993 showed that about 20 per cent of all hard drug addicts (heroin and cocaine users) are responsible for nearly all hard drug nuisance and some 50 per cent of criminal acts against property (Grapendaal, Leuw and Nelen 1995). Alcohol nuisance consists predominantly of aggression and road traffic accidents. Coffee shops cause more or less the same type of nuisance as pubs and bars do: noise, traffic and parking.

Due to the nuisance caused in part by coffee shops, the government decided that local governments should decrease their numbers. This policy is not designed to decrease the use of cannabis as it is, neither are there high expectations in this direction, but rather to decrease public nuisance of coffee shops. This is because the shops are responsible for only a part of the total sale of cannabis (more or less one-third) and it has been shown that the increased use of cannabis is not caused by coffee shops. The increase in cannabis use preceded the increase in coffee shops and a (sometimes steeper) increase in cannabis use is seen in many other countries where there are no coffee shops and often a more repressive policy (Spruit, Kuipers and Stam 1997). Furthermore the government has no wish at all to nullify the aims of the expediency principle policy which are: decriminalisation of small sales, prevention of young cannabis users being drawn into criminal circles, separation of hard drugs and soft drugs markets. There are various indications that the aims are being achieved to a large extent, although more research in this area is required.

The integral approach to decrease nuisance dates back to 1993, but the 1995 Paper provided a stronger impetus. The three central premises of this policy are: further development of an accessible supply of assistance and care facilities, a strong impetus to social rehabilitation, and better use of the criminal law system. Improved integration of the judicial system and more inpatient care were established within the 'care under pressure' (pressure and compulsion) programmes of addiction clinics and more detox facilities in prison. A new forensic addiction clinic is being constructed and is scheduled to open in 1997. New methods have been developed in the field of 'Early Assistance and Intervention' including education and work projects, employment, assisted daycare and nightcare; social boarding houses and sheltered living; and outreach work. Also new is the application of the system of 'tasksentences'(kindred to UK Community Service Orders). When con-

victed for a relatively small offence (a maximum sentence of six months imprisonment) the judge may replace imprisonment by a tasksentence, which can be an
educational or work sentence (or a combination of them). During 1995, the first
year of operation, 900 such sentences were given and in 1996 3800 were planned.
It is considered that tasksentences are useful for first offenders, because they substantially prevent re-offence.

Conclusion

Whether or not Dutch policy really is so deviant is a question more easily put than
answered. Dutch policy has met with national and international praise as well as
criticism. As regards social acceptability within the country, the current policy is
regularly under discussion with regard to drug-related nuisance. Developments at
the European level do influence Dutch policy, if only because there is co-operation
between several nations, including the Netherlands, within police investigations.
Because of national as well as international developments the Netherlands have
tightened up the control of regulations. There is a tendency towards more repres-
sion, although an impressive effort is made to maintain a balanced approach. Another remarkable thing in the international context is that at the level of
professionals working in addiction care and prevention, there often appear to be
more similarities in policy and approach than one would believe from national
governments and politicians.

References

European Monitoring Centre for Drugs and Drug Addiction (EMCDDA) (1996) *Annual
Report on the State of the Drugs Problem in the European Union.* Lisbon: EMCDDA.
Grapendaal, M., Leuw, E. and Nelen, J.M. (1995) *A World of Opportunities. Lifestyle and
Economic Behaviour of Heroin Addicts in Amsterdam.* Albany, New York: State University
of New York Press.
Laar, M.W. van, Zwart, W.M. de and Mensink, C. (1996) *Addiction Care and Assistance.*
Factsheet no. 4. Utrecht: Trimbos-institute
Ministerie van VWS (1995) Government Paper: *Stadhuis en House. Handreikingen voor
gemeentelijk beleid inzake grootschalige manifestaties en uitgaansdrugs. (City Hall and House.
Assistance to municipal policy regarding large-scale festivities and party drugs).* Rijswijk.
Ministerie van WVC (1985) Government Paper: *Alcohol en samenleving: nota over een
samenhangend. (Alcohol and society: paper on a coherent alcohol policy).* Rijswijk.

Ministerie van WVC (1985a) Government Paper: *Hulpverlening met inbegrip van preventie op het gebied van verslaving: een nadere vormgeving (Care and Assistance, including prevention in the area of addiction).* Rijswijk.

Ministerie van WVC (1986) Government Paper: *Nota 2000: over de ontwikkeling van gezondheidsbeleid: feiten, beschouwingen en beleidsvoornemens. (Note 2000: on the development of public health policy: facts, considerations and policy intentions).* Rijswijk.

Ministerie van WVC (1993) Government Paper: *inzake het beleid gericht op het verminderen van de door verslaafden veroorzaakte overlast. (Paper on the policy aiming to decrease the public nuisance caused by addicts).* Rijswijk.

Ministry of Health, Welfare and Sport, Ministry of Justice, Ministry of the Interior (1995) Government Paper: *Drugs Policy in the Netherlands. Continuity and Change.* Rijswijk: Ministry of Foreign Affairs.

Ministry of Health, Welfare and Sport (January 1997) Documentation The Netherlands, Rijswijk, No. 1.

Ministerie van WVC (1995) Government Note: *Gezond en Wel. Het Kader van het volksgezondheidsbeleid 1995–1998. (Healthy and well. Outline of the public health policy 1995–)1998,* Den Haag: SDU

Spruit, I.P., Kuipers, S.B.M. and Stam, H. (1997) 'Beleid.' (Policy) In *Jaarboek Verslaving (Dutch Annals of Addiction)* 1996. Houten: Bohn Stafleu van Loghum.

Spruit, I.P. and Laar, M.W. van (1996) *Education and Prevention Policy Alcohol and Drugs.* Factsheet no. 5. Utrecht: Trimbos-institute.

Spruit, I.P. and Laar, M.W. van (1997) *Cannabispolicy, an update.* Factsheet no. 7. Utrecht: Trimbos-Institute.

Spruit, I.P. and Zwart, W.M. de (1997) 'Epidemiologie van alcohol, drugsgebruik en gokken.' ('Epidemiology of alcohol and drug use and gambling'). In *Jaarboek Verslaving (Dutch Annals of Addiction)* 1996. Houten: Bohn Stafleu van Loghum.

(1972) *Rapport van de werkgroep verdovende middelen (Baan). Achtergronden en risico's van druggebruik. (Report of the narcotics advisory committee. Reasons and risks of drug use).* Den Haag: Staatsuitgeverij.

Stam, H., Spruit, I.P. and Laar M.W. van (1997) *Drugs Nuisance Policy.* Factsheet no.6. Utrecht: Trimbos-institute

STIVA, Jaarverslag 1995 (1996) (Annual Report 1995, Foundation of responsible alcohol use). Rotterdam: STIVA

WHO (1993) *European Alcohol Action Plan.* Alcohol, Drugs and Tobacco Unit, Lifestyles and Health Department, Regional Office for Europe. Copenhagen: World Health Organisation.

Zwart, W.M. de (1997) 'Ontwikkelingen in de hulpverlening.' ('Developments in care and assistance'). In *Jaarboek Verslaving (Dutch Annals of Addiction)* 1996. Houten: Bohn Stafleu van Loghum.

Zwart, W.M. de, and Mensink, C. (1996) *Dutch Annals of Addiction 1995, Statistics.* (Jaarboek Verslaving 1995; gebruik en zorg in cijfers). Houten: Bohn Stafleu van Loghum.

PART IV

The Impact of HIV

CHAPTER 7

Injecting Drug Use and the HIV Epidemic

Fiona Wood

Introduction

A Cheshire drug treatment clinic attracted national attention in 1995 because of its policy of providing drug users with crack cocaine and heroin. The policy was intended to reduce the number of crimes committed by users to serve their drug habit; moreover it also allowed users who could not give up to lead relatively normal lives. The clinic's policy received the approval of the police and other groups because of the reduction in drug-related crime; it also gained the approval of drug users themselves. However, in 1995, the clinic's contract to treat drug users was removed by the health authority. The health authority's reasons were twofold: they argued that prescribing heroin for patients was too costly, and that it created the possibility that the drugs they prescribed could leak onto the streets. The contract was given instead to doctors whose practice was to prescribe methadone. The resulting dispute was bitter, with opponents questioning the clinic's ethical imperatives and arguing that medical treatments should lead to, at least some, health gain for the patient.

People who talk about a 'war on drugs' view drug use as an alien, minority activity which must be stamped out. Those who wish to appear tough on crime are at the forefront of this process. But what happens when a sub-culture becomes mainstream? AIDS in Britain remains a highly politicised disease with its favourite topic being the allocation of blame. Society has responded to HIV and AIDS by stigmatising, by scapegoating and by attempting to identify 'guilty and innocent victims'. Prejudice, fear and loathing have been fostered through the popular media's representation of the disease as a threat to social stability centred on moral and physical corruption.

This chapter reviews recent research on the transmission of HIV amongst injecting drug users. The intent is to concentrate on risk behaviour in relation to intravenous drug use rather than to provide the reader with information on clinical aspects of the disease (more detailed accounts are available in clinical texts, for example, Houweling and Coutinho 1991). The chapter provides information on the size and nature and likely future trends of the HIV epidemic and discusses the uncertainty surrounding the epidemiology of drug injection. Risk behaviour amongst injecting drug users will be examined in relation to equipment-sharing, prison populations, young injectors and hepatitis infection along with the changing behavioural response among injectors. Finally the changing policy responses to the epidemic will be discussed.

Size and nature of the HIV epidemic

The epidemiology of HIV is not constant over space but varies dramatically both between and within countries. A distinction has been drawn between the epidemic in the developing world and that of the developed world. Pattern I countries (the developed world) are characterised by transmission being mainly though injecting drug use and homosexual men. Pattern II countries (the developing world) are characterised by more heterosexual transmission, and consequently more female and paediatric sufferers, and prevalences are generally considered to be high. Within the developing world epidemiological importance is given to the 'core group' hypothesis. This hypothesis proposes that small numbers of highly sexually active individuals with large numbers of partners, for example sex workers, mix with individuals who might otherwise be deemed at low risk of infection (Plummer *et al.* 1991).

Within Europe, injecting drug users are the transmission category with the largest number of HIV positive cases; the greatest concentrations are located in Italy, Spain, Southern France, Ireland and Scotland (Bloor 1995). Within the UK, homosexual transmission constitutes the largest number of HIV cases. The best known example of unequal prevalences within the UK is that of Edinburgh and Glasgow. In Edinburgh 50 per cent of a sample of injecting drug users attending a General Practice in 1985 were found to be HIV positive (Robertson *et al.* 1986), yet in Glasgow levels of HIV among injecting drug use remained low and stable at 1.8 per cent in 1990 (Taylor *et al.* 1994).

Prevalence of injecting drug use

The prevalence of HIV is dependent on the number of susceptible individuals which in turn is dependent on the pool of active injectors. It is difficult to obtain reliable estimates of the number of people at risk of infection from current injecting drug use because of the secrecy that surrounds this illegal and stigmatised activity. However, such estimates are needed in order to plan drug services and to interpret the surveillance data collected on infectious disease in injecting drug users (Durante and Heptonstall 1995). Injecting behaviour is not limited to a minority of heroin users nor are drug patterns constant over time and space. Typically drug use occurs in successive waves. In the early 1980s much of the UK had seen an increase in heroin use and by the mid-1980s many areas had experienced an epidemic of amphetamine injecting with associated outbreaks of hepatitis. More recently there have been reports of steroid injection associated with body-building and an increase in the use of heroin.

Prevalence of HIV

Official data on HIV prevalence is obtained from the voluntary confiden ial reporting of AIDS cases and HIV infections to the Public Health Laboratory Service by medical practitioners. The reporting scheme is not without its problems including reporting delays, and issues of case definition. The limitations of the HIV Reporting Scheme have led to the need to supplement this information with special studies; most notable amongst these is the Unlinked Anonymous HIVPrevalence Monitoring Programme.

The Public Health Laboratory Service estimated that at the end of 1993 21,900 adults in England and Wales were infected with HIV with a confidence interval range of 20,400 to 23,400 (Day 1996). This included 12,350 people infected through male homosexual exposure; 6800 men and women infected through heterosexual exposure, and 2050 men and women infected through injecting drug use (see Table 7.1). To June 1995, 370 of the 9651 (3.8 per cent) AIDS case reports in England and Wales had been ascribed to injecting drug use

(PHLS AIDS Centre 1995). In comparison to other European countries this could be considered a low rate of infection.

Table 7.1: Prevalence of HIV infection and AIDS in adults at the end of 1993

Exposure Category	Cumulative deaths of people infected with HIV	Estimated AID cases alive	Estimated number of HIV infected people alive
Homosex-ual exposure	5725	2260	12,350
Injecting drug users	320	135	2050
Heterosex-ual exposure	695	505	6800
Blood or blood factor recipients	590	100	700

The unlinked anonymous HIV seroprevalence monitoring programme aims to monitor the prevalence of risk factors for infection for adults whose behaviour makes them vulnerable. The programme includes a survey of injecting drug users and takes voluntary saliva samples from attenders to drug treatment and support agencies. Saliva specimens are irreversibly unlinked from any patient identification so that individual test results cannot be traced back to the patient. The programme for 1994 found prevalence of HIV infection among injecting drug users was 3 per cent for men and 4 per cent for women in London and the South East and 0.3 per cent and 0.6 per cent for men and women elsewhere (PHLS AIDS Centre 1995).

Research on subjects voluntarily tested for HIV antibody between 1986-1987 in England indicated that the main focus of infection was still in homosexual and bisexual men in London. Outside London prevalence remained low. Prevalence of HIV antibody in intravenous drug users in and outside London was 5.7 per cent and 1.5 per cent respectively (PHLS Working Group 1989), substantially lower than in Edinburgh where rates of 50 per cent were reported (Robertson *et al.* 1986).

The clandestine nature of drug injecting poses difficulties in identifying and recruiting representative samples of injecting drug users for prevalence studies. In the UK many prevalence studies of injecting drug users have included samples recruited from drug treatment clinics. It is likely that patients attending clinics show a concern for their health that is not present in other populations of drug users. The result of this may be that clinic samples produce lower rates of HIV than community samples. Multi-site community-wide surveys have sought to reduce this potential bias. Research by Stimson *et al.* (1996) using a multiple-site survey of treatment and community samples found that HIV prevalence was declining at a de-accelerating rate from 13 per cent in 1990 to 6.9 per cent in 1993. However, declining prevalence rates can mask substantial incidence (new cases) in a population through migration, death and cessation of injecting as only current injecting drug users are included in the sample. If incidence has declined, then behaviour change would seem a likely explanation.

The progress of the epidemic

Assessing the past and present prevalence of HIV infection and AIDS is a difficult task, made more difficult by factors such as the long latent period before symptoms appear. But predictions of the future spread are still more uncertain, because they are dependent on variables such as the willingness of people to change their risk behaviour.

At the 1991 International AIDS Conference in Florence, James Chin, the WHO chief AIDS epidemiologist, suggested that in Western counties the incidence of HIV had peaked in the mid-1980s. Due to the long dormancy period before the onset of AIDS, the incidence of AIDS cases were projected to reach a peak before the middle of the 1990s. What the headlines at the time failed to convey from Dr Chin's speech was that these trends only applied to the 'first wave', mainly gay men and intravenous drug users whose behaviour puts them at high risk of infection. However there remains the concern of the slow building epidemic of heterosexually transmitted HIV.

Projections for England and Wales in the revised Day Report (Day 1996) estimate that there will be approximately 2010 new cases of HIV by 1999 with 155 of those cases being attributable to injecting drug use. The Day Report goes on to estimate that between 1995 and 1999 new cases of AIDS in homosexuals and bisexuals will fall by 7 per cent; but there will be a 25 per cent increase for heterosexual transmission and a 29 per cent increase for injecting drug users.

Cohort studies which follow a defined group of individuals, such as patients in STD clinics, may have their drawbacks for studying HIV incidence partly because such cohorts may not accurately represent their own subset of the population. For example, researchers believe that injecting drug users who agree to participate in studies may be more motivated to change their behaviour than other injecting drug users. The course of the injecting drug users epidemic appears to be following the same pattern for gay men but with a three-year time lag.

The UK data indicate that HIV prevalence rates among injectors may be stabilising. Stabilisation has also been reported in other countries albeit at much higher levels than in the UK. The decline in new infections for injecting drug users can, in part, be attributed to a change in risk behaviour through a reduction in equipment sharing and restrictions on sharing circles following HIV-prevention interventions. Reductions could also be a result of disproportionate attrition of the drug-using population due to the relatively high mortality rate through suicides, overdoses or through cessation of injecting (Bloor *et al.* 1994). At least part of the decrease in infection rates may be explained by the characteristic pattern by which new infections spread through a population. When a new sexually transmitted infection appears in a previously unexposed population it spreads rapidly among those whose behaviour puts them at most risk and then diffuses into the larger proportion of the population whose behaviour puts them at moderate risk. Among those at highest risk the virus spreads rapidly and may eventually run out of new people to infect–a situation that epidemiologists call saturation. Eventually the overall level of infection in the saturated population may stabilise. Research undertaken in Europe and in the United States has indicated an overall increase in the age at which AIDS is diagnosed among the main transmission categories (Zellweger *et al.* 1996). It is suggested by the authors of the research that this may be a result of a decrease in HIV incidence brought about by saturation, behavioural risk reduction or prevention interventions or it may be due to clinical advances delaying the onset of AIDS.

Although levels of HIV infection among injecting drug users in many parts of the UK remain low, there is always the potential for an HIV epidemic as long as drug users continue to inject their drugs. Once HIV has entered a previously unin- fected injecting drug user population it can spread extremely rapidly given a cer- tain level of HIV infection and risk behaviour. Such explosive epidemics have occurred in Edinburgh and in Bari (Italy) in the mid-1980s, in Bangkok in 1987 and in Manipur (India) in 1989. The rapid epidemic spread may be associated with the biology of HIV transmission as newly infected people are more infectious dur- ing the 'window of infection' period before sero-conversion when antibodies de- velop. Antibodies are usually formed within three months of infection and so after this period infectiousness remains relatively low until viral loads increase with the progression to AIDS.

Risk behaviour in injecting drug users

As HIV-infected individuals become progressively more immunocompromised they will experience increased rates of infections such as pneumonia, septicaemia, endocarditis and tuberculosis. Furthermore, impurities in the drug and poor inject- ing techniques can lead to abscesses, septicaemia, and gangrene. Injecting drug us- ers have traditionally been a group at high risk from early mortality and the AIDS epidemic has increased this risk. It is thought that official prevalence figures for AIDS amongst injecting drug users may be an underestimate because injectors are dying of drug-associated complications before they fulfil the surveillance defini- tion of AIDS.

Equipment sharing

Injecting drug users who share equipment may transmit and acquire blood-borne virus infections including HIV, Hepatitis B virus and Hepatitis C virus. The term 'sharing' actually represents a number of different activities with varying risks of infection. Even without sharing, injection with non-sterile equipment or mixing agents may result in infection due to bacteria. Chin (1991) has estimated that transmissibility rates through sharing of injecting equipment are between 3 to 10 infections per 1000 exposures but the level of transmissibility will depend on the particular sharing activity. In 1994 about 1 in 5 injectors reported recent sharing

of equipment (PHLS AIDS Centre 1995) with young injectors and women reporting significantly higher rates of sharing.

Sharing can be dependent on a number of issues: whether clean equipment is
available; the nature of the relationship between sharers; the local cultural norms;
the need to inject; an assessment of risk; and potential inadvertent sharing (McKeganey and Barnard 1992). Bloor (1995) asserts that sharing is not a random behaviour but that it is largely confined to the immediate social circle of the injector.
Consequently equipment sharing is associated with intimacy and trust. Social cohesion between drug injectors may vary geographically and over time and therefore could partly explain variations in needle-sharing behaviour. However, Hart *et
al.* (1989) found that drug injectors were more likely to share due to the unavail-
ability of equipment rather than the community feeling it engendered. Research in
Glasgow indicated that only a small proportion of drug injectors would be prepared to make a switch from injecting to non-injecting drug use, the main reason
being that other methods such as snorting and smoking were not able to produce
the same 'rush' effect associated with injecting drug use (McKeganey, Barnard and
Watson 1989). Equipment sharing is also likely to be related to patterns of drug
use. Some drugs, such as heroin, are more addictive and therefore would be injected more frequently. Other drugs, for example tranquillisers, diminish caution
and clarity of thought and consequently safe injecting practices are less likely to be
practised.

Prison populations

Prison populations constitute a group at high risk of HIV infection mainly because
a high proportion are injecting drug users and a large proportion of drug users
spend some time in custody. Turnbull *et al.* (1992) found that of 168 ex-prisoners
who inject drugs, 27 per cent had continued to inject whilst in prison and 75 per
cent had shared equipment whilst in custody. Turnbull also found 4.7 per cent of
the prison population in the sample were HIV positive with injecting drug users
comprising the largest proportion of people HIV positive at 10.1 per cent. Research by Maden *et al.* (1992) found 9 per cent of a sample of 1751 prisoners had
used heroin or amphetamines prior to prison and 3 per cent sedatives. Prison environments mix drug-using populations from different geographical areas and social

networks and consequently at the end of a custodial sentence the injecting drug user may then go on to transmit infection to their own network.

The Young Offender Institute in Glenochil, Scotland was an example of how an arrival of a carrier of HIV within a needle-sharing network in any prison is all that is required to initiate an outbreak of HIV (Gore *et al.* 1995). Given that drug use in prison is extremely difficult to eradicate there is concern that prisoners are cut off from community health programmes that aim to minimise harm through, amongst other things, the provision of clean injecting equipment. Imprisonment could offer an opportunity to provide education and preventive programs to this specific group that might otherwise be difficult to reach. If little help is available to dependent drug injectors whilst in custody there will be less incentive to identify themselves and consequently more sharing of drugs and equipment.

Young injectors

Research has shown that schoolchildren routinely experiment with illicit substances. A survey conducted in Wales (Roberts *et al.* 1995) found that between 1990 and 1994 the proportion of pupils aged 15–16 reporting to have ever used drugs increased from 24 per cent to 40 per cent for boys and from 20 per cent to 40 per cent for girls. If drug use amongst teenagers is becoming normalised within youth culture, policy-makers and enforcement agencies will be required to adopt a more realistic approach to the drug experience of today. Currently there are few services aimed at teenage drug users. Many drug workers are reluctant to refer children to adult clinics and argue that specific services should be developed for their younger clients.

Hepatitis

Hepatitis types B and C are associated with high risk sexual and drug use behaviour. Research in Sydney, Australia found that 59 per cent of injecting drug users tested were found to have hepatitis C antibodies (van Beek *et al.* 1994) and research in Nottingham found that 53 per cent of hepatitis C-infected blood donors reported previous use of injected drugs (Neal *et al.* 1994). The high prevalence of hepatitis B and C antibodies in injectors is another indicator that injecting drug users are engaging in high risk practices and therefore remain vulnerable to HIV infection. The prevalence of hepatitis in injecting drug users is sometimes used as a marker or proxy measure of HIV.

Behavioural changes amongst injectors

There is considerable evidence for the hypothesis that prevalence rates have remained low and relatively stable because risk behaviours have changed. In the late 1980s the UK HIV/AIDS awareness campaign was underway and needle and syringe distribution had gained public support. The multi-site evaluation of the syringe-exchange programmes in England and Scotland reported past month sharing levels of 28 per cent in 1987 down to 21 per cent by 1990 (Stimson 1995). Qualitative studies have also indicated that equipment sharing has become more selective with the number of sharing partners falling (Burt and Stimson 1993). While many of the older injecting drug users with longer injecting careers may have since stopped sharing, effective interventions are still required to prevent the creation of new transmission networks among younger, less experienced injectors. As drug use is characterised by waves of drug patterns, often with limited population overlap between each wave, the lessons of harm-reduction need to be re-taught.

Once HIV is established in an injecting drug using population it can become a major source of infection for heterosexual and perinatal transmission. There is evidence that the reduction in equipment-sharing amongst injecting drug users has been paralleled by an increase in condom use with casual partners, but there is no evidence of an increase in condom use with regular partners (Taylor *et al.* 1993). Prostitutes working within the high HIV prevalence areas are at considerable risk of contracting and spreading HIV infection. Injecting drug users may turn to prostitution to finance their habit and the private sexual partners of prostitutes are often injecting drug users. The importance of other sexually transmitted diseases in facilitating HIV transmission has been widely documented (Chirgwin *et al.* 1991). Women injecting drug users are more likely than male injecting drug users to have a sexual partner who is also an injecting drug user and are therefore more likely to share equipment with their partner.

Policy responses to the epidemic

By the mid-1980s the potential threat to public health, the financial cost and the human suffering resulting from HIV infection had been recognised. Since then there have been major changes in the working philosophy and practices of drug services with the development of goals of harm minimisation, flexibility and accessibility. The organisational response to HIV has traditionally been led by the National Health Service involving the Health Authorities (Health Boards in Scotland), hospital, community and the primary health care sectors. The role of the voluntary sectors, particularly from groups such as the Terrence Higgins Trust and London Lighthouse, have been the buttress of health education, care and support.

The development of harm minimisation has centred mainly on needle and syringe exchange and with the distribution of literature and advice on harm minimisation. In addition to targeting current injectors for risk education, potential injectors should also be identified to discourage recruitment to injecting and the diffusion of injecting to new populations. Drug injectors have also become a target for sexual behaviour change. Effective outreach is an important component of a strategy which aims to reach greater numbers of drug users at an earlier stage in their drug-using career. It is acknowledged that the majority of drug users are not in contact with drug services and outreach or 'detached work' can play a vital role by attracting people to existing services or by providing condoms and clean injecting equipment to those who are not using those services. Comprehensive discussion of the developments of needle exchange and outreach work are provided in the chapters by Lawrie Elliott and Tim Rhodes and Gerry Stimson.

The 1988 Advisory Council on Drugs identified methadone prescribing as an important contribution to the reduction of HIV risk behaviour arguing that the goal of substitute prescribing is to attract drug users to services, to keep them in contact and to facilitate change away from HIV risk practices. The emphasis is therefore on the adoption of a range of goals in addition to abstinence.

There are a vast array of problems, both medical and social, that HIV infection and injecting drug use can produce. Typically general practitioners have been reluctant to become involved in the management of injecting drug users either because they feel inappropriately trained to do so or because of competing work demands. Furthermore for many young people with chaotic lifestyles access to conventional primary care services may be impossible. Consequently management of injecting drug users usually remains the domain of the statutory drug agencies although a significant number of drug users can be managed in the primary care setting.

It is likely that care provision for people with AIDS will need to increase because there will be more cases and those cases will be living longer. Consequently the need to develop community care options for this client group is becoming increasingly apparent. The needs of people with AIDS cared for in the community are no different from those of other sick people, where services of home-helps, aids and adaptations, nursing care and medication, friendship and respite care, amongst others, are provided.

Conclusion

Drug users may be in contact with social services or probation staff at a stage before they present to drug treatment services. It is therefore necessary for staff working in generic services, such as social services, housing, probation and youth services, to be aware of drug and HIV issues and how these might apply to their client. With the prevalence of HIV remaining geographically very uneven, the highest concentrations being in London and the central belt of Scotland, many social workers will not have regular contact with people living with HIV and AIDS.

In order to keep HIV prevalences for injecting drug users at a low level, both a continued reduction of risk behaviour plus an absence of large scale increase in drug use is required. The future pattern of epidemic-spread among injecting drug users is extremely difficult to predict partly due to the uncertainty surrounding the future size and nature of the population at risk. The extent and patterns of drug-using behaviour, the prevalence of HIV infection and the prevalence of other blood-borne viruses in injecting drug users require continual monitoring. Whilst there is ongoing research to provide more reliable prevalence estimates, to date patterns of injecting drug use have been very unstable. The message from all this is that health educators and drug agencies still have more hard work ahead if a slow but substantial injecting drug use epidemic is to be averted in the UK.

References

Bloor, M. (1995) *The Sociology of HIV Transmission.* London: Sage.

Bloor, M., Frischer, M., Taylor, A., Covell, R., Goldberg, D., Green, S., McKeganey N. and Platt S. (1994) 'Tideline and Turn: Possible reasons for the continuing low HIV prevalence among Glasgow's injecting drug users.' *The Sociological Review 42,* 4, 738–757.

Burt, J. and Stimson, G.V. (1993) *Drug Injectors and HIV Risk Reduction: Strategies for Protection.* London: Health Education Authority.

Chin, J. (1991) 'Keynote address.' Seventh International Conference on AIDS, Florence, July 1991.

Chirgwin, K., Dehovitz, T., Dillon, S. and McCormack, S. (1991) 'HIV infection, genital ulcer disease and crack cocaine use among patients attending a clinic for sexually transmitted disease.' *American Journal of Public Health 81,* 1576–1579.

Day, N. (1996) 'The incidence and prevalence of AIDS and prevalence of other severe HIV disease in England and Wales for 1995–1999: projections using data to the end of 1994.' Summary Report of an Expert Group convened by the Director of the Public Health Laboratory Service. *Communicable Disease Report 6,* 1, R1–R24.

Durante, A. and Heptonstall, J. (1995) 'How many people in England and Wales risk infection from injecting drug use?' *Communicable Disease Report 5,* 3, R40–R44.

Gore, S., Bird, G., Burns, S., Goldberg, D., Ross, A. and Macgregor, J. (1995) 'Drug injection and HIV prevalence in inmates of Glenochil prison.' *British Medical Journal 310,* 293–296.

Hart, G., Sonnex, C., Petherick, A., Johnson, A., Geinmann, C. and Adler M. (1989) 'Risk behaviours for HIV infection among injecting drug users attending a drug dependency clinic.' *British Medical Journal 298,* 1081–1083.

Houweling, H. and Coutinho, R. (1991) 'Acquired immune deficiency syndrome (AIDS).' In W. Holland *et al.* (eds) *Oxford Textbook of Public Health.* Oxford: Oxford University Press.

McKeganey, N., Barnard, M. and Watson, H. (1989) 'HIV-related risk behaviour among a non-clinic sample of injecting drug users.' *British Journal of Addiction 84,* 1481–1490.

McKeganey, N. and Barnard, M. (1992) *AIDS, Drugs and Sexual Risk: Lives in the Balance.* Buckingham: Open University Press.

Maden, A., Swinton, M. and Gunn, J. 'A survey of pre-arrest drug use in sentenced prisoners.' *British Journal of Addiction 87,* 27–33.

Neal, K., Jones, D., Killey, D. and James, V. (1994) 'Risk factors for hepatitis C virus infection. A case-control study of blood donors in the Trent Region (UK).' *Epidemiology and Infection 112,* 3, 595–601.

PHLS Working Group (1989) 'Prevalence of HIV antibody in high and low risk groups in England.' *British Medical Journal 298,* 422–423.

PHLS AIDS Centre (PHLS Virus Reference Division, PHLS Statistics Unit) (1995) *Unlinked Anonymous HIV Seroprevalence Monitoring Programme in England and Wales. Report from the Unlinked HIV Surveys Steering Group.* London: Department of Health.

Plummer, F., Nagelkerke, N., Moses, S., Ndinyaachola, J., Bwayo, J. and Ngugi, E. (1991) 'The importance of core groups in the epidemiology and control of HIV-1 infection.' *AIDS 5,* (suppl. 1), S169–S176.

Roberts, C., Moore., Blakey, V., Playle, R. and Tudor-Smith, C. (1995) 'Drug use among 15–16 year olds in Wales 1990–1994.' *Drugs: Education, Prevention and Policy 2,* 3, 305–316.

Robertson, R., Bucknall, A. Welsby, P., Roberts, J., Inglis, J., Peutherer, J. and Brettle, R. (1986) 'Epidemic of AIDS-related virus among intravenous drug users.' *British Medical Journal 292,* 527–529.

Stimson, G.V. (1995) 'AIDS and injecting drug use in the United Kingdom, 1988 to 1993: the policy response and the prevention of the epidemic.' *Social Science and Medicine 41,* 5, 699–716.

Stimson G., Hunter, G., Donoghoe, M., Rhodes, T., Parry J. and Charmers C. (1996) 'HIV-1 prevalence in community-wide samples of injecting drug users in London, 1990–1993.' *AIDS 10,* 657–666.

Taylor, A., Frischer, M., McKeganey, N., Goldberg, D., Green, S. and Platt S. (1993) 'HIV risk behaviour among females prostitute drug injectors in Glasgow.' *Addiction 88,* 1561–1564.

Taylor, A., Frischer, M., Green, S., Goldberg, D., McKeganey, N. and Gruer, L. (1994) 'Low and stable prevalence of HIV among Glasgow drug injectors.' *International Journal of STD and AIDS 5,* 105–107.

Turnbull,P., Stimson, G. and Dolan, K. (1992) 'Prevalence of HIV infection among ex-prisoners in England.' *British Medical Journal 304,* 90–91.

van Beek, I., Buckley, R., Stewart, M., MacDonald, M. and Kaldor, J. (1994) 'Risk factors for hepatitis C virus infection among injecting drug users in Sydney.' *Genitourinary Medicine 70,* 5, 321–324.

Zellweger, U., Wang, J., Heusser, R. and Somaini, B (1996) Trends in age at AIDS diagnosis in Europe and the United States: evidence of pronounced "ageing" among injecting drug users.' *AIDS 10,* 9, 1001–1007.

Further Reading

Advisory Council on the Misuse of Drugs (1988) *Aids and Drug Misuse.* London: Department of Health and Social Security.

Advisory Council on the Misuse of Drugs (1993) *AIDS and Drug Misuse: Update Report.* London: Department of Health.

Strang, J. and Stimson, G. (eds) (1990) *AIDS and Drug Misuse.* London: Routledge.

CHAPTER 8

Ten Years of Needle Exchange Provision, But Do They Work?[1]

Lawrie Elliott

Introduction

The late 1990s marked the end of the first decade of needle exchange provision in the UK. This also applied to many other countries, notably Holland, Denmark, Germany, Australia, New Zealand, USA and Canada. Its implementation and subsequent growth have been affected by a number of factors, including anti-paraphernalia legislation, public resistance and lack of proper funding. However, no matter on which side of the sociopolitical debate you happen to find yourself, the question of effectiveness is always raised. When this happens, people turn to research for the answer.

Like other issues, the answer to the question posed in the title of this chapter is complex. Studies have produced contradictory findings. These contradictions may be explained by the various scientific methods employed by researchers. They may also be related to the type of service provision or different populations of drug injectors who use needle exchanges. Needless to say, the political advocates and adversaries of needle exchange use these findings to substantiate their own arguments, sometimes overlooking the caveats which accompany them.

What I want to do in this chapter is to take two key questions of needle exchange provision and examine these in the light of existing research. I will also explain why research findings are contradictory and, using this evidence, give my

1   I would like to thank Laurence Gruer and all the Glasgow needle exchange staff for their guidance and assistance in putting this chapter together.

own answer to the question of whether needle exchanges work. I would also urge you to draw your own conclusions once you have weighed up the evidence. In doing so, you will come to appreciate how research can help make informed decisions and how service provision should be based upon that decision-making process. I will also explain the possible impact of these decisions on needle exchange provision and research. First a brief 'world history' of needle exchange.

The history of needle exchange

In 1986, the World Health Organisation suggested that supplying sterile needles and syringes to drug injectors could contribute to the prevention of HIV. Some countries took this advice and established needle exchanges as one way of tackling the problem of shortages of sterile injecting equipment among drug injectors, but this was not to happen in every country affected by HIV. In America, for instance, it is still illegal in many states to distribute needles and syringes to injecting drug users. Many other countries which now supply injecting drug users with injecting equipment had to overcome either adverse legislation or social norms. Swedish laws initially prevented the sale of injecting equipment to drug injectors; Australia had laws preventing the carrying of injecting equipment for the purpose of drug use; and in Scotland common laws regarding reckless conduct could have been used against suppliers.

The availability of injecting equipment, therefore, varied between countries. Needle exchange programmes were generally introduced after supplies of injecting equipment were made available through pharmacies. In Holland, Denmark, Germany and the UK, needles and syringes were available to a greater or lesser extent in pharmacies prior to 1984. In fact, pharmacies have played an increasing role in the provision of injecting equipment to drug injectors in the UK (Sheridan *et al.* 1996). However, needle exchanges, which generally provide a more extensive range of services, were set up in Holland in 1984, Denmark and Sweden in 1986, and in Germany and the UK in 1987. In Australia and New Zealand the first needle exchanges were opened in 1987, in the USA 1988, and in Canada 1989. Although there is evidence of widespread injecting and HIV in other areas of the world, especially Asia and Latin America, there have been few reports of needle exchanges operating in these regions with notable exceptions in Brazil, Thailand and Nepal.

The structure and operation of needle exchanges differ widely across the world according to local conditions, funding and staffing levels. For instance, in San Francisco a needle exchange was set up by volunteers in 1988 on a street corner using a baby perambulator to deliver supplies of injecting equipment (Watters *et al*. 1994), whilst in Paris in 1989 the first needle exchange operated out of a medical centre staffed by a multi-disciplinary medical and social work team offering a wide range of services. This was later housed in a mobile van which toured the city. Differences were also apparent among the first programmes in the UK, although these tended to operate out of fixed sites either in medical centres or drugs projects (Stimson *et al*. 1988). Funding for the needle exchange in Peterborough covered only injecting equipment costs, whilst in Middlesex equipment was supplied and exchanged by two full-time staff. In Liverpool, the first exchange was run from a converted toilet in the Regional Drug Training and Information Centre, whilst in St. George's, London, they operated at three health centres. In Scotland needle exchanges are relatively well staffed. Each of the seven health-centre-based exchanges in Glasgow is staffed by two nurses and one or more drug workers.

Although the range of services differ at each exchange, at a general level, the list of services offered worldwide is impressive. This includes: needles, syringes, bleach, sterile water, alcohol wipes, injecting paraphernalia (cookers, filters), gloves, safe return containers, tourniquets, sterile dressings, non-prescribed medicines, condoms, lubricant and spermicides. Other services offered include: education and counselling for HIV; drugs advice and counselling; HIV testing; TB, pneumonia and influenza screening; tetanus inoculation; abscess and wound care; social, financial and legal advice; and even bible study classes.

Research and evaluation of needle exchange programmes

Research in this area has generally concentrated on answering questions which relate to the service delivery and impact, among which are two key questions:

Question 1. Do needle exchanges reduce the likelihood of contracting HIV and Hepatitis?

Question 2. Do needle exchanges reduce the sharing of injecting
equipment?

*Question 1: Do needle exchanges reduce the likelihood of
contracting HIV and Hepatitis?*

EVIDENCE THAT NEEDLE EXCHANGES MAY PROTECT AGAINST HIV

Evidence has emerged from studies to support the argument that needle exchanges
have a protective effect against HIV. In Tacoma (USA), 3 per cent of needle exchange attenders are HIV positive compared with 8 per cent of non-attenders (Hagan *et al.* 1992) and in Seattle, 5 per cent of attenders are HIV positive compared
with 11 per cent of non-attenders (Bley *et al.* 1991). Low seroconversion rates have
also been reported among single samples of needle exchange attenders. For instance, in New York, where approximately 52 per cent of injectors are estimated to
be HIV positive (Des Jarlais *et al.* 1994), there have been no reported seroconver-
sions among attenders between 1992 and 1993 (Paone *et al.* 1994). In London,
there was a low rate of seroconversion among attenders over a one-year period
(Hart *et al.* 1989). In New Haven (USA) the prevalence of HIV in syringes returned
to needle exchanges decreased from 65 per cent in 1990 to 40 per cent in 1992
and further possible reductions were noted in 1993 (Kaplan and Heimer 1994).
The authors argue that needle exchanges reduced the number of infected needles
circulating among injectors and therefore the likelihood of infection.

EVIDENCE THAT EXCHANGES MAY NOT PROTECT AGAINST HIV

A study from Montreal found that the HIV prevalence among attenders between
1989 and 1993 was 18 per cent compared with 6 per cent among non-attenders,
and the annual incidence of new infections was 11.6 and 3.5 respectively. Seroconversion was strongly related to needle exchange attendance (Bruneau *et al.*
1994a, 1994b, 1995). In another cohort study, carried out in Chicago, long-term
exchange attenders exhibited slightly higher but non-significant seroincidence
rates of HIV infection (O'Brien *et al.* 1995). Cohorts of attenders and non-
attenders were followed up from 1992 to 1994. The annual incidence rate of new
infections for attenders was 3 compared with 0.75 among non-attenders. Unlike
other research both of these are longitudinal cohort studies using multi-site sampling and, as such, represent fairly sophisticated designs.

INCONCLUSIVE EVIDENCE

Several studies, although providing some evidence that needle exchange has a contributory role in reducing or containing the spread of HIV infection, remain inconclusive. Approximately 1 per cent of Glasgow drug injectors (including needle exchange attenders) are HIV positive and this has remained so since 1991 (Taylor *et al.* 1994). In Amsterdam, injectors who seroconverted between 1985 and 1991 were compared with those who remained HIV negative. The annual incidence rate fell from 9.5 in 1985 to 3.3 in 1991. Needle exchange attendance had a protective role earlier in the study but not in the longer term (Van Ameijden *et al.* 1992). In San Francisco, 14 per cent of attenders were HIV positive compared with 19 per cent of non-attenders, a non-significant difference (Watters and Cheng 1991). In each of these studies the authors are unable to comment on the *exclusive* role of needle exchange in reducing or stabilising HIV infection.

HEPATITIS – EVIDENCE FOR AND AGAINST

Needle exchanges' ability to control hepatitis is more controversial. High rates of hepatitis have been noted among injectors in many countries where needle exchanges operate and where HIV prevalence is low, including the UK (Gruer *et al.* 1991; Rhodes *et al.* 1996), Canada (Bruneau *et al.* 1994b, 1995), Australia and New Zealand (Robinson, Reynolds and Robinson 1995; Van Beek *et al.* 1994). There is some evidence that needle exchanges have a partial effect on the incidence of hepatitis B, although this is weak. For instance, in Tacoma (USA) the number of drug injectors newly infected with HBV reduced from approximately 45 in 1986 to 5 in 1990. Needle exchanges were opened in 1988 (Hagan *et al.* 1991b). Additional evidence from the same city suggests that non-use of a needle exchange is attributed to a greater risk of acquiring hepatitis B or C (Hagan *et al.* 1995). In Amsterdam, the number of injectors with acute hepatitis B reduced from 26 in 1984 to 5 in 1988. Needle exchanges began in 1984 (Buning 1991). However, most of the evidence relating to the effect of needle exchange on hepatitis B and C infection remains anecdotal. It is possible that needle exchanges may not make a significant impact on these infections. This may be related to the increased relative efficiency of transmission of hepatiti compared with HIV (Rhodes *et al.* 1996) or the widespread prevalence of these diseases prior to needle exchanges opening. As such, additional measures may have to be used to reduce the spread of these diseases, such as encouraging non-injecting methods of drug administration.

Question 2: Do needle exchanges reduce the sharing of injecting equipment?
EVIDENCE THAT EXCHANGES MAY REDUCE SHARING

This is probably the most important and contentious issue relating to needle exchange provision. The availability of equipment through exchanges should reduce the necessity to share equipment. Needle exchanges supply injecting equipment, and through the exchange mechanism, theoretically, reduce the amount of used equipment circulating in the injecting population, thus decreasing the likelihood of sharing (circulation theory) (Kaplan and Heimer 1994). Evidence from studies supports this argument. For instance, the proportion of injectors who share in areas where clean injecting equipment is available is lower (78 per cent) than areas where there is restricted access to sterile equipment (98 per cent) (Calsyn *et al.* 1991). In Connecticut, sharing reduced from 52 per cent to 31 per cent among injectors after the repeal of prescription and paraphernalia laws (Groseclose *et al.* 1995).

More detailed studies involving needle exchange attenders lend weight to the argument that needle exchange attendance is associated with a reduction in sharing. Longitudinal comparative research from the UK and Holland suggests that needle exchange attenders will reduce sharing more than non-attenders. In Amsterdam in 1987, 10 per cent of exchangers borrowed used injecting equipment compared with 23 per cent of non-exchangers. In 1988 this reduced to 0 per cent and 10 per cent respectively (Hartgers *et al.* 1989). In the UK, the proportion of needle exchange attenders sharing injecting equipment decreased from 28 per cent in 1987 to 22 per cent in 1988, whilst among non-attenders it fell from 52 per cent to only 49 per cent (Donoghoe *et al.* 1989). In Wales, 10 per cent of attenders shared injecting equipment compared with 40 per cent of non-attenders over a one-year period (Keene *et al.* 1993).

Three cross-sectional studies which compared attenders with non-attenders reach similar conclusions. Injectors in the UK who use needle exchanges are less likely to share compared with those who obtain injecting equipment from other sources (Durante *et al.* 1995). Needle exchange attenders in Glasgow are less likely to inject with used (borrowed) injecting equipment than non-attenders (Frischer and Elliott 1993). A total of 39 per cent of attenders compared with 47 per cent of non-attenders injected with used equipment on average 4.5 and 9.2 times a month respectively. Needle exchange attenders at the Tacoma exchange (USA) injected on average 19 times per month with borrowed injecting equipment compared with 46 times per month for non-attenders (Hagan *et al.* 1991a).

Finally, studies involving samples of needle exchange attenders where baseline and post-entry measures are taken also support the argument that needle exchange attendance is associated with reduced levels of both borrowing and lending. Approximately 30 per cent of new attenders at a New York exchange borrowed used equipment in the 30-day period prior to their first visit. This fell to 11 per cent after a year (Paone *et al.* 1994). At the Tacoma needle exchange participants were asked about sharing in the four-week period prior to their first visit and a 'typical' four-week period since attending the exchange. The average number of injections with borrowed used equipment prior to their first visit was 56 and after their first visit 30. The average number of times a syringe was lent prior to their first visit was 100 and after their first visit 62 (Hagan *et al.* 1993). In London 15 per cent of attenders had shared injecting equipment upon entry to the exchange and 11 per cent did so after one year's attendance (Hart *et al.* 1989).

EVIDENCE THAT NEEDLE EXCHANGES MAY NOT REDUCE SHARING

Work from one cross-sectional study in Manchester suggested that needle exchange attenders pass on injecting equipment more frequently than non-attenders. In Manchester, 59 per cent of needle exchange attenders lent used needles compared with 42 per cent of non-attenders in the two weeks prior to interview (Klee *et al.* 1991). One reason for passing on used injecting equipment was pressure from non-attending friends. Different groups attending exchanges are also more likely to share equipment especially those using amphetamines and those with injecting partners or friends (Klee and Morris 1995).

INCONCLUSIVE EVIDENCE

A substantial number of papers report little or no association between needle exchange attendance and sharing injecting equipment. A large cohort study carried out in Amsterdam between 1985 and 1991 concluded that the effect of needle exchange on sharing may diminish over a long period of time (five years) with only some effect during earlier contacts (Van Ameijden *et al.* 1992). Updated reports from the same study reported a reduction in borrowing and lending in the injector population as a whole. However, the reduction in sharing was not strongly associated with needle exchange attendance (Van Ameijden *et al.* 1994). A recent cohort study carried out in Chicago from 1992 to 1994 found that needle exchanges had no observable effect on sharing (O'Brien *et al.* 1995). There was also no significant difference in sharing levels between attenders and non-attenders in another cohort study conducted in Montreal between 1989 and 1993 (Bruneau *et al.* 1994a, 1994b). Higher rates of sharing among needle exchange attenders in this study may be attributed to the high risk behaviours exhibited by the study cohort and not necessarily the failure of the exchange service. In a longitudinal study from San Francisco which used two cross-sectional comparisons, there was a reduction in sharing from 66 per cent of injectors in 1987 to 35.5 per cent in 1992. Only those who used an exchange more than 20 times a year were less likely to share (Watters *et al.* 1994).

Discussion

Why such contradictory findings to both questions?

Although most of the research worldwide supports the argument that needle exchanges protect against HIV (and to a lesser extent hepatitis), and help reduce risk behaviour, not all research studies concur. How can these findings be explained? There are important methodological issues which must be considered when interpreting the results of this research.

Methodological problems

Methodological and moral constraints prevent the use of randomised controlled studies in this area of research and, as a result, researchers use a wide variety of study designs. For instance, comparisons have been made between needle exchange attenders and non-attenders, sampled from drugs or HIV testing services. These groups are used in either a 'snapshot' or in serial longitudinal comparisons, and in some instances followed up as cohorts over time. Sampling methods vary and include ethnographic snowballing and systematic multi-site sampling. Some studies, however, used no comparison groups, taking samples only from needle exchanges. These are used in either single cross-sectional, or follow-up studies. Other researchers have used epidemiological data to monitor the impact of needle exchanges. For instance, attempting to estimate the prevalence of drug injecting or HIV/HBV in various drug-using populations prior to and after the introduction of an exchange.

The problem with using non-randomised designs and epidemiological data is that arguments regarding impact of needle exchange rest on grounds of association rather than cause and effect. However, study methods have improved in recent years. Longitudinal cohort studies, especially those which compare needle exchange attenders with non-attenders, are probably the most rigorously designed research in this field, notably those conducted by Van Ameijden (Amsterdam) between 1985 and 1992, O'Brien (Chicago) between 1992 and 1994, and Bruneau (Montreal) between 1989 and 1994 (Bruneau *et al.* 1994b; O'Brien *et al.* 1995; Van Ameijden *et al.* 1994). Even here there are problems of sample bias. Needle exchange attenders entering these studies could be a self-selected low-risk group, or in the case of Montreal, a high-risk group. Thus, sample characteristics may explain the differences found between attenders and non-attenders.

So at best, the differences in behaviour between needle exchange attenders and non-attenders can only be interpreted as possible indicators of needle exchange performance and not directly caused by needle exchanges. However, as Alex Wodak points out:

> HIV prevention policies are widely regarded as having successfully prevented the spread of HIV among IDUs, although rigorous scientific proof of their effectiveness is unavailable and wisely not regarded as a prerequisite for adoption and   expansion of prevention programmes. Attributing benefit to any single intervention is impossible when multiple strategies have been implemented at about the same time. The intensity of implementation is difficult if not impossible to measure and the effect of interventions is in all likelihood synergistic. In a categorical sense, these methodological problems cannot be resolved without a controlled trial of communities randomly allocated to a single intervention or no intervention. The ethical, logistical, financial and public health problems of attempting such a study are such that there is no alternative, especially in the urgency of the epidemic, to making a judgement on the grounds of plausibility, feasibility, cost and international experience. At issue is whether authorities in a particular country prefer to be roughly right or precisely wrong. (Wodak 1995)

It could also be argued that quantitative research largely based upon assessing an individual's risk behaviour has dominated this field, possibly at the expense of qualitative work. Quantitative techniques can identify relationships between a complex number of behavioural, attitudinal, cognitive and social factors but do not constitute an explanation of these relationships. Qualitative data on the other hand can provide contextualisation and further interpretation, and should lead to a greater understanding of the determinants behind these relationships (Barnard and Frischer 1995)–for instance, identifying the complex social relationships which determine sharing behaviour among injectors. Indeed the key to future research in the area of needle exchange evaluation may lie in combining both quantitative and qualitative techniques. Cross-sectional sampling of needle exchange attenders and non-attenders over time provides an alternative method to the randomised control trial. There is no reason why detailed serial ethnographic and quantitative analysis of risk behaviour could not be combined to provide evidence of change at a community level. Although this does not provide absolute proof of the exclusive role of needle exchange in bringing about this change, it would provide more persuasive evidence of some of the links between this type of service provision and impact. This is surely an argument for developing both techniques in the field of needle exchange evaluation.

Despite these methodological problems the large majority of studies in the field lend support to the idea that needle exchanges have worked. A substantial number of drug injectors have been attracted to the service and have been provided with a range of services which cannot be suitably offered by other health services. The service has also made some contribution to continued low, or reduced, spread of HIV among the injecting population in many countries and has probably helped those who attend to maintain low levels of risk behaviour, most notably reduced levels of sharing. Close liaison with the public has also meant that needle exchanges are widely accepted, at least in some European countries, and, because they reduce the circulation of used injecting equipme, they provide a very important and effective public health service. It is, therefore, difficult to argue against this weight of evidence. However, other studies have pointed to some weaknesses, including the ability of needle exchanges to reduce risk in the longer term and control hepatitis infection. These findings will have an impact on future service provision.

The future of needle exchange

Needle exchanges are primarily based upon a model of health intervention which is essentially individual-centred and not one which deals with groups or communities of injecting drug users. In some instances social factors may prevent further behavioural change among injectors and, as such, needle exchanges may have failed to make significant headway in motivating social change. The influence of social and cultural norms on sharing has been well documented in a number of ethnographic studies. Sharing will occur despite the general levels of supply. Of particular interest is sharing which takes place between sexual partners: a situation where women may rely on their male partners for injecting equipment (Bloor *et al.* 1994). As a result, female injectors may be more exposed to sharing situations (Barnard 1993). Certain types of drug users also engage in higher-risk behaviours for example, amphetamine users may share injecting equipment more than other injectors (Klee *et al.* 1995). Thus, although in some instances sharing practices result from a lack of clean injecting equipment, other situational and social factors are clearly important.

Working with communities of drug users rather than individual drug users would perhaps tackle the social norms and influences which lead to continued risks. In many instances this would require structural change to the present form of needle exchange provision, perhaps requiring a shift in emphasis to one which included outreach work and possibly peer education (Stimson, Eaton, Rhodes and Power 1994). Outreach needle exchanges organised by drug injectors in Holland have been successful in attracting and maintaining contact with a number of 'hidden' drug injectors (Grund, Kaplan and Adriaans 1991). However, this does not mean that existing exchanges should be closed. Present exchanges are capable of offering a wide range of health and social services and are also able to refer clients to other more specialist services. Rather, both should work together to tackle the existing problems of risk behaviour and injecting-related harms. This model of service provision is not fully proven and would obviously require further research.

Needle exchanges, therefore, face new challenges from diseases like hepatitis which may only be tackled successfully by changing social norms. This poses new problems for service providers who will have to develop techniques which successfully prevent the spread of such diseases and for researchers who must evaluate the effectiveness of these interventions without the help of randomised control trials. I see these as new opportunities for needle exchange provision and research, and not as evidence against the effectiveness of existing service provision or research. Perhaps the next ten years of needle exchange provision will provide new ways of working and strengthen the links between service providers and researchers which have already crystallised in the preceding decade. I would argue that, so far, needle exchanges have survived the test, both politically and scientifically. They do work and are excellent examples of evidence-based health care.

References

Barnard, M. (1993) 'Needle sharing in context: patterns of sharing among men and women injectors and HIV risks.' *Addiction 88,* 805–812.

Barnard, M. and Frischer, M. (1995) 'Combining quantitative and qualitative approaches: researching HIV-related risk behaviours among drug injectors.' *Addiction Research 2,* 4, 351–362.

Bley, L., Harris, N.V., Gordon, D.C. and Fields, M.J. (1991) 'HIV and related risk behaviours among jail inmates and needle exchange and drug treatment clients.' Seventh International Conference on AIDS, 16–21 June, Florence, Italy. Abstract No: WC 3362.

Bloor, M., Frischer, M., Taylor, A., Covell, R., Goldberg, D., Green, S., McKeganey, N. and Platt, S. (1994) 'Tideline and turn: possible reasons for the continuing low HIV prevalence among Glasgow's injecting drug users.' *The Sociological Review,* 738–757, 42 (4), 8.

Bruneau, J., Lamothe, F., Lachance, N., Soto, J. and Vincelette, J. (1994a) 'Needle exchange users versus non-users in a population of IVDUs in Montreal.' Fifth International Conference on the Reduction of Drug Related Harm, 6–10 March, Toronto, Ontario, Canada.

Bruneau, J., Lamothe, F., Lachance, N., Soto, J. and Vincelette, J. (1994b) 'HIV prevalence and incidence in a cohort of IDUs in Montreal according to their needle exchange attendance.' Tenth International Conference on AIDS, 7–12 Aug, Yokohama, Japan. Abstract No: PD 0496.

Bruneau, J., Lamothe, F., Lachance, N., Vincelette, J. and Soto, J. (1995) 'Needle exchange programme attendance and HIV-1 infection in Montreal: report of a paradoxical association.' Sixth International Conference on the Reduction of Drug Related Harm, 26–30 March, Florence, Italy. Abstract No: SA9.

Buning, E. (1991) 'Effects of Amsterdam needle and syringe exchange.' *The International Journal of Addictions 26,* 12, 1303–1311.

Calsyn, D.A., Saxon, A.J., Freeman, G. and Whittaker, S. (1991) 'Needle-use practices among intravenous drug users in an area where needle purchase is legal.' *AIDS 5*, 187–193.

Des Jarlais, D., Friedman, S., Sotheran, J., Wenston, J., Marmor, M., Yancovitz, S., Frank, B., Beatrice, S. and Mildvan, D. (1994) 'Continuity and change within an HIV epidemic.' *JAMA 271*, 2, 121–127.

Donoghoe, M.C., Stimson, G.V., Dolan, K. and Alldritt, L. (1989) 'Changes in HIV risk behaviour in clients of syringe-exchange schemes in England and Scotland.' *AIDS 3*, 267–272.

Durante, A., Hart, G., Brady, A., Madden, P. and Noone, A. (1995) 'The Health of the Nation Target on syringe sharing: A role for routine surveillance in assessing progress and targeting interventions.' *Addiction 90*, 10, 1389–1396.

Frischer, M. and Elliott, L. (1993) 'Discriminating needle exchange attenders from non-attenders.' *Addiction 88*, 681–687.

Groseclose, S., Weinstein, S., Jones, S., Valleroy, A., Fehrs, J. and Kassler, J. (1995) 'Impact of increased legal access to needles and syringes on the practices of injecting drug users and police officers–Connecticut 1992–1993.' *Journal of Acquired Immune Deficiency Syndromes and Human Retrovirology 10*, 1, 82–89.

Gruer, L.D., Peedle, M., Carrington, D., Clements, G.B. and Follet, E.A. (1991) 'Distribution of HIV and acute hepatitis B infection among drug injectors in Glasgow.' *International Journal of STD & AIDS 2*, 356–358.

Grund, J.P., Kaplan, C. and Adriaans, N. (1991) 'Featuring high-risk behaviour: needle sharing in the Netherlands.' *American Journal of Public Health 81*, 12, 1602–1607.

Hagan, H., Des Jarlais, D.C., Purchase, D., Reid, T.R. and Friedman, S.R. (1991a) 'Lower HIV seroprevalence, declining HBV incidence, and safer injection in relation to the Tacoma syringe exchange.' International Conference on AIDS, 16–21 June, Florence, Italy. Abstract No: W.C. 3291.

Hagan, H., Reid, T., Des Jarlais, D.C., Purchase, D., Friedman, S. and Bell, T.A. (1991b) 'The incidence of HBV infection and syringe programs.' *JAMA 266*, 12, 1646–1647.

Hagan, H., Des Jarlais, D.C., Friedman, S.R., Purchase, D. and Reid, T.R. (1992) 'Multiple outcome measures of the impact of the Tacoma syringe exchange.' 8th International Conference on AIDS, 19–24 July, Amsterdam. Abstract No: POC4283.

Hagan, H., Des Jarlais, D.C., Purchase, D., Friedman, S., Reid, T. and Bell, T. (1993) 'An Interview study of participants in the Tacoma, Washington, syringe exchange.' *Addiction 88*, 1691–1697.

Hagan, H., Des Jarlias, D., Friedman, S., Purchase, D. and Alter, M. (1995) 'Reduced risk of Hepatitis B and Hepatitis C among injection drug users in the Tacoma Syringe Exchange Programme.' *American Journal of Public Health 85*, 11, 1531–1537.

Hart, G.J., Carvell, L.M., Woodward, N., Johnson, A.M., Williams, Parry. J.V. (1989) 'Evaluation of needle exchange in central London: behaviour change and anti-HIV status over one year.' *AIDS 3*, 261–265.

Hartgers, C., Buning, E., Van Santen, G.W., Vester, A.D. and Coutinho, R.A. (1989) 'The impact of the needle and syringe-exchange programme in Amsterdam on injecting risk behaviour.' *AIDS 3*, 571–576.

Kaplan, E. and Heimer, R. (1994) 'A circulation theory of needle exchange.' *AIDS 8*, 567–574.

Kaplan, E. and Heimer, R. (1995) 'HIV incidence among New Haven needle exchange participants: updated estimates from syringe tracking and testing data.' *Journal of Acquired Immune Deficiency Syndromes and Human Retrovirology 10*, 2, 175–176.

Keene, J., Stimson, G., Jones, S. and Parry-Langdon, N. (1993) 'Evaluation of syringe exchange for HIV prevention among injecting drug users in rural and urban areas of Wales.' *Addiction 88*, 1063–1070.

Klee, H., Faugier, J., Hayes, C. and Morris, J. (1991) 'The sharing of injecting equipment among drug users attending prescribing clinics and those using needle-exchanges.' *British Journal of Addiction 86*, 217–222.

Klee, H. and Morris, J. (1995) 'The role of needle exchanges in modifying sharing behaviour: cross-study comparisons 1989–1993.' *Addiction 90*, 1635–1645.

O'Brien, M.V., Murry, J., Ouellet, L. and Wayne, W. (1995) 'Needle exchanges in Chicago: the demand for free needles and the impacts of the exchange.' Sixth International Conference on the Reduction of Drug Related Harm, 26–30 March, Florence, Italy. Abstract No: SA9.

Paone, D., Des Jarlais, D.C., Caloir, S., Jose, B. and Friedman, S.R. (1994) 'New York city syringe exchange: expansion, risk reduction and seroincidence.' Tenth International Conference on AIDS, 7–12 Aug, Yokohama, Japan. Abstract No: PC0470.

Rhodes, T., Hunter, G., Stimson, G., Donoghoe, M., Noble, A., Parry, J. and Chalmers, C. (1996) 'Prevalence of markers for hepatitis B virus and HIV 1 among drug injectors in London: injecting careers, positivity and risk behaviour.' *Addiction 91*, 10, 1457–1467.

Robinson, G.M., Reynolds, J.N. and Robinson, B.J. (1995) 'Hepatitis C prevalence and needle/syringe sharing behaviours in recent onset injecting drug users.' *New Zealand Medical Journal 108*, 996, 103–105.

Sheridan, J., Strang, J., Barber, N. and Glanz, A. (1996) 'Role of community pharmacies in relation to HIV prevention and drug misuse: findings from the 1995 National Survey in England and Wales.' *British Medical Journal 313*, 272–274.

Stimson, G.V., Alldritt, L.J., Dolan, K., Donoghoe, M.C. and Lart, R.A. (1988) *Injecting Equipment Exchange Schemes: Final Report*. Monitoring Research Group, Goldsmiths College, University of London.

Stimson, G., Eaton, G., Rhodes, T. and Power, R. (1994) 'Potential development of community oriented HIV outreach among drug injectors in the UK.' *Addiction 89,* 1601–1611.

Taylor, A., Frischer, M., Green, S., Goldberg, D., McKeganey, N. and Gruer, L. (1994) 'Low and stable prevalence of HIV among drug injectors in Glasgow.' *International Journal of STD & AIDS 5,* 105–107.

Van Ameijden, E.J.C., Van den Hoek, J.A.R., Haastrecht, H.J.A. and Coutinho, R.A. (1992) 'The harm reduction approach and risk factors for Human Immunodeficiency Virus (HIV) seroconversion in injecting drug users, Amsterdam.' *American Journal of Epidemiology 136,* 236–243.

Van Ameijden, E.J.C., Anneke, M., Van den Hoek, J.A.R. and Coutinho, R.A. (1994) 'Injecting risk behaviour among drug users in Amsterdam, 1986 to 1992, and its relationship to AIDS prevention programs.' *American Journal of Public Health 84,* 2, 275–281.

Van Beek, I., Buckley, R., Stewart, M., Macdonald, M. and Kaldor, J. (1994) 'Risk factors for Hepatitis C virus infection among injecting drug users in Sydney.' *Genitourinary Medicine 70,* 321.

Watters, J. and Cheng, Y.T. (1991) 'Syringe exchange in San Francisco: preliminary findings.' International Conference on AIDS, June 16–21, Florence, Italy. Abstract No: TH. C 99.

Watters, J., Estilo, M., Clark, G. and Lorvick, J. (1994) 'Syringe and needle exchange as HIV/AIDS prevention for drug users.' *JAMA 271,* 2, 115–120.

Wodak, A. (1995) 'Needle exchange and bleach distribution programmes: the Australian experience.' *International Journal of Drug Policy 6,* 1, 46–57.

CHAPTER 9

Community Intervention Among Hidden Populations of Injecting Drug Users in the Time of AIDS

Tim Rhodes and Gerry V. Stimson[1]

Two key challenges face public health interventions targeting injecting drug users (IDUs) in the time of AIDS. The first is reaching the target population. The second is encouraging behaviour change.

A variety of innovative interventions have been introduced in response to these challenges. First, interventions have aimed to 'reach-out' to IDUs, the majority of whom are 'hidden' from contact with health agencies (Frischer 1992). Despite evidence of behaviour change, IDUs who are not in contact with services are often at highest risk of HIV and other infections (Stimson 1991). This has demanded the need for interventions which are oriented towards working directly in the community. Second, not only have interventions attempted to provide IDUs with the knowledge and means to reduce the risks associated with their drug use, they have experimented with intervention strategies designed to bring about community-wide changes in drug use norms and practices. This has demanded the need not only to work *in* the community but *with* the community so as to foster group-mediated community changes within IDU peer and social networks (Rhodes 1993; Stimson *et al.* 1994).

1   The authors are grateful to the Department of Health, Health Education Authority and National AIDS Trust who funded Tim Rhodes to make field visits to peer outreach projects in North America and Australia, and to North Thames Region who provide core funding to the Centre for Research on Drugs and Health Behaviour.

This chapter outlines the development of community HIV prevention responses among IDUs. Tracing the emergence of 'outreach' in the context of UK policy shifts towards a renewed emphasis on harm reduction, the chapter goes on to describe key models of community intervention designed to prevent HIV among hidden populations of IDUs. The chapter ends by identifying four emerging principles which are of key relevance to future intervention developments.

Public health pragmatism and outreach responses

The advent of HIV infection has been associated with a process of change in British drug policy characterised by a greater emphasis on public health pragmatism (see Chapter 5). The shift was from a singular emphasis on the prevention of drug misuse *per se* towards the prevention of harms, and particularly HIV infection, associated with drug use. In 1988, the Advisory Council on the Misuse of Drugs (ACMD)[2] report *AIDS and Drug Misuse* stated:

> We have no hesitation in concluding that the spread of HIV is a greater danger to individual and public health than drug misuse. (ACMD 1988/1989)

This shift in policy emphasis led to reorganisation in service delivery. First, drug users' access to services became less dependent on them actively seeking help (Hartnoll 1992). Instead, services shifted towards more egalitarian approaches whereby they attempted to actively seek out potential patients, now called 'clients'. Second, with the adoption of more egalitarian approaches, visions of 'expertise' to some extent shifted from the professional to those with 'indigenous' status. The shift was from 'business suits to grassroots' (Patton 1990), where '"street credibility" took over from professional credentials' (Stimson and Donoghoe 1996, p.19).

'Outreach' epitomised these shifts in policy and practice.[3] Recognising that agency-based initiatives, such as syringe exchange, are reliant on drug users seek-

---

2   The Advisory Council on the Misuse of Drugs (ACMD) is an independent advisory
      group of experts, established as a result of the 1974 UK Drug Misuse Act, which
      provides policy recommendations to government departments on drug misuse.
3   Outreach can be defined as 'a community-based activity with the overall aim of
      facilitating improvement in health of individuals and groups who are not effectively
      reached by existing services or through traditional health education channels' (Rhodes,
      Holland and Hartnoll 1991).

ing help, outreach was envisaged as a way of reaching-out to 'hidden' populations of IDUs (ACMD 1988). While not a new phenomenon (outreach can be traced back to the philanthropic work with 'down and outs' in Britain in the 1920s), outreach was eagerly embraced as an 'innovative' method of providing IDUs with both the knowledge (via street education) and the means (via condoms and injecting equipment) to risk avoidance. Now a staple component of UK drugs work, outreach is viewed as the key strategy by which agencies 'broaden the constituency' of drug users they contact so as to 'influence greater numbers of drug users at an earlier stage in their drug using career' (ACMD 1993).

Community intervention approaches among IDUs

All behavioural interventions make assumptions about the processes which influence behaviour change. One commonly drawn distinction is between 'individualistic' interventions which target changes in individuals' beliefs and behaviours, and 'community' interventions which aim to encourage collective changes among community groups of IDUs. While individualistic interventions emphasise links between individuals' risk awareness, risk perceptions and self-efficacy to avoid risk, they do not, like collective appoaches, emphasise links between individual behaviours, group social norms and practices and the wider social environment (Friedman, Des Jarlais and Ward 1994; Rhodes 1997).

While the individual–collective distinction represents something of a divide in competing theoretical paradigms, effective health promotion is known to benefit from a combination of individual and community-oriented approaches (WHO and Canadian Public Health Association 1986; Bunton and MacDonald 1992). While individualistic intervention paradigms remain dominant within the field of HIV prevention (such approaches have been termed 'traditional AIDS prevention'; see Broadhead *et al.* 1995), researchers and practitioners increasingly have advocated the need for integrated 'health promotion' approaches which recognise the need for combining individualistic 'knowledge and means' interventions with collective models of social change (Rhodes 1993; Friedman *et al.* 1994). As a consequence, a burgeoning research literature has debated the relative merits of 'model' intervention approaches among IDUs. These range from 'provider–client' models of 'individual outreach', to community-oriented models of 'peer outreach' and 'social diffusion', to models of 'community development' and 'collective action'. Each of these are in some way distinct in the theoretical and practical assumptions they make about intervention strategy and behaviour change. In an attempt to clarify these distinctions, we outline below a typological description of models of community intervention among IDUs.

Provider–client models of individual outreach

Provider–client models of outreach consist of a small number of professionally employed outreach workers (OWs) who 'reach out' to individual drug users with the aim of providing health education and prevention materials directly in the community (Broadhead *et al.* 1995; Grund *et al.* 1996). By far the most common form of outreach in Europe and the USA, most provider–client interventions target changes in individual clients' health beliefs and risk behaviour. Based on one-to-one interactions between provider and client, outreach contacts proceed in an 'arithmetic' fashion throughout target populations (Stimson *et al.* 1994). Outreach providers, usually a combination of 'professionally' trained and 'indigenous' workers (i.e. former/current drug users), aim to bring about changes in clients' behaviour either directly in the community by *in situ* health education or indirectly by referral to agency-based health services (Des Jarlais 1989; Rhodes *et al.* 1991).

Provider–client outreach has had considerable success in reaching IDUs with no history of previous contact with helping services, and in distributing prevention materials (condoms, needles, syringes, bleach) (Booth and Wiebel 1992; Buning 1990; Des Jarlais 1989; Rhodes *et al.* 1991; Watters *et al.* 1990). Studies also associate outreach with increases in clients' risk awareness and reductions in injecting risk behaviour (McCoy, Rivers and Khoury 1993; Stephens, Feucht and Roma 1991; Neaigus *et al.* 1990). In some cases, controlled or comparative evaluations associate risk reduction changes brought about as a result of outreach with a levelling in HIV incidence among target IDUs (Watters *et al.* 1990; Wiebel *et al.* 1994).

But provider–client models of outreach are not without their problems. First, they are limited by the numbers of IDUs reached by OWs. One-to-one provider–client contacts 'allows only arithmetic progression into the target population, limiting the numbers who can be effectively reached' (Stimson *et al.* 1994). UK evaluation suggests that it is 'easier-to-reach' IDUs who are most likely to be contacted, and that those most in need of services often remain uncontacted by OWs (Rhodes *et al.* 1991).

Second, provider–client models are limited by their over-reliance on individualistic modes of behaviour change. Ethnographic work indicates that drug users' risk behaviour is not simply the product of individuals' beliefs and intentions, but is dependent on a variety of influences, such as the types of social relationships in which risk behaviours occur, and the social norms and values common to particular peer groups, social networks and subcultures (Grund 1993; Koester 1996; Sibthorpe 1992; Zule 1992). The individualised nature of provider–client contacts limits the possibilities for targeting wider social relationships within IDU networks as a means of facilitating group-mediated 'community change' (Rhodes 1993). An over-reliance, particularly in the UK, on provider–client models of individualised change has meant that 'outreach has not yet reached its full potential' (ACMD 1993).

Third, research suggests that provider–client models of outreach are associated with a number of organisational problems. Broadhead and Heckathorn (1994) have identified a range of agency problems associated with managing OWs within a provider–client model. These include problems associated with supervision, occupational hazards, relapse, lack of career structure, conflicts between the local culture and the outreach project, and political conflicts between OWs and managers. While the extent to which these problems are also associated with other modes of outreach delivery is unclear, it is likely that many UK outreach projects have suffered as a consequence of inappropriate or ineffective management (ACMD 1993; Stimson *et al.* 1994).

Models of peer outreach and social diffusion

The success of any behavioural intervention is in some way dependent on how it is received by its target population. This has led to the realisation that IDUs are not merely reactive or passive receivers of providers' HIV prevention messages, but that they are effective prevention advocates in their own right (Wiebel 1988; Rhodes 1994). The restrictive and dependent status of drug users as 'clients' in provider–client models limits the possibilities for IDUs to work as independent agents of HIV prevention and change within their peer groups and social networks. In response, recent developments in community outreach among IDUs emphasise the need for interventions to foster peer support.

Peer outreach models make two assumptions. First, that IDUs make effective advocates for HIV prevention, and second, that changing peer group norms and practices are an effective method for facilitating individual and collective behaviour change. There is considerable evidence to support the first of these contentions, and increasing evidence to support the second. As ethnographic observations of peer outreach indicate:

> ...we have found that as addicts become aware of the threat that AIDS poses, they are quite capable of assimilating a strong sense of social responsibility which can be readily channelled to include an assumed role of prevention advocacy. (Wiebel 1988, p.147)

While only a minority of outreach projects in the UK employ 'indigenous' OWs (approximately 10 percent in 1989: see Hartnoll *et al.* 1990), evaluation studies in the United States suggest that former or current IDUs, and OWs working within peer outreach projects, are more effective in making contacts with hidden IDUs than conventional provider–client projects (Broadhead *et al.* 1995; Friedman *et al.* 1992; Grund *et al.* 1996). Overcoming the inherent limitations of 'arithmetic progression', IDUs working as prevention advocates among their peers, allow for 'geometric progression' throughout IDU networks (Stimson *et al.* 1994). Similar to 'pyramid selling', peer education aims to bring about a cascade of change, like a domino effect, along pre-existing channels of communication within IDU social networks.

This makes for a different type of behaviour change strategy than that commonly employed by outreach initiatives. Change becomes a process of social diffusion–not unlike that championed by diffusion of innovation theory (Rogers and Shoemaker 1971) – where ideas of risk reduction are 'communicated through certain channels over time among members of a social system' (Rogers 1983, p.5). This shifts the intervention target and unit of change from individuals to their social relationships. The vision shared by peer interventions is that they aim to mobilise changes in the risk norms and practices of communities as a whole (Friedman *et al.* 1992; Rhodes 1993, 1994). In viewing drug users' risk behaviours as 'social actions' which take shape through the course of group interactions, peer outreach aims to influence the social relations of risk by modifying how risk is defined and managed within different social groups of IDUs. The rationale for this is that group-mediated changes help to create the social conditions where individual and group behaviour-changes become easier to initiate and maintain (Rogers 1983).

In the UK, there is a lack of evidence about the effectiveness of peer outreach (ACMD 1993). Despite recent policy recommendations that clients of drug services should become 'peer educators' (ACMD 1993, p.79), there has yet to be a systematic evaluation of a peer intervention among UK IDUs (Hunter *et al.* 1997). In the United States, where the National Institute on Drug Abuse (NIDA) has funded over 40 evaluations of outreach demonstration projects (Fisher and Needle 1993), there is an ongoing debate about which models of peer intervention are preferred and which are most likely to yield the greatest levels of behaviour change. Two models at the centre of this debate are outlined below.

Indigenous Leader models (ILM)

The Indigenous Leader Outreach Intervention Model (IL) was developed at the University of Illinois at Chicago by Wayne Wiebel and colleagues (1988, 1996). Evolving out of earlier experiments to develop a multi-method approach to contain community outbreaks of heroin use (Hughes and Crawford 1972), the IL model combines community ethnography with medical epidemiology to target reductions in HIV risk behaviour within community networks of IDUs (Wiebel 1988, 1996).

The IL model aims to do this by first identifying, and then encouraging, pre-existing 'leaders' within IDU social networks to advocate risk reduction among their peers. First, ethnographers, working from 'field-stations' in different parts of the city, identify key leaders within different IDU social networks. Second, indigenous OWs, who also work as ethnographers, aim to make contact with IDUs. Third, the targeting of key 'natural' leaders by indigenous OWs, and their subsequent recruitment as AIDS Prevention Advocates, aims to generate network diffusion of socially responsible beliefs about risk reduction and, over time, a collective response to behaviour change (Wiebel 1988).

The idea of 'indigenous leaders' and network diffusion draws on the principles developed in communication of innovations theory (Rogers and Shoemaker 1971; Rogers 1983). By using ethnography, the model identifies how the characteristics of networks influence the desire and parameters for change. By using indigenous workers/leaders it recognises the importance of ownership over the intervention, accepts the importance of homophily[4] between community members and change agents, and acknowledges that the community governs the likelihood of adopting and sustaining change (Rogers 1983). Epidemiological monitoring of the IL project suggests the intervention has brought about reductions in risk behaviour and a decline in new HIV infections within targeted IDU networks (Wiebel *et al.* 1994; Booth and Wiebel 1992).

Peer Driven Intervention models (PDI)

The East Connecticut Outreach Project (ECHO) provides an example of peer outreach where the pre-existing structure of IDU networks is defined less by ethnographic research than by IDUs themselves (Broadhead *et al.* 1995; Grund *et al.* 1996). This 'peer driven intervention' model (PDI) employs ethnography and OWs to make initial contact with IDUs and to develop appropriate intervention messages, but thereafter encourages IDUs, by a coupon system of peer-referral, to contact and educate their peers (Broadhead *et al.* 1995). Once having been contacted and educated by agency OWs, IDUs are given three 'recruitment coupons' to give to their peers. For every peer contact who receives education and a coupon from the IDU, and who returns to the agency for an interview, the IDU receives $10 (i.e. $30 for three peer recruits). In addition, the IDU can earn a further $30 depending on how well their three peer recruits perform in a risk reduction knowledge test conducted at the agency (i.e. a total of $60 for three recruits who return to the agency and 'pass' the knowledge test). Once peer recruits have undertaken their knowledge test, they too can be trained to work as peer educators, and are given $20 as an incentive and three 'recruitment coupons' to give to peer contacts of their own. This is a form of 'geometric' progression where all IDUs contacted by the project are given incentives to act as peer educators and to 'sell on' the intervention message to others.

Whereas the IL model targets intervention on the basis of ethnographic observations of network structures and intra-group leadership potential, the PDI is 'peer driven' in that it simply taps into pre-existing channels of communication and in-

4   Homophily is defined as 'the degree to which pairs of individuals who interact are
     similar in certain attributes, such as beliefs, values, education, social status' (Rogers and
     Shoemaker 1971).

fluence as they 'naturally occur' within IDU networks (Broadhead and Heckathorn 1994). The IL model 'ethnographically' guides innovation diffusion by identifying which IDUs appear to have most influence in 'policing' network norms, while the PDI diffuses innovation through a cue system of 'group-mediated social control' (Heckathorn 1990) where individuals are given 'positive reinforcements' to 'police' others' risk behaviour:

> A PDI works by strengthening the regulatory interests of members of the drug-using community by providing direct rewards to members for eliciting positive responses from their peers. (Broadhead *et al.* 1995, p.543)

While it is questionable the extent to which there are differences associated with the selection of indigenous leaders as 'prevention advocates' (as with the IL model) and the opportunity for any IDU to work as a peer educator (as with the PDI), the PDI aims for greater points of communication entry into IDU networks. Evaluation findings to date–which are not tailored to assessing differences in outcome between PDI and IL models–suggest that PDIs achieve a greater level of contact with IDUs, at less cost per contact, than traditional provider–client models of outreach, and that contacts of PDIs achieve higher knowledge scores on risk reduction than contacts of OWs (Broadhead *et al.* 1995). No data are yet available on IDUs' risk behaviour. In the absence of behavioural data it is difficult to conclude how effective the model is as HIV prevention. While the possibility of earning $60 may act as an incentive for IDUs to become involved in the project, and to pass on risk reduction knowledge to their peers, the PDI has yet to demonstrate that it is in any way more effective than provider–client or IL interventions in encouraging and sustaining greater levels of behaviour change. The emphasis on monetary incentives may also be inappropriate in some cultural and economic contexts.

Models of community development and collective action

The use of peer influence as a method of diffusing and reinforcing change in IDUs' social relationships can be viewed as a first step towards encouraging community change. Yet peer interventions–which are invariably organised by outside agents–are distinct from models of intervention which explicitly aim to encourage 'collective action'.

Following the principles of 'community action'–which involves 'deliberate organisation of community members to accomplish some objective or goal' (Brown 1991, p.446)–and 'community organisation'–which involves attempts to 'form temporary or permanent organisational structures involving members of a community' (Brown 1991, p.446)–community development aims to foster collective action among IDUs (Friedman *et al.* 1987; Friedman, De Jong and Wodak 1993; Jose *et al.* 1996). These interventions promise to 'work through collective community action' with 'communities having their own power and having control of their own initiatives and activities' (Ashton and Seymour 1990, p.26).

While there is a strong advocacy of community development among professionals working with IDU populations (Friedman *et al.* 1993), there are few documented examples of collective action among IDUs. It has been said that 'organisations of injecting drug users are part of the backdrop' (Crofts and Herkt 1995, p.599), but it is also the case that community development has rarely been attempted among IDUs.

A number of factors may limit the efficacy of collective action among IDUs. First, IDU networks lack pre-existing organisational infrastructures for mobilising collectively. Drug use, though an ostensibly 'social' activity, does not necessarily encourage a shared sense of community or political identity among drug users. While social relationships within IDU networks can, and do, encourage peer support, the functionality of these networks often works against the creation of any meaningful sense of 'community' as might be the case among some other social groups, such as gay men (Kayal 1993; Patton 1990).

Second, many attempted IDU collective action groups suffer managerial problems. Evidence, which is primarily anecdotal, points to a lack of shared or sustained interest, and internal conflict, among community members (Jose *et al.* 1996). While no collective action group is immune from internal conflict or intra-community difference (ACT-UP and GMHC provide examples: see Kayal 1993), the 'hustling' culture said to be common to many drug use lifestyles may impede the organisation and management of collective action groups among active IDUs (Booth and Koester 1996). Examples do exist where drug user organisations temporarily folded because 'the treasurer ran away with the money' (Crofts and Herkt 1995).

Third, in many countries the political and legal status of injecting drug use impedes the creation of collective action groups with any meaningful power. Not only is injecting drug use commonly marginalised outside the health service, IDUs may also be marginalised within health services as both 'difficult to manage' and 'manipulative'. There are, regrettably, few health organisations which would outwardly champion the idea of collective action among their IDU clients.

Non-assisted collective action

The earliest known example of an 'autonomous' (i.e. initially established without assistance from outside agencies) drug users' organisation is the Dutch Junkiebonden (Friedman *et al.* 1993). Established in the 1970s, and with little opposition from law enforcement authorities, the Junkiebonden helped form the first syringe exchange in the Netherlands in 1984 (Kools and Buurman 1984). There are few other documented examples of non-assisted user groups, although such groups exist across a number of European countries, the United States, New Zealand and Australia (Burrows and Price 1993; Friedman *et al.* 1993).

The development of drug user organisations in Australia has been unique. Thought to be the first country, in 1992, to have included the words 'harm reduction' in a national drug policy document (Crofts and Herkt 1995), the National AIDS Strategy gave considerable emphasis to the importance of peer education and community development as early as 1989 (Commonwealth Department of Health 1990). From the outset, national policies were developed and implemented in close consultation with representatives of HIV-affected communities (Crofts and Herkt 1995). By 1988, and as a direct result of the Strategy, a national umbrella organisation, the Australian IV League, was established with responsibility for coordinating user groups in the six states of Australia.

Most state user groups were established around 1987 (for a full description see Crofts and Herkt 1995). The Victorian Intravenous AIDS Group (VIVAIDS), which consisted of approximately 30 members in 1987, established the state's first peer-based syringe exchange. Monitoring showed the exchange to be effective in reaching hidden IDUs and in encouraging secondary distribution among exchange attenders and their peers (Herkt 1993). Similar to evaluation findings of a peer-based syringe exchange in Rotterdam (Grund *et al.* 1992), the VIVAIDS exchange was said to be more effective in distributing equipment than non peer-based exchanges in Victoria (Herkt 1993). In the neighbouring state, the South Australian Voice for Intravenous Equity (SAVIVE) also ran a peer-based exchange.

This had the largest client attendance and distribution network of any exchange in South Australia (Crofts and Herkt 1995).

Both the New South Wales Users and AIDS Association (NUAA) and the Queensland IV AIDS Association (QuIVAA) have had considerable success as lobby groups for IDUs (Burrows and Price 1993; Crofts and Herkt 1995). But as the projects became more successful in their political lobbying activities, and in forging links with other health professionals and policy development agencies, the organisations' identity as peer projects diluted, and the direct involvement of current street IDUs in service management and planning diminished. This highlights the tensions which may arise between working independently as a user-led provider of street outreach (such as syringe exchange) and working in collaboration with non-drug users and health professionals so as to gain the funding and organisational base from which to undertake lobbying activities (see below).

Assisted collective action and community development

Assisted collective action groups are those which are organised 'from the outside' (Jose *et al.* 1996). One of the earliest documented examples in the field of HIV prevention is New York's Association for Drug Abuse Prevention and Treatment (ADAPT) (Friedman and Casriel 1989). Encouraged by the support of interested health professionals, and with initial funding from the New York City Department of Health, ADAPT consists primarily of former IDUs who undertake street outreach and community organising initiatives with IDUs (Des Jarlais 1989; Friedman *et al.* 1992).

One such initiative, funded as part of NIDA community outreach research, was undertaken in Williamsburg, Brooklyn (Friedman *et al.* 1992; Jose *et al.* 1996). This aimed to identify community leaders with a view to establishing a drug user organisation and to provide street outreach distributing bleach kits.[5] The initiative was unsuccessful in forming a user group or in identifying permanent leadership, in part because of conflicts over whether the intervention should emphasise individually oriented counselling or collective organising. Despite this, evaluation associ-

---

5   Bleach, which is commonly distributed in cities without adequate syringe exchange
     distribution, provides a method for IDUs to disinfect used needles and syringes.
     Research indicates that injecting equipment must be exposed to full-strength bleach for
     at least 30 seconds to inactivate residual HIV (Shapshak.MDBR/et al..MDNM/ 1993).

ates the intervention with increased risk reduction among IDUs in the target neighbourhood, and suggests that the greatest risk reduction changes were made among IDUs participating in peer support meetings (Jose *et al.* 1996).

Assisted models are by far the most common form of community organising in the United States. Operating on a similar model to the New York initiatives is a research–provider collaboration in San Francisco known as Prevention Point (Moore and Wenger 1995). Prevention Point, which is an illegal syringe exchange–Californian state laws prohibit syringe exchange (Watters 1996)–was established in 1988 through a collaboration between interested IDUs, former IDUs, health professionals and researchers. Despite state paraphernalia laws, Prevention Point gained informal support from local police throughout 1989, and clandestine City funding as early as 1990 (Moore and Wenger 1995). In 1993, when the San Francisco Department of Public Health called a state of emergency in a City attempt to challenge state paraphernalia laws, the City agreed, for the first time, to fund legal supplies of injecting equipment and three full-time positions at the exchange.

Now the largest syringe exchange in the United States, there has been a shift towards more bureaucratic forms of management and Prevention Point's status as a user-led intervention has become confused. Operating in 'legal limbo' at the state level, and thus dependent on the City for support, Prevention Point is 'not mandated to encourage IDUs to self-organise' yet if it should 'play a progressive role in organising IDUs, it may find itself...in the politically murky territory of "hating the sin but loving the sinner"' (Moore and Wenger 1995, p.595). In a legal and political climate not unlike other US cities, this makes for a very precarious position for some assisted models of collective action:

> If...the organisation attempts to reconcile internal desires to empower IDUs and work collaboratively with them, as opposed to a service agency that administers to them, it will find itself in direct opposition to both the national orientation toward abstention and the personal orientation of some volunteers. (Moore and Wenger 1995, p.595)

Emerging principles governing effective intervention

Community interventions are a key component of effective HIV prevention strategy. The underlying principles of health promotion, as outlined in the World Health Organization Ottawa Charter for Health Promotion, recognise the need to balance individual and community action as a means of facilitating changes in individual and collective health status (WHO and Canadian Public Health Association 1986). The prevention of adverse health conditions not only requires changes in individuals' health beliefs and awareness but also re-orientation in service delivery, community action, social environments supportive of risk reduction, and pragmatic public policy (WHO and Canadian Public Health Association 1986). Risk reduction among IDUs demands a strategic approach to intervention which encourages change at the levels of the individual, the community and the wider social environment (Rhodes 1996; Ball 1998).

For the most part, intervention responses among IDUs have evolved out of a public health realism about the dangers associated with the uncontrolled spread of HIV. In many countries, this has led to rapid re-orientation in service delivery towards 'lower threshold' interventions emphasising the prevention of harm associated with the continued injection of drugs (Stimson 1995). Yet while many HIV prevention interventions are community-based, few are community-oriented. Most interventions are individually-oriented, and adopt a 'knowledge and means' approach to individual behaviour change (Friedman *et al.* 1994). Despite increasing advocacy for community action and collective models of change, such approaches are rarely applied among IDUs (Rhodes 1993). Even less likely are interventions which explicitly aim to foster 'political action' as a means of creating the social and policy conditions supportive of risk reduction.

This chapter has provided a typological description of community interventions targeting IDUs. While not an exhaustive review, and based on limited evaluation data, taken together these initiatives provide useful pointers to some emerging principles which may govern the effectiveness of future community interventions among IDUs.

First, effective HIV prevention among IDUs requires a community-based response. Outreach has been found to be an effective method for reaching hidden populations of IDUs and for distributing the 'means' for individuals to make risk reduction changes. While outreach to some extent has gained mythological status as an intrevention panacea in the field of HIV prevention, it is best viewed as a pragmatic method of public health intervention delivery. Outreach, particularly in the absence of pre-existing infrastructures for community organising, provides a cost-efficient method of reaching and providing services directly in the community (Des Jarlais 1989).

Second, effective HIV prevention among IDUs requires community participation. The effectiveness of outreach is to a large extent dependent on the active involvement of IDUs themselves. In provider–client models of outreach, the relative success that 'providers' have had in reaching 'clients' has been dependent on the extent to which clients actively assist providers in their work. An over-reliance on provider–client models may limit the effectiveness and efficiency of interventions, whereas outreach which explicitly aims to foster peer support and community involvement may have greater success in reaching IDUs and in bringing about lasting behaviour change (Broadhead *et al.* 1995; Friedman *et al.* 1994; Wiebel 1996).

Third, effective HIV prevention among IDUs requires community change. Individually-oriented interventions, which target changes in individual beliefs and behaviours, are only partially effective. There is a concomitant need for 'community changes' towards risk reduction within peer groups and social networks of IDUs. Individually- and community-oriented interventions are theoretically and methodologically distinct, but each are part of an integrated community intervention response to enabling change. This highlights the importance of 'peer driven' and 'indigenous leader' approaches which explicitly aim to bring about group-mediated changes within IDU social networks. Future HIV prevention among IDUs not only demands action among individual IDUs, but also demands community action among IDUs (Rhodes 1993). A key underlying principle of effective health promotion, as well as of HIV prevention, is the need to strengthen community action and peer support among target populations themselves (WHO 1996; Canadian Public Health Association 1996, Ball 1998).

Fourth, effective HIV prevention among IDUs may require changes in public policy and attitudes. It is misleading to assume that by targeting individuals alone interventions will create the social conditions necessary for behaviour change. At the outset, interventions require an appreciation of how individual and group attempts at risk reduction can be encouraged or constrained by the wider social and political environment. In the same way as individual actions operate within the constraints and boundaries of group and community norms, community actions operate within the constraints and boundaries of the political and legal environment. The relative success of community organising initiatives among IDUs are to a large extent dependent on there being pre-existing infrastructures for organising within the community (Jose *et al.* 1996) and public policy which is supportive, rather than repressive, of such actions (Crofts and Herkt 1995; Moore and Wenger 1995). The instability of many IDU collective action groups can be related to the lack of community identity and organisational infrastructure within IDU communities which in turn bears some relation to the wider social, political and legal environment as far as injecting drug use is concerned.

Future HIV prevention initiatives among IDUs need to continue to provide the 'knowledge and means' for behaviour change, but such an approach not only demands individually-oriented behaviour change strategies, but also concomitant changes in the community and wider social environment. If the principles of effective health promotion as outlined by the World Health Organization are to be followed, effective HIV prevention demands a multi-oriented intervention strategy which emphasises the central importance of community interventions alongside interventions targeting political and social change (WHO and Canadian Public Health Association 1986). The second decade of AIDS prevention among IDUs will need to consolidate community intervention approaches as part of mainstream HIV prevention.

References

Advisory Council on the Misuse of Drugs (ACMD) (1988/1989) *AIDS and Drug Misuse. Parts One and Two.* London: HMSO.

Advisory Council on the Misuse of Drugs (ACMD) (1993) *AIDS and Drug Misuse: Update.* London: Department of Health.

Ashton, J. and Seymour, H. (1990) *The New Public Health.* Milton Keynes: Open University Press.

Ball, A. (1998) 'Overview: policies and interventions to stem HIV-1 epidemics associated with IDU'. In G.V. Stimson, D.C. Des Jarlais and A. Ball (eds) *Drug Injecting and HIV Infection: Global and Local Responses.* London: Taylor and Francis.

Booth, R. and Koester, S.K. (1996) 'Issues and approaches to evaluating HIV outreach interventions.' *Journal of Drug Issues 26*, 3, 525–539.

Booth, R.E. and Wiebel, W.W. (1992) 'The effectiveness of reducing needle-related risks for HIV through indigenous outreach to injection drug users.' *American Journal on the Addictions 1*, 277–288.

Broadhead, R.S. and Heckathorn, D.D. (1994) 'AIDS prevention outreach among injection drug users: agency problems and new approaches.' *Social Problems 41*, 473–495.

Broadhead, R.S. Heckathorn, D.D, Grund, J.P, Stern, L.S. and Anthony, D.L. (1995) 'Drug users versus outreach workers in combating AIDS: preliminary results of a peer-driven intervention.' *The Journal of Drug Issues 25*, 3, 531–564.

Brown, E.R. (1991) 'Community action for health promotion: a strategy to empower individuals and communities.' *International Journal of Health Services 21*, 441–456.

Buning, E. (1990) 'The role of harm reduction programmes in curbing the spread of HIV by drug injectors.' In J. Strang and G.V. Stimson (eds) *AIDS and Drug Misuse*. London: Routledge.

Bunton, R. and MacDonald, G. (1992) (eds) *Health Promotion: Disciplines and Diversity*. London: Routledge.

Burrows, D. and Price, C. (1993) 'Peer education among IDUs in Baltimore (US) and Sydney (Australia): similarities and differences within a model of peer education.' Paper presented to Ninth International Conference on AIDS, Berlin.

Commonwealth Department of Health (1990) *National AIDS Strategy*. Canberra: Australian Government Publishing Service.

Crofts N, and Herkt, D. (1995) 'A history of peer-based drug-user groups in Australia.' *The Journal of Drug Issues 25*, 3, 599–616.

Des Jarlais (1989) 'AIDS prevention programs for intravenous drug users: diversity and evolution.' *International Review of Psychiatry 1*, 1, 101–108.

Fisher, D. and Needle, R. (eds) (1993) AIDS and Community-Based Drug Intervention Programs. New York: Harrington Park Press.

Friedman, S.R. and Casriel, C. (1989) 'Drug users organizations and AIDS policy.' *AIDS and Public Policy 3*, 30–36.

Friedman, S.R., De Jong, W. and Wodak, A. (1993) 'Community development as a response to HIV among drug injectors.' *AIDS 7* (Supp. 1), S263–9.

Friedman, S.R., Des Jarlais, D.C. and Ward, T. (1994) 'Social models for changing risk behaviour.' In J. Peterson and R. DiClemente (eds) *Preventing AIDS*. New York: Plenum.

Friedman, S.R., Des Jarlais, D.C. *et al.* (1987) 'AIDS and self-organization among intravenous drug users.' *Health Education Quarterly 13*, 383–394.

Friedman, S.R., Neaigus, A., Des Jarlais, D.C., Sotheran, J.L., Woods, J. and Sufian, M. (1992) 'Social intervention against AIDS among injecting drug users.' *British Journal of Addiction 87*, 393–404.

Frischer, M. (1992) 'Estimated prevalence of injecting drug use in Glasgow.' *British Journal of Addiction 87*, 235–243.

Grund, J-P.C. (1993) *Drug Use as a Social Ritual: Functionality, Symbolism and Determinants of Self-Regulation.* Rotterdam: Erasmus University.

Grund, J.P.C., Blanken, P., Adriaans, N.F.P. *et al.* (1992) 'Reaching the unreached: an outreach model for "on the spot" AIDS prevention among active, out of treatment drug addicts.' In P.A. O'Hare *et al.* (eds) *The Reduction of Drug Related Harm.* London: Routledge.

Grund, J.P.C., Broadhead, R., Heckathorn, D.D. and Stern, L.S. (1996) 'Peer-driven outreach to combat HIV among IDUs: a basic design and preliminary results.' In T. Rhodes and R. Hartnoll (eds) *AIDS, Drugs and Prevention: Perspectives on Individual and Community Action.* London: Routledge.

Hartnoll, R. (1992) 'Research and the help-seeking process.' *British Journal of Addiction 87,* 429–437.

Hartnoll, R., Rhodes, T., Jones, S. *et al.* (1990) *A Survey of HIV Outreach Intervention in the United Kingdom.* University of London: Birkbeck College.

Heckathorn, D. (1990) 'Collective sanctions and compliance norms: a formal theory of group-mediated social control.' *American Sociological Review 5,* 366–384.

Herkt, D. (1993) 'Peer-based user groups: the Australian experience.' In N. Heather *et al.* (eds) *Psychoactive Drugs and Harm Reduction.* London: Wurr Publishers.

Hughes, P. and Crawford, G. (1972) 'A contagious model for researching and intervening in heroin epidemics.' *Archives of General Psychiatry 27,* 149–155.

Hunter, G., Ward, J. and Power, R. (1997) Research and Development focusing on peer intervention for drug users. *Drugs: Education, Prevention and Policy,* 4: 259-278.

Jose, B., Friedman, S.R., Neaigus, A. et al. (1996) 'Collection organisation of injecting drug users and the struggle against AIDS.' In T. Rhodes and R. Hartnoll (eds) *AIDS, Drugs and Prevention: Perspectives on Individual and Community Action.* London: Routledge.

Kayal, P.M. (1993) *Bearing Witness: Gay Men's Health Crisis and the Politics of AIDS.* Oxford: Westview Press.

Koester, S. (1996) 'The process of drug injection: applying ethnography to the study of HIV risk among IDUs.' In T. Rhodes and R. Hartnoll (eds) *AIDS, Drugs and Prevention: Perspectives on Individual and Community Action.* London: Routledge.

Kools, J. and Buurman, J. (1984) Notitie MDHG spuitenomruilsysteem, 5 June.

McCoy, C.B., Rivers, J.E. and Khoury, E.L. (1993) 'An emerging public health model for reducing AIDS-related risk behavior among injecting drug users and their sexual partners.' *Drugs and Society 7,* 3, 143–159.

Moore, L.D and Wenger, L.D. (1995) 'The social context of needle exchange in user self-organisation in San Francisco: Possibililties and pitfalls.' *The Journal of Drug Issues 25,* 3, 583–598.

Neaigus, A., Sufian, M., Friedman, S.R., Goldmith, D., Stepherson, B., Mota, P., Pascal, J. and Des Jarlais, D.C. (1990) 'Effects of outreach intervention on risk reduction among intravenous drug users.' *AIDS Education and Prevention 2*, 253–271.

Patton, C. (1990) *Inventing AIDS.* London: Routledge.

Rogers, E. M. (1983) *Diffusion of Innovations* (3rd edition). New York: Free Press.

Rogers, E.M. and Shoemaker (1971) *Communication of Innovation* (2nd edition). New York: Free Press.

Rhodes, T. (1993) 'Time for community change: what has outreach to offer?' *Addiction* 88, 1317–1320

Rhodes, T. (1994) 'HIV outreach, peer education and community change: developments and dilemmas.' *Health Education Journal 53*, 92–99.

Rhodes, T. (1996) Individual and community action in HIV prevention, in Rhodes, T. and Hartnoll, R. (eds) *AIDS, Drugs and Prevention: Perspectives on Individual and Community Action,* London: Routledge.

Rhodes, T. (1997) 'Risk theory in epidemic times: sex, drugs and the social organisation of "risk behaviour"'. *Sociology of Health and Illness 19*, 208–227.

Rhodes, T. and Hartnoll, R. (1996) (eds) *AIDS, Drugs and Prevention: Perspectives on Individual and Community Action.* London: Routledge.

Rhodes, T., Holland, J. and Hartnoll, R.L. (1991) *Hard to Reach or Out of Reach? An Evaluation of an Innovative Model of HIV Outreach Health Education.* London: Tufnell Press.

Shapshak, P., McCoy, C., Rivers, J. et al. (1993) 'Inactivation of HIV-1 at short time intervals using undiluted bleach.' *Journal of Acquired Immune Deficiency Syndromes 6*, 218–219.

Sibthorpe, B. (1992) 'The social construction of sexual relationships as a determinant of HIV risk perception and condom use among injection drug users.' *Medical Anthropology Quarterly 6*, 255–270.

Stephens, R.C., Feucht, T.E. and Roma, S.W. (1991) 'Effects of an outreach intervention among intravenous drug users.' *American Journal of Public Health 81*, 568–571.

Stimson, G.V. (1991) 'Risk reduction by drug users with regard to HIV infection.' *International Journal of Psychiatry 3*, 401–415.

Stimson, G.V. (1995) 'AIDS and injecting drug use in the United Kingdom, 1987–1993: the policy response and the prevention of the epidemic.' *Social Science and Medicine 41*, 699–716.

Stimson, G.V. and Donoghoe, D.C. (1996) 'Health promotion and the facilitation of individual change: the case of syringe distribution and exchange.' In T. Rhodes and R. Hartnoll (eds) *AIDS, Drugs and Prevention: Perspectives on Individual and Community Action.* London: Routledge.

Stimson, G.V., Eaton, G., Rhodes T. and Power, R. (1994) 'Potential development of community oriented HIV outreach among drug injectors in the UK.' *Addiction 89,* 1601–1611.

Watters, J. (1996) 'Americans and syringe exchnage: roots of resistance.' In T. Rhodes and R. Hartnoll, R. (eds) *AIDS, Drugs and Prevention: Perspectives on Individual and Community Action.* London: Routledge.

Watters, J.K., Downing, P., Case J. et al. (1990) 'AIDS prevention for intravenous drug users in the community: street-based education and risk behavior.' *American Journal of Community Psychology 18,* 587–596.

Wiebel, W. (1988) 'Combining ethnographic and epidemiological methods in targeted AIDS interventions: the Chicago model.' In R. Battjes and R. Pickens (eds) *Needle Sharing Among Intravenous Drug Abusers: National and International Perspectives.* Rockville: NIDA Monograph 80.

Wiebel, W. (1996) 'Ethnographic contributions to AIDS interventions.' In T. Rhodes and R. Hartnoll (eds) *AIDS, Drugs and Prevention: Perspectives on Individual and Community Action.* London: Routledge.

Wiebel, W., Jimenez, A., Johnson, W. et al. (1994) 'Prevention of new HIV infections among out-of-treatment injection drug users: a four year prospective study' (in press).

World Health Organisation (WHO) and Canadian Public Health Association (1986) 'Ottawa Charter for Health Promotion.' *Health Promotion 1,* iii–v.

Zule, W.. A. (1992) 'Risk and reciprocity: HIV and the injection drug user.' *Journal of Psychoactive Drugs 24,* 243–249.

PART V

Providing and Assessing Services

CHAPTER 10

Working with Androgenic Anabolic Steroid Users

Andrew J. McBride, Trudi Petersen and Kathryn Williamson

Introduction and background

The use of performance enhancing (ergogenic) drugs, real and placebo, has been recorded in sport since the ancient cultures of Asia, the Americas, Australia and Europe (Cszaky 1972; Nelson 1989). The first major step towards the scientific understanding of today's most widely used drugs, androgenic anabolic steroids (AAS), was the synthesis of the human hormone, testosterone, in 1935 (Windsor and Dumitri 1988).

The nature of AAS

AAS are a group of more than 16 drugs closely related to testosterone, some naturally occurring, others synthetic. All share androgenic (masculinising) and anabolic (nitrogen-retaining, muscle-promoting) effects which result from activity at specific receptor sites. In the United Kingdom, AAS are covered by the Medicines Act (1968) and not by the Misuse of Drugs Act (1971). Possession of the drug for personal use is therefore legal, but supply to others is prohibited. The Act gives no guidance on how the courts are to distinguish between these reasons for possession. AAS users commonly also take other drugs including diuretics, tamoxifen, clenbutarol, human chorionic gonadotrophin, growth hormone and nalbuphine. It is beyond the scope of this chapter to give details of these other drugs, but complications of their use can be equally problematic.

How are AAS used?

AAS are taken either orally or by deep intramuscular injection. A recent study by Lenehan, Bellis and McVeigh (undated) showed that 49 per cent used both routes of ingestion, 32 per cent only injected and 19 per cent only took orally. AAS are usually 'cycled' so that periods of abstinence are interspersed with periods of use. The times spent on and off drugs should be equal, cycles varying usually from 4 to 12 weeks. AAS users believe that drug holidays allow natural hormonal systems to recover, minimise side effects and avoid drug detection in competition (Brower 1993), but periods of abstinence are frequently shortened and there is little evidence for or against any protective effect on health.

Two common beliefs among AAS users are that different AAS have different effects, and that the higher the dose the greater the effect. Experienced users therefore usually take two or more AAS together ('stacking') and greatly exceed medical doses. Another common technique is 'pyramiding,' which involves increasing and then decreasing doses during a cycle, rather than using the same doses throughout.

Why do people take AAS?

Testosterone and other AAS have very limited legitimate, therapeutic uses. Medical indications in adolescents include some cases of micro penis, delayed puberty, hypogonadism and retarded growth; and in adults, some cases of aplastic anaemia, disseminated breast cancer, intractable itching in chronic biliary obstruction and osteoporosis in post-menopausal women (Moore 1988).

Outside medical settings people take AAS in the belief that they will improve physique, strength and performance. It is not difficult to understand the reasons for the use of AAS among top-class athletes. They devote their lives to training and competing, and are highly rewarded socially and financially. For the successful but not world-beating athlete early in a sporting career, and for the champion in decline, AAS may be viewed as the only method of achieving that vital one per cent improvement. For those who will never reach the top of their chosen sport, or who never compete (such as the majority of bodybuilders), cultural, social and psychological factors may all contribute to the use of AAS.

In the UK, bodybuilding and AAS use appear to be more prevalent in areas of deprivation that previously housed traditional, heavy industry. This would fit with suggestions that AAS might compensate for uncertainties about men's role in post-industrial society. Following Harlow (1951) and Thune (1949), Mishkind *et al.* (1986) suggest that weightlifters and bodybuilders, in comparison with those engaging in other sports, might be trying to compensate for a lowered sense of masculinity. They conclude that 'one of the only remaining ways that men can express and preserve traditional male characteristics may be to literally embody them.'

Film stars such as Schwarzenegger, Stallone and Van Damme, all former competitive bodybuilders, and television shows such as *Gladiators*, have all brought 'built' bodies to the public's attention. No longer viewed as 'freakish', the very heavily muscled body has increasingly been seen as aesthetically pleasing and desirable. In bodybuilding, the Mr Universes of the 1950s could not compete with today's physiques, which are at the very limits of possibility. This shift, and the changing emphasis of women's bodybuilding towards more masculine shapes, have been made possible because of AAS.

Several studies (Schwerin and Corcoran 1992; Van Raalte, Cusimano and Brewer 1993) have shown that known AAS users are viewed negatively by the public. But when drug status is unknown, mesomorphic males are seen as less vulnerable, more efficacious, and as having greater 'mastery over the environment,' mirroring the psychological benefits AAS users describe themselves (Mishkind *et al.* 1986). In Perry *et al.*'s (1990b) survey of users, the prime reasons cited for taking AAS were to 'build better bodies' and to 'get people to look at you'. Attractive people accrue social benefits, ranging from greater co-operation in social interactions and more satisfying interpersonal relationships to better education and employment prospects. Mishkind *et al.* (1986) found that 95 per cent of male college students were dissatisfied with some aspect of their bodies. Tucker (1982) demonstrated that the majority of men would prefer a mesomorphic physique, and many a hyper-mesomorphic or 'muscleman' figure. Marketers of men's products are content to exploit men's vulnerability to this ideal image in advertising; as female stereotypes become ever thinner, male stereotypes become larger. The possession of a superhero's body may be ever more desirable, but fewer young people than ever before are actively involved in sport and most men undertake only sedentary activities.

AAS have become very much a part of the male gym culture. Experienced bodybuilders may adopt the role of guru, handing down advice and instruction to novices. Peer pressure to conform can be strong and AAS use, as an 'underground' activity, can be seen as a right of passage to a secret society with its own rules and pseudoscientific beliefs. Once started on AAS, reasons for continued use include involvement in gym culture and utility for work; among clinic attenders, those employed in 'macho' jobs, such as night club doormen, are over-represented. Pharmacological effects of euphoria (Haupt and Rovere 1984) and dependence on AAS can also be important. Brower *et al.* (1991) found at least one DSM III R symptom of dependence in 94 per cent of 49 AAS users, and three or more symptoms in 57 per cent. They conclude that AAS dependence is driven by negative reinforcement—a wish to avoid feeling 'not' big.

Do AAS really work?

For many years the medical profession doubted the effects of AAS on muscle mass and performance. It was only in 1984 that the American College of Sports Medicine admitted that AAS produce strength gain (Landry and Primos 1990). This medical scepticism has probably contributed significantly both to the mistrust between medical professionals and AAS users and to the lack of good quality scientific research. Review articles looking at the efficacy of AAS in improving performance have failed to resolve these uncertainties definitively. Haupt and Rovere (1984) found inconsistent effects on human strength and no improvement in athletes' aerobic performance. Cicero and O'Connor (1990) describes equal numbers of positive and negative findings in the literature regarding athletic performance, but notes that many of the positive findings are probably too small to be relevant. The reasons for the discrepant results between different studies lie in the differing and inadequate methodologies employed. Athletes are able to distinguish between AAS and placebo which reduces the value of studies employing crossover designs (Crist, Stackpole and Peake 1983; Freed *et al.* 1975; Smith and Perry 1992). Athletes take AAS in doses 10 to 200 times those used in medical treatment (Narducci *et al.* 1990), so that studies of medical doses do not reflect likely effects in the real world. The value of much of the research is further reduced by the failure to pay attention to the physical state of the athletes prior to investigation, exercise regimes and diet, the duration of treatment, the interpretation of complex data (Lombardo 1993) or the potential for athletes involved taking extra AAS during the study. Psychological factors are also important to AAS efficacy.

Ariel and Saville (1972) gave placebo 'AAS' to experienced weightlifters, who then demonstrated improved performance, confirming the importance of placebo-controlled designs. Haupt and Rovere (1984) highlight the euphoria and reduction in fatigue which AAS produce, allowing more productive training irrespective of any metabolic effects.

Perhaps the clearest evidence of efficacy comes from a randomised, placebo-controlled trial of the effects of testosterone enanthate (600mg weekly) over 10 weeks, with and without three times weekly weightlifting, on 43 normal male volunteers (Bhasin *et al.* 1996). Testosterone increased muscle size and strength with and without exercise, but weightlifting significantly further improved results. It remains safest to conclude with Haupt and Rovere (1984) that significant strength-increases occur only if the user trains before and throughout AAS use and maintains an adequate diet.

AAS use in sport

AAS were introduced into competitive sports in the early 1950s. The team physician for the US weightlifters at the 1954 World Championships conducted the first US case studies of testosterone, following the example of his Russian counterpart (Cowart 1984). In 1956 the drug company Ciba developed the first oral AAS, methandrostenolone (Windsor and Dumitri 1988) and many US athletes used this before the Melbourne Olympics in Australia that year (Brierly 1987). During television coverage of the Olympic Games in 1960, viewers became accustomed to seeing competitors whose gender needed to be announced (Cowart 1987). Many competitors admitted using AAS at the 1972 Olympic Games (Bahrke, Yesalis and Wright 1990). 'State Plan 14.25', a drug programme for lite athletes, has been credited for East Germany having won more gold medals than the USA with less than 5 per cent of the population, and 120 medals in total at the Moscow Olympic games (British Broadcasting Corporation 1992). Maximum media attention for AAS awaited the disqualification of Ben Johnson, after he had won the 100 metre Olympic gold medal in 1988.

Drug use to improve competitive performance is generally considered both unfair and dangerous and is outlawed by most sporting bodies. That most sports are intrinsically unfair, and many dangerous (Fost 1986), and that drug use at the highest levels in sport has been national policy for many countries over long periods appear to have been conveniently forgotten. Within bodybuilding, drug-free competitions now exist for those who do not take drugs, but such honesty is unusual. Most other sports maintain, contrary to the evidence, that prohibition and testing will ultimately prevent drug use, not simply generate more sophisticated means of evasion.

The 1980s saw AAS become increasingly available to amateurs at all levels, and the 'typical' male user in his twenties was joined by adolescents, older age groups (Buckley *et al.* 1988; Williamson 1993) and women (Durant *et al.* 1993; Strauss, Liggett and Lanese 1985; Yesalis *et al.* 1993). Although there are dissimilarities between psychoactive and AAS drug-using cultures, two studies from the United States have demonstrated positive correlations between these forms of drug misuse among young people (Durant *et al.* 1993; Yesalis *et al.* 1993). Much of this crossover use may simply reflect youthful risk-taking behaviour, and this may be furthered by the evolution of common black market dealership networks, AAS being sold and used as 'just another drug'. More specifically, AAS are sometimes used to counter the catabolic effects of stimulant drugs, and AAS users sometimes turn to opioid and stimulant drugs for other effects (e.g. McBride, Williamson and Petersen 1996). We have anecdotal evidence of all these phenomena, although the extent of crossover use in Britain has not been investigated.

The extent of AAS use

Information about the extent of use of AAS use derives from several sources. Data from drug testing only reflect detected use among those affiliated to official bodies at the highest levels and are greatly influenced by policies on out-of-competition testing (Sports Council 1995). The percentages of positive test results for all banned drugs, including AAS, in recent international athletics competitions, have varied between 1.7 per cent and 3.2 per cent (MacAuley 1996). More reliable data derive from surveys of the general population and those at risk. In a recent UK survey of 15- and 16-year-olds 2.2 per cent of male and 1 per cent of female respondents said that they had used AAS (Miller and Plant 1996). American surveys of young people of school age have shown levels of lifetime exposure as high as 3 to 7.6 per cent (Komoroski and Rickert 1992; Nelson 1989; Terney and McLain 1990; Whitehead, Chillag and Elliott 1992; Windsor and Dumitri 1989). Self-report surveys of bodybuilders show the highest rates of AAS use. A questionnaire study of 1669 clients at 21 gyms in England, Scotland and Wales reported a 7.7 per cent (range across gyms 0 per cent to 46 per cent) lifetime prevalence of AAS use. Five per cent were using currently (Korkia and Stimson 1993). A South Wales survey in gyms found a 39 per cent rate of AAS use (Perry *et al.* 1992), which compares with 19.5 per cent in the West of Scotland (McKillop 1987) and 54 per cent of men and 10 per cent of women in one American study (Tricker *et al.* 1989). Supportive evidence for such high levels of use comes from unannounced laboratory screening programmes at competitions, in which 38 to 58 per cent of bodybuilders tested positive (Delbeke *et al.* 1995).

Side effects

Most AAS users probably take them for only a short period, at modest doses and with little risk to health. A minority goes on to use complex, high-dose regimes, increasing the risks without necessarily increasing the effects (Millar 1994). Potentially serious side effects of AAS are both medical and psychological. The more prevalent, minor side effects, such as acne, are generally reversible.

The best-known side effects of AAS are the feminising effects–gynaecomastia (breast development) and testicular atrophy–in men (Pope and Katz 1994), and the masculinising effects–voice lowering, hirsuteness, reduced breast size, clitoral enlargement, amenorrhoea and male-pattern baldness–in women (Strauss, Liggett and Lanese 1985). Some of these effects are irreversible and have longer-term psychological consequences. Enlargement of the prostate gland (Wemyss-Holder, Hamdy and Hastie 1994), and possibly increased risk of prostatic cancer (Roberts and Essenhigh 1986) may come to be seen as the most significant long-term health problems for men. Libido may be increased or decreased and erectile dysfunction in men has been reported. Lowered sperm counts and subfertility, with recovery taking between one and three years, are reported (Knuth, Maniera and Nieschlag 1989; Lloyd, Powell and Murdoch 1996). Acute effects on liver function are common. Haupt and Rovere (1984) conclude that almost 50 per cent of users studied showed liver function tests in the abnormal range. Serious liver disease, including liver tumours and peliosis hepatis, have been linked to AAS, particularly oral drugs, which appear to be more toxic (Kibble and Ross 1987). AAS reverse the 'healthy' pattern of blood lipids, normally promoted by exercise, increasing the low- and decreasing the high-density lipoprotein fractions. These changes predispose users to coronary artery disease, as do changes in the chemistry of blood clotting, which also increases the risk of other thromboses (Ferenchick *et al.* 1995). These risks are further compounded by AAS-induced high blood pressure (Graham and Kennedy 1990). There have been case reports of many other possible medical complications including Wilms tumour (Pratt *et al.*1977) and severe muscular injury (Visuri and Lindholm 1994) but such associations are unproven.

Evidence of associations between AAS and psychological abnormalities also originally derived from case reports. Wilson, Prange and Lara (1974) reports the acute onset of paranoid delusional states in four AAS users, within days of their starting 15 mg of methyltestosterone daily. More recently there have been reports of links between AAS and a schizophrenia-like episode (Annitto and Layman 1980), mania and hypomania (Freinhar and Alvarez 1985; Pope and Katz 1987, 1988, 1990), and depression (Pope and Katz 1987). Pope and Katz (1990) also report detailed case histories of violent crimes, including murder, committed by AAS users with no previous forensic or psychiatric history, and propose a causal link. The notion of AAS-induced irritability and anger, 'roid rage,' is accepted as fact by AAS users, and understood by partners of users, some of whom have established a 'Steroid Abused Wives Association' (Choi 1993). In the United States a 'dumbbell defence' of AAS-induced insanity has been successfully employed (Moss 1988).

Clearer evidence of links between AAS use and psychological change derives from three controlled studies. Perry, Yates and Andersen (1990a) conclude that although symptoms of depression, anxiety, hostility, paranoid thinking and somatisation occurred, these were of insufficient severity to achieve psychiatric caseness. Su, Pagliaro and Scmidt (1993), studying changes during high-dose methyltestosterone use, report euphoria, increased energy, anger, hostility, distractibility, forgetfulness and confusion. Three subjects met diagnostic criteria for major depression, hypomania or mania. In the third study, Pope and Katz (1994) report that during the 'on' phase of cycles 23 per cent of AAS users suffered major mood disturbance including depression, hypomania or mania.

Problems of injecting

There are various hazardous injecting practices. The use of inappropriate equipment or poor injecting technique can lead to failure to reach muscle, with the risk of local reactions and scarring, and the possibility of needles snapping. All injecting carries the risk of injury to underlying structures such as blood vessels, nerves and joints. Poor sterile technique risks sepsis at the site of injection. The use of shared injecting equipment carries the risk of transmitting blood-borne disease. Two cases of HIV infection associated with AAS use have been reported (Scott and Scott 1989; Sklarek *et al.*, 1984) and significant numbers of HIV-infected AAS users predicted (Nemechek 1991). Injectors of psychoactive drugs represent one of the largest reservoirs of HIV and hepatitis B and C infections. Any association of AAS users with this population places them at increased risk of contracting these viruses, and the non-AAS user at potential risk of Creutzfeldt-Jakob disease from contaminated growth hormone (Williamson 1994).

Changes in legislation and greater vigilance over prescribing have restricted the availability of legally manufactured AAS. This has encouraged the diversion of veterinary products, and the manufacture of black market drugs, the quality of whose contents is unknown (Millar 1994). A South Wales study of drugs marketed as AAS (Perry 1995) sampled five different drugs from several suppliers. Most drugs carried no registered pharmaceutical company name and drug content varied from 0 to 168 per cent of the stated dose. This clearly has implications for those giving advice about safer use.

Services

Should there be services?

Societies which value the health and welfare of their young citizens must identify and seek to ameliorate the effects of high-risk behaviours. They also need to be aware of the consequences of the unfettered promotion of role models of implausible physique. In personal health and social terms, failure to act in this way in connection with AAS may turn out to be short-sighted.

The obvious place for AAS users to seek health advice is primary care but many users avoid general practitioners, fearing disapproval and the leaking of information to family and employers. The Drugs and Sport Information Service survey (Lenehan .MDBR/et al..MDNM/ undated) shows that only one third of AAS users tells their general practitioner. Specialist drug services are viewed as inappropriate to AAS users' health needs, because AAS users, quite properly, view themselves as 'different' from most substance misusers attending services. The exceptions to this general rule are needle exchange services. In a survey of 88 UK needle exchanges (a response rate of 68 per cent) 51 (59 per cent) had had contact with AAS users (Korkia and Stimson 1993).

We became involved with AAS users when running a Community Drug Team, targeting illicit drug injectors in the South Wales valleys. The first AAS user attended our needle exchange during March 1990, requesting needles and syringes suitable for AAS (only u100 insulin syringes were available through community pharmacists). The Well Steroid User clinic (Williamson, Davies and McBride 1992) evolved from our rapidly growing awareness of the high local prevalence of AAS use, and users' limited knowledge of safer injection techniques and other risks. The clinic allows regular contact with a large number of AAS users, permits some understanding of the local AAS-using culture, a sharing of knowledge with users and the systematic collection of some data. Elsewhere in the UK, Morrison (1994) briefly describes the development of services for AAS users within a needle exchange. Similar services have been discreetly established elsewhere, but, because developments have resulted from individual initiatives with no central strategic drive, there is no register of what services are available. Below are brief descriptions of some service elements.

Philosophy

Clients' priority will be to achieve size, strength and performance improvements, whilst the service's priority will be for reductions in high-risk behaviour. Abstinence is not the clients' goal. Services for AAS users, like most of those for other drug problems, must therefore focus on harm minimisation. The drug service ethos of 'user friendliness' and strict confidentiality need to go hand in hand with staff enthusiasm to learn both in and out of the clinic.

Staffing

Some form of medical input is necessary because of the clinical monitoring required, but most of the work can be undertaken by anybody with relevant knowledge and skills. Primary care has clear advantages as the provider, but requires staff education, enthusiasm for working within a harm minimisation framework, and initiatives to overcome the predictable low rate of uptake. Drug services have experience in working with 'difficult to reach' groups, using a harm minimisation framework and motivating change from risk behaviours. Although most have neither specific contracts nor funding, all UK services we know of arise from drug agencies. Millar (1994, p.79) concurred with Perry *et al.* (1990b) that '[i]t will only be when Sports Medicine Specialists become experts in [AAS]...that athletes will...turn away from underground sources towards medical counselling', but there are too few sports medicine specialists in the UK to deal with the numbers of AAS users. The solution could be a tripartite service, bringing together the widespread availability of primary care, the confidentiality and accessibility of substance misuse services and the credibility of sports medicine.

Setting

Gym owners and sports bodies do not wish to be associated with AAS use. Detached work with users at such venues or even publicity, such as posters for a new service, are therefore invariably unwelcome. In our experience, new clients are introduced by other clients, the cheapest form of outreach work, and perhaps a measure of the extent to which the service is valued.

Any accessible, discreetly located rooms will suffice. If premises are shared, specific time set aside (perhaps in the evening for the majority who work) demonstrates that the service is solely for this client group. A confidential record-keeping system, accurate instruments for measuring weight, height and blood pressure, and facilities for phlebotomy are the only resources needed and are easily transportable. Funding for pathology testing is required. Millar (1994) offered testing of lean/fat body composition by electrical impedance using a BIA 103 Analyser (Manufactured by RJL systems, Detroit, Michigan, USA), but this will be beyond the resources of most UK services. An informal, drop-in needle exchange and health screening service is probably the most practicable model for most would-be service providers in the UK, but regular attenders could clearly be given appointments for mutual convenience.

Information

Just as the risks of tobacco fail to deter smokers, education about the risks of AAS use is insufficient, in itself, to deter athletes from continued use (Perry *et al.* 1990b; Van Raalte *et al.* 1993). Nevertheless, up-to-date, accurate scientific information should be circulated to counteract misinformation from elsewhere and forewarn users of potential hazards of new or unusual drugs as they arrive on the scene

(McBride *et al.* 1996; Williamson 1994). Users take pride in their knowledge of AAS, but this is often gleaned from unreliable sources such as underground handbooks promulgating high-dose regimes (e.g. Ducheine 1989), other gym users and suppliers. By contrast, most health and other professionals lack even basic knowledge about AAS. MacAuley (1996) identifies 620 recent medical papers on 'doping in sports', but few of these are of practical value to clinicians. Rectifying the dearth of written information for users is problematic because of the false assumptions and widely differing levels of knowledge among users. Two booklets for users (Petersen and Angulatta 1994; Baines undated) which outline ways to minimise harm when taking AAS have been widely circulated.

Psychological tests

Simple pen and paper self-completion tests for aggression (e.g. The Buss-Durke Inventory: see Buss 1961) and anxiety and depression (e.g. The Hospital Anxiety and Depression scale: see Zigmond and Snaith 1983) provide useful objective feedback on any potentially deleterious effect that drug use may be having.

Physiological measures

Accurate measurement and recording of weight and other variables of interest to users, such as lean body mass, may encourage regular attendance. Regular monitoring of blood pressure is desirable on medical grounds.

Laboratory testing

Screening tests are justified when there is a relatively high likelihood of detecting abnormality and when possible interventions are cost-effective (Wilson 1968). Full blood count, liver function, renal function, blood sugar and high density lipoprotein cholesterol are the tests usually advocated (Williamson *et al.* 1992; Millar 1994; Morrison 1994). In individuals considered at risk, pre-test counselling and testing for HIV and hepatitis B and C should be given, with hepatitis B immunisation for those still at risk.

Advice on training

Beneficial effects of AAS are greatest in those who eat and train appropriately, but this is not always understood by users, who should be directed to clear, expert ad-

vice relevant to their sport (e.g. Hemery, Ogden and Evans 1990). For bodybuilders Millar (1994) advises a balanced diet including 1.5 to 2g per kilogram of
protein per day, without dietary supplements. Millar recommends training at least
four days per week, all body parts to be stressed at least twice, using progressive
'sets' of 12–15 repetitions to failure, increasing resistance and decreasing the repetitions until only two or three are possible. Millar commenced his prescribing programme only when this regime had been followed and weight and strength
increases had stopped. Similar advice should be given to those attending non-
prescribing services, so that improvements in performance are not misattributed to
starting AAS.

Advice on drug use and effects

Clients who reject advice to stop may accept advice about the lack of evidence for
high-dose poly-drug use, and advocacy of a low-dose single-drug regime. Discussion with clients, using motivational interviewing techniques (Miller 1983),
should include detailed objective feedback about the impact of the drugs on blood
pressure, laboratory indices and psychological screening.

Needle exchange

Needle exchange for AAS users involves the availability of packs of appropriately
sized, sterile needles and syringes, with an information leaflet about safer injecting. This should be available through all tiers of existing needle exchange: auto-
mated dispensers, community pharmacists, outreach teams, and drugs agencies as
well as specific AAS user services. If the AAS user attends a needle exchange, advice on safer injecting can be given and demonstrated, including checking the
drugs, basic anatomy to avoid injury, sterile technique, safer disposal of sharps,
and first aid.

Prescribing

Only Millar (1994) has written of an AAS prescription programme designed to
minimise harm. A first, seven-week course was subject to strict entry criteria and
the 169 enrolled users were monitored closely both on and off drugs. Fifteen per
cent dropped out because they thought their doses were too low. A further 35 per
cent stopped after one course because of caution, success or disappointment. Millar

concludes that low doses of AAS, by black market standards, can be used success-fully by athletes, without significant problems for up to five years, if accompanied by correct education, advice and medical supervision.

Possible future options

Possibilities for future work with AAS are many and various. Better health educa-tion through information in 'muscle' magazines, and more varied written informa-tion through agencies for those who will never attend specialist services, merit attention. Wider availability of services through drug agencies and primary health care clinics, perhaps run by specially trained practice nurses, would require rela-tively little expenditure. Greater interest from sports medicine is probably over-due. Peer-led harm minimisation programmes are an interesting possibility for AAS users, because information networks are already well developed and correct information and advice might be more readily accepted from other users than from health professionals. We hope that some such initiatives might be prompted by this chapter.

Evaluation

Clinical and cost effectiveness, in terms of illness prevention and health gain, in-creasingly need to be demonstrated and expenditure on AAS services justified (Morrison 1995). Strang (1990) suggests three criteria for measuring success: at-tracting relevant clients, maintaining their contact with the service, and changing their behaviour. Process measures (such as the numbers of people attending, tak-ing away information, receiving advice, and using needle exchange; the numbers returning to the service; information from client appraisal forms; and calculations of cost per contact) are easy to monitor and indicate the quality of the service.

To evaluate changes in behaviour, one appropriate methodology is to compare outcomes in two groups of AAS users, one attending the service, the other, con-tacted through a detached research worker, acting as a control group. This allows a single blind, non-randomised controlled trial of the services on offer. The principle problem of such an approach is that the comparability of the two groups cannot be assumed. Help-seeking behaviour among other service users suggests that the clinic group will have different health experiences, making comparison difficult (e.g. Goldberg and Huxley 1980). An alternative is to randomly assign clinic attenders either to intervention or to no-intervention/placebo-intervention groups. Ethical issues, the difficulty of obtaining informed consent and the likely high immediate drop-out from the control group probably precludes such an approach.

Measures of outcome reflect the goals of the service, which might include: use of appropriate training and diet, reduced high-risk injecting, simplified drug regimes, and reduced AAS and other drug use. Users' accounts of change can be corroborated by physiological and laboratory measures of toxicity and hair analysis for recent use of AAS. Little is understood about which factors—dose, duration, poly-pharmacy, or drug holidays—prevent or lead to long-term morbidity and mortality. Determining the extent of long-term health effects, and any differences resulting from service intervention, require long-term follow up of service users and controls.

Conclusions

Steps to prevent the spread of AAS have failed inside and outside professional sport and AAS use is increasingly prevalent among young people. Awareness of the more common effects of AAS will become increasingly important for a range of professionals, be they a social worker investigating child abuse or a general practitioner uncovering hypertension. We have sought to give an overview of the subject with a focus on possible services to minimise the harm caused by AAS. Awareness of cultural and motivational factors underlying AAS use should increase understanding, empathy and, for those dealing with users, the possibility of having good advice accepted. It would be usual to suggest that interested professionals learn where to turn for further advice, information or help, but in 1997, across most of the UK such resources are simply not available.

References

Annitto, W.J. and Layman, W.A. (1980) 'Anabolic steroids and acute schizophrenic episode.' *Journal of Clinical Psychiatry 41,* 4, 143–144.

Ariel, G. and Saville, W. (1972) 'Anabolic steroids; the physiological effects of placebos.' *Medicine and Science in Sports and Exercise 4,* 124–126.

Bahrke, M.S., Yesalis, C.E. and Wright, G.E. (1990) 'Psychological and behavioural effects of endogenous testosterone levels and anabolic-androgenic steroids among males.' *Sports Medicine 10,* 5, 303–337.

Baines, J. (undated) *Anabolic Steroids: Hardcore Info.* Manchester: Lifeline Publications.

Bhasin, S., Storer, T.W., Berman, N., Callegari, C., Clevenger, B., Phillips, J., Bunnell, T.J., Tricker, R., Shirazi, A. and Casaburi, R. (1996) 'The effects of supraphysiologic doses of testosterone on muscle size and strength in normal men.' *New England Journal of Medicine 335*, 1, 1–7.

Brierly, J.R. (1987) 'Use of anabolic steroids by athletes–do the nots outweigh the benefits?' *Postgraduate Medicine 82*, 3, 67–74.

British Broadcasting Corporation (1992) *A Question of Sport.* London: Broadcasting Support Services.

Brower, K.J. (1993) 'Anabolic steroids.' *Recent Advances in Addictive Disorders 16*, 1, 97–103.

Brower, K.J., Blow, F.C., Young, J.P. and Hill, E.M. (1991) 'Symptoms and correlates of anabolic androgenic steroids dependence.' *British Journal of Addiction 86*, 759–768.

Buss, A.H. (1961) *The Psychology of Aggression.* New York: Wiley.

Choi, P.Y.L. (1993) 'Alarming effects of anabolic steroids.' *The Psychologist*, 258–260.

Cicero, T.J. and O'Connor, L.H. (1990) 'Abuse liability of anabolic steroids and their possible role in abuse of alcohol, morphine and other substances.' In G.C. Lin and L. Erinoff (eds) *NIDA Research Monograph 102.* Rockville, USA: National Institute on Drug Abuse.

Cowart, V. (1987) 'Steroids in sport: after four decades, time to return these genies to the bottle?' *Journal of the American Medical Association 257*, 4, 421–427.

Crist, D.M., Stackpole, P.J. and Peake, G.T. (1983) 'Effects of androgenic anabolic steroids on neuromuscular power and body composition.' *Journal of Applied Physiology 54*, 366–370.

Cszaky, T.Z. (1972) 'Doping.' *Journal of Sports Medicine and Physical Fitness 12*, 117–123.

Delbeke, F.T., Desmet, N. and Debackere, M. (1995) 'The abuse of doping agents in competing bodybuilders in Flanders (1988–1993).' *International Journal of Sports Medicine 16*, 66–70.

Ducheine, D. (1989) *Underground Steroid Handbook.* Venice, California, USA: ALR Technical Books.

Durant, R.H., Rickert, V.I., Ashworth, C.S., Newman, C. and Slavens, G. (1993) 'Use of multiple drugs among adolescents who use anabolic steroids.' *The New England Journal of Medicine 328*, 922–926.

Fost, N. (1986) *Banning Drugs in Sports: A Skeptical View.* Hastings Centre Report 16, 5-10.

Freed, D.L.J., Banks, A.J., Longson, D. and Burley, D.M. (1975) 'Anabolic steroids in athletics: crossover double blind trial on weightlifters.' *British Medical Journal 2*, 471–473.

Freinhar, J.P. and Alvarez, W. (1985) 'Androgen-induced hypomania.' *Journal of Clinical Psychiatry 46*, 8, 354–355.

Goldberg, D. and Huxley, P. (1980) *Mental Illness in the Community: The Pathway to Psychiatric Care.* London: Tavistock Publications.

Graham, S. and Kennedy, M. (1990) 'Recent developments in the toxicology of anabolic steroids.' *Drug Safety 5,* 6, 458–476.

Harlow, R. (1951) 'Masculine inadequacy and the compensatory development of physique.' *Journal of Personality 19,* 312–333.

Haupt, H.A. and Rovere, G.D. (1984) 'Anabolic steroids: a review of the literature.' *The American Journal of Sports Medicine 12,* 6, 469–484.

Hemery, D., Ogden, D. and Evans, A. (1990) *Winning Without Drugs: The Natural Approach to Competitive Sport.* London: Collins.

Kibble, W. and Ross, M.B. (1987) 'Adverse effects of anabolic steroids on athletes.' *Clinical Pharmacy 6,* 9, 686–692.

Knuth, U.A., Maniera, H. and Nieschlag, E. (1989) 'Anabolic steroids and semen parameters in bodybuilders.' *Fertility and Sterility 52,* 6, 180–192.

Komoroski, E.M. and Rickert, V.I. (1992) 'Adolescent body image and attitudes to anabolic steroid use.' *American Journal of Diseases in Childhood 146,* 823–828.

Korkia, P.K. and Stimson G.V. (1993) *Anabolic Steroid Use in Great Britain: An Exploratory Investigation.* London: Centre for Research on Drugs and Health Behaviour.

Landry, G.L. and Primos, W.A. (1990) 'Anabolic steroid abuse.' *Advances in Paediatrics 37,* 185–205.

Lenehan, P., Bellis, M. and McVeigh, J. (No publishing date on document but the research was carried out in c. 1995) *Anabolic Steroid Use in the North West of England. A Summary.* Liverpool: The Drugs and Sport Information Service.

Lloyd, F.H., Powell, P. and Murdoch, A.P. (1996) 'Lesson of the week: anabolic steroid abuse by bodybuilders and male subfertility.' *British Medical Journal 313,* 100–101.

Lombardo, J.A. (1993) 'Anabolic-androgenic steroids.' In G.C. Lin and L. Erinoff (eds) *NIDA Research Monograph 102.* Rockville, USA: National Institute on Drug Abuse.

MacAuley, D. (1996) 'Drugs in sport.' *British Medical Journal 313,* 211–215.

McBride, A.J., Williamson, K. and Petersen, T. (1996) 'Three cases of nalbuphine hydrochloride dependence associated with anabolic steroid use.' *British Journal of Sports Medicine 30,* 69–70.

McKillop, G. (1987) 'Drug abuse in bodybuilders in the west of Scotland.' *Scottish Medical Journal 32,* 39–41.

Miller, W.R. (1983) 'Motivational interviewing with problem drinkers.' *Behavioural Psychotherapy 11,* 147–172.

Millar, A.P. (1994) 'Licit steroid use–hope for the future.' *British Journal of Sports Medicine 28,* 2, 79–83.

Miller, P.M. and Plant, M. (1996) 'Drinking, smoking, and illicit drug use among 15 and 16 year olds in the United Kingdom.' *British Medical Journal 313*, 394–397.

Mishkind, M.E., Rodin, J., Silberstein, L.R. and Striegel-Moore A. (1986) 'The embodiment of masculinity.' *American Behavioural Scientist 29*, 5, 545–562.

Moore, W.V. (1988) 'Anabolic steroid use in adolescence.' *Journal of the American Medical Association 260*, 3484–3486.

Morrison, C. (1995) 'The cost of running a well steroid user service.' *Relay 1*, 3, 10.

Morrison, C.L. (1994) 'Anabolic steroid users identified by needle and syringe exchange contact.' *Drug and Alcohol Dependence 36*, 153–156.

Moss, D.C. (1988) 'And now the steroid defence?' *American Bar Association Journal,* October 1, 22–24.

Narducci, W.A., Wagner, J.C., Hendrickson, T.P. and Jeffrey, T.P. (1990) 'Anabolic steroids–a review of the clinical toxicology and diagnostic screening.' *Clinical Toxicology 28*, 3, 287–310.

Nelson, M.A. (1989) 'Androgenic-anabolic steroid use in adolescents.' *Journal of Paediatric Health Care 3*, 4, 175–180.

Nemechek, P.M. (1991) 'Anabolic steroid users–another potential risk group for HIV infection.' *New England Journal of Medicine 325*, 357.

Perry, H. (1995) 'Counterfeit–fake anabolic steroids and hazards of their use.' *Relay 1*, 4, 9–11.

Perry, H.M., Wright, D. and Littlepage, B.N. (1992) 'Dying to be big: a review of anabolic steroid use.' *British Journal of Sports Medicine 26*, 259–261.

Perry, P.J. Yates, W.R. and Andersen, K.H. (1990a) 'Psychiatric symptoms associated with anabolic steroids: a controlled retrospective study.' *Annals of Clinical Psychiatry 2*, 1, 11–17.

Perry, P.J., Andersen K.H. and Yates, W.R. (1990b) 'Illicit anabolic steroid use in athletes. A case series analysis.' *American Journal of Sports Medicine 18*, 4, 422–428.

Petersen, T.J. and Angulatta, L. (1994) *Mid Glamorgan C.D.A.T. Harm Reduction Booklet–Steriods.* Mid Glamorgan: Rhondda NHS Trust.

Pope, H.G. and Katz, D.L. (1987) 'Bodybuilders' psychosis.' *Lancet 1*, 863.

Pope, H.G. and Katz, D.L. (1988) 'Affective and psychotic symptoms associated with anabolic steroid use.' *American Journal of Psychiatry 145*, 4, 487–490.

Pope, H.G. and Katz, D.L. (1990) 'Homicide and near-homicide by anabolic steroid users.' *Journal of Clinical Psychiatry 51*, 1, 28–31.

Pope, H.G. and Katz, D.L. (1994) 'Psychiatric and medical effects of anabolic androgenic steroid use.' *Archives of General Psychiatry 51*, 375–382.

Pope, H.G. and Katz, D.L. (1994) 'Psychiatric and medical effects of anabolic androgenic steroid use.' *Archives of General Psychiatry 51*, 375–382.

Pratt, J., Gray, G.F., Stolley, P.D. and Coleman, J.W. (1977) 'Wilms tumour in an adult associated with androgen abuse.' *Journal of the American Medical Association 237,* 2322–2323.

Schwerin, M.J. and Corcoran, K.J. (1992) 'What do people think of male steroid users? An experimental investigation.' *Journal of Applied Social Psychology 22,* 10, 833–840.

Scott, M.J. and Scott M.J. (1989) 'HIV infection associated with injection of anabolic steroids.' *Journal of the American Medical Association 262,* 207–208.

Sklarek, H.M., Mantovani, R.P., Erens, E., Heisler, D., Neiderman, M.S. and Fein, A.M. (1984) 'AIDS in a bodybuilder using anabolic steroids.' *New England Journal of Medicine 311,* 1701.

Smith D.A. and Perry P.J. (1992) 'The Efficacy of ergogenic agents in athletic competitions. Part I: Androgenic-anabolic steroids.' *The Annals of Pharmacotherapy 26,* 520–528.

Sports Council (1995) *Doping Control in the UK. A Survey of Experiences and Views of Elite Competitors.* London: Sports Council.

Strang, J. (1990). 'Intermediate goals and the process of change.' In J. Strang and G. Stimson (eds) *AIDS and Drug Misuse: The Challenge for Policy and Practice in the 1990s.* pp.211–221. London: Routledge.

Strauss R.H., Liggett M.T. and Lanese R.R. (1985) 'Anabolic steroid use and perceived effects in ten weight trained women athletes.' *Journal of the American Medical Sssociation 253,* 19, 2871–2873.

Su, T. Pagliaro, R.N. and Scmidt, P.J. (1993) 'Neuropsychiatric effects of anabolic steroids in male normal volunteers.' *Journal of the American Medical Association 269,* 21, 2760–2764.

Terney, R. and McLain, L.G. (1990) 'The use of anabolic steroids in high school students.' *American Journal of Diseases in Childhood 144,* 99–103.

Thune, J. (1949) 'Personality of weightlifters.' *Research Quarterly of the American Physical Education Association 20,* 296–306.

Tricker, R., O'Neill, M.R. and Cook, D. (1989) 'The incidence of anabolic steroid use among competitive bodybuilders.' *Journal of Drug Education 19,* 313–325.

Tucker, L.A. (1982) 'Relationship between perceived somatotype and body cathexis of college males.' *Psychological Reports 50,* 983–989.

Van Raalte, J.L., Cusimano, K.A. and Brewer, B.W. (1993) 'Perceptions of anabolic steroid users.' *Journal of Applied Social Psychology 23,* 15, 1214–1225.

Visuri, T. and Lindholm, H. (1994) 'Bilateral distal biceps tendon avulsions with use of anabolic steroids.' *Medicine and Science in Sports and Exercise 26,* 941–944.

Wemyss-Holder, S.A., Hamdy, F.C. and Hastie, K.J. (1994) 'Steroid abuse in athletes, prostatic enlargement and bladder outflow obstruction–is there a relationship?' *British Journal of Urology 74,* 476–478.

Whitehead, R., Chillag, S. and Elliott, D. (1992) 'Anabolic steroid use among adolescents in a rural state.' *Journal of Family Practice 35,* 401–405.

Williamson, K. (1993) 'Misuse of anabolic drugs.' *British Medical Journal 306,* 459.

Williamson, K. (1994) 'Creutzfeldt-Jakob disease: another avenue?' *British Journal of Hospital Medicine 51,* 7–8.

Williamson, K., Davies, M. and McBride, A.J. (1992) 'A well steroid user clinic.' *Druglink 7,* 15.

Wilson, J. (1968) *Principles and Practice of Screening for Disease.* Geneva: World Health Organisation.

Windsor, R. and Dumitri, D. (1989) 'Prevalence of anabolic steroid use by male and female adolescents.' *Medicine and Science in Sports and Exercise 21,* 5, 494–497.

Windsor, R.E. and Dumitri, D. (1988) 'Anabolic steroid use by athletes.' *Postgraduate Medicine 84,* 4, 37–48.

Yesalis, C.E., Kennedy N.J., Kopstein A.N. and Bahrke, M.S. (1993) 'Anabolic androgenic steroid use in the United States.' *Journal of the American Medical Association 270,* 10, 1217–1221.

Zigmond, A.S. and Snaith, R.P. (1983) 'The hospital anxiety and depression scale.' *Acta Psychiatrica Scandinavica 67,* 361–370.

Further Reading

Buckley, W., Yeastis, C., Freide, K. et al. (1988) 'Estimated prevalence of anabolic steroid use among male high school seniors.' *Journal of the American Medical Association 260,* 3, 3441–3445.

Ferenchick, G.S., Hirokawa, S., Mammen, E.F. and Schwartz, K.A. (1995) 'Anabolic-androgenic steriod abuse in weight lifters: evidence for activation of the hemostatic system.' *American Journal of Hematology 49,* 282–288.

Roberts, J.T. and Essenhigh, D.M. (1986) 'Adenocarcinoma of the prostate in a 40 year old bodybuilder.' *Lancet 2,* 742.

Williamson, D.J. (1993) 'Anabolic steriod use among students at a British college of technology.' *British Journal of Sports Medicine 279,* 30, 200–201.

Wilson, I.C., Prange, A.J. and Lara, P.P. (1974) 'Methyltestosterone with imipramine in men: conversion of depression to paranoid reaction.' *American Journal of Psychiatry 131,* 1, 21–24.

CHAPTER 11

Effective Interventions for Problem Drinkers
Is Matching the Answer?

Jan Keene

Introduction

Researchers have failed to find differences in outcome between alcohol treatment interventions which are based on very different theoretical models and in which the majority of clients have relapsed within two years whichever treatment model is used. A possible interpretation of this research evidence is that individual differences are important in determining response to different treatment models and that this should be taken into account by matching clients to different models.

This chapter will review the research evidence for matching and then consider the possibility of an alternative interpretation, in essence that theoretical perspectives actually have little influence on practice. This may be because all clinicians use similar treatment methods irrespective of the theoretical model, or simply that non-treatment variables such as social support and life skills are more important than treatment variables. It will be suggested that instead of the foundation for practice being provided by scientific research and theory development, practice is developed by clinicians working from experience of the practical utility of particular methods with individual clients. As a consequence clinicians all use similar methods independently of the particular theory espoused. Data from a recent study will be used to illustrate these similarities.

Brief summary of research

Outcome researchers in the alcohol field have been unable to distinguish between one treatment model and another in terms of effectiveness. All models seem to be equally effective in reducing severity of dependence and/or drinking behaviour. Any one model results in a successful treatment outcome for between a third and a half of cases (Lindstrom 1992). In the light of this information, researchers have tried to identify individual differences or characteristics which predispose some people to do better with particular treatments. They have failed to identify significant individual or personality differences.

It is interesting that, whilst models of alcohol dependency and treatment are radically different, in practical terms they tend to lead to similar methods. Recent reviews of outcome studies suggest that some methods may be more successful than others. Lindstrom (1992) and Hodgson (1994) identify aspects of treatment that appear to be more useful than others, particularly social factors and improved social functioning, which prove significant in terms of pre-treatment characteristics and treatment outcome.

Comparative outcome studies in the substance-misuse field as a whole are handicapped by problems in the identification of relevant criteria for baseline, outcome and follow-up measures. There has been much controversy about the identification of predictors of treatment outcome and indeed its usefulness as a measure at all (Edwards 1988). Emphasis on follow-up studies indicates that, although specific treatment variables may be significant for immediate drinking behaviour change, many other variables mediate treatment effect itself. This is further complicated by variables influencing maintenance of change at follow-up, such as personal and social functioning (Lindstrom 1992; Moos, Finney and Cronkite 1990). The absence of conclusive outcomes in comparative studies has led to an interest in the interactive effects of treatment and a wide range of individual and social variables (Glaser 1980; Lindstrom 1992). In order to pursue these new directions in general treatment research there is a growing need to identify, define and eventually quantify treatment methods or components.

But there has been less success in defining and comparing different treatment methods than in measuring other variables, largely due to an inability to identify the core components which differentiate between them. Although much is known of the theory and practice of cognitive/behavioural treatment models, very little is known about the core components of other models and less is known about the significant variables or core components of successful maintenance of change.

Different models of alcohol treatment

Psychological models of alcohol dependency apply cognitive and behavioural theories to alcohol treatment and relapse prevention (Marlatt and Gordon 1985; Raistrick and Davidson 1985; Wilson 1992). A shorter version of these interventions has also been developed under the title of minimal or brief interventions (Heather and Robinson 1986). A comprehensive review of early intervention strategies is provided by Babor *et al.* (1986) and Chick, Lloyd and Crombie (1985). The theory of a 'continuum of dependence' refers to a biopsychosocial dependence syndrome (Edwards 1986; Edwards and Grant 1977; Edwards and Gross 1976). This concept has been developed with the WHO and utilised for both clinical and screening purposes (Edwards 1986).

The motivational and process theories of Prochaska and DiClemente (1982, 1983, 1986, 1994), Miller, Sovereign and Krege (1987) and Davidson, Rollnick and MacEwan (1991) emphasise the importance of process and the need for a sequentially structured counselling process. The Minnesota, or Twelve Step, model of dependency understands addiction as a disease, for which abstinence is the only recovery (Cook 1988). Evaluative studies have been carried out by Laundergan (1982), Rossi, Stach and Bradley (1963) and Spicer and Barnett (1980).

It can be seen that there are several major approaches to alcohol problems: the cognitive behavioural model, the brief interventions model, the dependency syndrome, the process of change model and the disease model. Research has not produced enough evidence to demonstrate that any one approach is superior but instead has indicated that these treatment models are all equally successful in reducing severity of dependence and/or drinking behaviour.

Methodological issues

Within the alcohol field the traditional emphasis on experimental method and outcome data derives from the particular theories and research methodology of medicine and the behavioural sciences. Positivist research in effect presupposes that the phenomenon can be defined and isolated, all peripheral variables controlled and experimental comparisons made. There is also a further presupposition that data inaccessible to this approach (concerning individual differences, subjective inter-pretations and the treatment process itself) are, in effect, largely superfluous.

Positivist studies comparing outcome statistics do not however help clarify what actually happens in treatment interventions nor do they convey information concerning the individual change process within therapeutic change programmes. This type of research tends to overlook individual differences and ignore what ac-tually happens in treatment, in an attempt to compare and contrast different treat-ment intervention outcomes.

While there are clear limitations to the phenomenological approach underpin-ning qualitative analysis (as the methods derived from this methodology do not confer scientific credibility), this approach does serve a descriptive and interpretive purpose, examining subjective interpretations and individual change processes. The qualitative approach therefore offers data describing both the individual treat-ment process and the treatment components.

Methodological constraints can also be compounded by the limitations of par-ticular theoretical perspectives; many of the basic underlying theoretical beliefs of a particular discipline are taken for granted, thus the initial definition of addiction will influence both how treatment is undertaken and how it is evaluated. For exam-ple, previous attempts by scientists to explain and understand the theory underly-ing the Alcoholics Anonymous (AA) disease model have often been made within the context of psychological (behavioural) theory (Fingarette 1988; Heather and Robinson 1981, 1986). This theoretical framework is limited by its basic premises that 'addiction' can be adequately understood as an objective phenomenon and as a behavioural disorder (Gorman 1989). In contrast to the behavioural model, the disease model is based on the premises that subjective interpretation and treatment process are critical factors and thus makes no attempt to assess this approach within a scientific framework.

It can be seen therefore that two separate bodies of knowledge exist, based on different methodologies. These different types of knowledge have resulted in the formation of different theories of addiction or alcohol dependence.

The clinicians' perspective: advantages and disadvantages of different methodologies

It is important to emphasise that research methods in the medical and psychological fields are not the equivalent of clinical methods. Although quantitative methods are essential for social researchers to attain scientific status, they are less essential or useful to clinicians. Donald Schon (1990) argues that practitioners themselves do not utilise scientific knowledge as it is seen as less useful than task-based, experiential, 'knowledge in action.' Although clinicians may find scientific research less useful, they may be more dependent than academics on qualitative data derived from individual case studies. For example, concepts such as 'loss of control' and 'craving' are not accessible to scientific experiment as they owe much to subjective interpretation. Yet, if discarded, it would be difficult for the clinician or the client to interpret and communicate, that is to 'recognise' or make sense of certain phenomena or experiences.

Clinicians are also more concerned with the actual methods used in an intervention, rather than simply the outcome. Treatment interventions are often based as much on individual clinical casework experience of the efficacy of particular methods as on research findings or theories. So many clinicians may view both diagnosis and treatment as professional crafts, rather than scientific procedures. The lack of qualitative data in academic research means a lack of descriptive accounts of the methods used within treatment process. It is therefore often unclear to academics what clinicians actually do. This has serious implications when drawing conclusions from comparative outcome studies.

The clinicians' perspective: advantages and disadvantages of using any one model or theoretical perspective

It is possible that a clinician or practitioner will prefer to work with only one approach. There is evidence that it is important that counsellors believe in the particular approach within which they are working (Frank 1974). However, it seems clear that within the field at the present time there are theories of the aetiology of dependence, treatment and relapse prevention. It cannot be taken for granted that clinicians use corresponding theories for each stage. It may be that they can select several different theories for each   client, describing the development of the problem in terms of a particular theoretical perspective, and then, perhaps independently of this initial understanding of the aetiology of the problem, choose a particular treatment process to structure their practical response. While it is no doubt true that academics would require some degree of 'fit' between a theory of aetiology and one of treatment, it is not necessarily true for either clinicians or clients. It seems possible for clients to work both with therapists who take a cognitive/behavioural approach and those who work with the disease perspective; it is also possible for 'eclectic' clinicians to use both. The cognitive dissonance which would be generated in many academics is also problematic for some clinicians and clients, but for many people these discrepancies are not of any importance, if they are recognised at all.

The limitations of particular theoretical perspectives on academic research are reflected in their limitations on clinical practice. The disadvantages of using one particular theoretical perspective are of course the constraints that each places on alternative options. The basic premise of AA rules out possible courses of action which theoretically may be equally viable and perhaps have a greater 'fit' for some individual experience. If these basic beliefs are accepted, alcohol problems cannot be seen as a disorder of behaviour, so excluding methods which involve teaching individuals to control and modify their own behaviour. The same is true for the behavioural approach. If clients accept the initial premise that they can control their own behaviour, they cannot then admit powerlessness. It should, however, be noted that while logical contradictions present obstacles for academics, this may, again, not be the case for clients themselves, some of whom seem quite happy combining different perspectives such as cognitive/behavioural during the day and AA at night.

There are practical advantages to each different model. Whilst the disease perspective often requires more intensive input than a behavioural or social learning approach (see Goldfried and Bergin 1978; Mash and Terdal 1976), proponents of this model effectively utilise a network of self-help groups and volunteers, who provide more ongoing support than most professionals could ever afford to give. The average attendance at Alcoholics Anonymous self-help support groups is two to three times a week or more for an average four to five years. AA support is of course free. At present, to take full advantage of these self-help groups, professionals would apparently need to work with similar concepts in their own therapy and counselling. It would therefore seem that the rationale of providing a service working on the same model, to enable a link in to AA, has a good deal of sense. On the other hand, the cognitive/behavioural approach is likely to be more accessible to a wider range of clients with drinking problems and to generic professionals such as health care workers and social workers in Britain, as a Social Learning approach to alcohol abuse and treatment often forms part of their basic training. These workers may have difficulties in integrating the disease concept with their own working practices.

Should all clients with alcohol problems be treated in the same way or should clients be matched to different models?

Whilst advocates of each treatment model often argue that their approach is suitable for all clients with alcohol problems, a substantial group of theorists argue that it will be more effective to match clients to different models.

There has been little useful research on treatment matching. The effectiveness of this approach is disputed; some studies indicate no positive outcomes from attempted matches, whereas others suggest that individual differences may be significant and that different models are more effective for particular clients.

Perhaps the most famous study demonstrating equivalence between different treatment models was completed by Edwards and Orford (1977). They found little difference between treatment approaches and this work is often cited as the best example of an outcome study illustrating no difference between the two options of 'treatment' and 'advice'. This work has been reflected in many similar studies over the last 20 years (Lindstrom 1992). However, there are several studies that indicate the positive potential of matching.

Orford, Oppenheimer and Edwards (1979) carried out a two-year follow up of the famous Edwards and Orford study. This confirmed the authors' initial hypothesis, finding that the long-term results were different for different categories of client. Those clients considered more seriously dependent achieved better results in the treatment group and others (suffering only disability) did better in the group receiving only advice. There was an interaction between the types of client and the goals they achieved, with the seriously addicted clients achieving better results through abstention and the others tending to achieve good results through controlled drinking. Edwards believed that if the dependence syndrome were severe, then the chances of returning to controlled drinking were low. If the syndrome were mild, then controlled drinking would be possible. He felt it essential, but problematic, to group subjects in terms of degrees of dependence rather than in terms of disability. Edwards and Orford concluded:

> For people who are disabilitated simple strategies of social adjustment or psychotherapy (coping mechanisms) might be useful in reversing the 'dependence syndrome'. There is an important contrast here with the benefits of such general strategies for severe dependence, where similar approaches may be expected to lead to remission. (Edwards and Orford 1977, p.149)

That is, what is good for someone not heavily addicted may be a disaster for someone who is heavily addicted, and vice versa (see also Edwards 1988 and 1989). The problem of deciding whether dependency has caused certain disabilities or whether certain disabilities have led to and aggravated dependency has not been resolved. It seems very difficult, if not impossible, to discover simple objective criteria for assessing this, for professionals and clients alike.

Whilst Edwards has argued that the distinction between dependency and non-dependency is critical in matching clients to treatments, several authors have suggested that it is more complicated than this. The most influential of these 'matching theorists' is Glaser (1980). Glaser highlighted the possibilities of matching clients to different services, stating:

> The question is not whether similarities and differences between individuals exist—they do, but which is prepotent in determining the outcome of treatment? (p.178)

He makes the point that

> In most circumstances at the present time, the similarities between individuals are assumed to be prepotent, and hence all individuals presenting are dealt with in the same way…which is perhaps why the matching hypothesis in most fields remains a hypothesis (p.178).

He continues:

> Yet in certain circumstances, such as with respect to alcohol problems, controlled experimentation has suggested that the results of uniform experimen-

tation applied across the board are no better than those achieved with minimal interventions (p.178).

Edwards and Orford's 1977 study illustrates this point well. Glaser (1980) argues that

> In addition to being generally ineffective, uniform approaches to complex problems may compound therapeutic pessimism by disguising or obscuring significant interactions between sub-groups and the treatment provided (p.80).

This point is of particular importance, as many studies are limited to surveys of fairly large populations or to comparisons between groups of subjects. Glaser suggests that if a heterogeneous group is treated as if it were homogeneous, the significant variables in client–treatment interactions will tend to be uniformly distributed in the differing conditions, and the results in each condition will appear to be the same. Marlatt (1988) concurs with this conclusion, also emphasising that most research is based on the assumption that alcoholics are a homogeneous group and therefore individual differences obscure any major effects due to treatment type.

Several authors have followed Glaser and argued that individual differences are of relevance in treatment outcome, for example, Caddy and Block (1985), McCrady and Sher (1983), and Miller and Hester (1986). However, few can cite evidence in support and comparative studies matching clients to different treatments have been rare. Despite the lack of research evidence, several authors propose that, as the population of people with alcohol problems is multivariate, treatment services should be diverse (Pattison *et al.* 1977) and that the potential implications of matching should be considered in terms of improved assessment and better treatment matches (Schwartz 1982). These conclusions lead many towards what Glaser refers to as a 'growing consensus' in accord with the belief 'that the differences between groups of people are of the greatest importance in terms of outcome of various kinds of interventions, and hence that these interventions should not be uniform.'

It is open to debate whether or not this 'growing consensus' has led to any changes in basic research or practice in the field, as it is now many years since Edwards produced his initial results and 50 years since Jellinek and Bowman (1946) first commented on the significance of individual differences. There is still very little work, either in terms of theories or development of methods, to suggest that these initial ideas have been taken seriously and despite an academic interest in matching, there has been little concrete guidance for clinicians (Miller and Hester 1986).

Discussion of client matching has remained largely abstract and the practical implications for treatment allocation remain vague. Research in the 1990s is as yet as inconclusive as that in the 1970s/1980s, with perhaps one exception, the large American study of alcohol treatment, 'Project MATCH'. MATCH should give much needed information about the possibilities of matching clients to different treatment regimes. This large multi-centre trial compares client characteristics and treatment outcome across three distinct models: Minnesota, Motivational Interviewing and Relapse Prevention. Rather than focus on testing the matching hypothesis itself, this study compares different methods. It follows the tradition of medical and epidemiological research using a randomised controlled trial to allow for demonstration of a statistically significant effect. A problem generally encountered in comparison studies is the wide range of conflicting standardised outcome measures and the continuing controversy as to which are most appropriate. This is of course due to the different theoretical understandings underlying different treatment methods; definitions of the problem and of success are different. These issues are often not addressed in outcome studies. This is apparent in the MATCH study, which is based on the taken-for-granted premise that abstinence can be the only realistic aim for any treatment.

> Since abstinence from alcohol is the ultimate aim of all three therapeutic interventions, the primary statistical analyses will test treatment matching hypotheses in relation to two key measures of alcohol consumption, percentage days drinking and percentage days heavy drinking in three months. (Project MATCH Research Group 1993)

This underlying assumption reflects the American emphasis on abstinence and would not be the case in Britain where controlled drinking is often the treatment goal. Perhaps a more significant problem in the MATCH study was the difficulty in distinguishing between the different methods (treatment protocols) used by each model. MATCH researchers used approximately 1600 subjects within eight centres. The researchers needed to develop independent process measures of treatment distinctiveness and specificity prior to the study in order to develop some form of quality control process measure. This reflects a deficiency in all alcohol treatment research as, apart from specialised cognitive behavioural interventions, treatment protocols are seldom specified in the alcohol field.

Discussion: Why is there so little evidence for the efficacy of matching and what is the relevance of common treatment (and 'non-treatment') methods?

The previous section has highlighted the possible gains from matching if individual differences could be identified and appropriate criteria developed for allocating clients to models. It has also noted the fact that nothing has been produced in the last 20 years to substantiate claims for the usefulness of matching. This section considers possible reasons for this lack of progress and alternative explanations for the research evidence, considering the possibility that treatment methods (and non-treatment variables) identified in qualitative work on treatment and recovery processes may be common to all work with clients, independent of the theoretical model used.

For example, it is possible that all models use methods which have an equivalent effect such as providing a socialising process with successful socialisation as an integral (necessary if not sufficient) part of each approach. Socialisation is just one of many variables often ignored or trivialised in research into treatment and maintenance of treatment gains. Other variables that may be significant include a range of practical help, from social skills to developing social support systems in the community, one-to-one counselling, cognitive behavioural control techniques, stress management and relaxation, health care, social support and skills training.

The question raised earlier was whether all clients with alcohol problems should be treated in the same way. Perhaps a precursor to this should be the question of whether they are not already being treated in the same way, independent of the theoretical model used?

A case study of methods in different alcohol treatment models

The following study was carried out in substance misuse services (including alcohol) with radically different theories of dependency: the disease model and the cognitive behavioural model (Keene and Trinder 1995; Trinder and Keene 1997).

The study used the concept of 'cause maps' (Moos, Finney and Cronkite 1990) to identify the different methods used within each theoretical model, in order to develop protocols for matching. This involved clearly distinguishing each method and identifying the relevant rationales used by staff for using each method.

In practical terms the programmes studied used similar methods, offering treatment packages based on client-centred, task-orientated counselling or therapeutic models. These included assessment, goal setting, activities designed to facilitate behaviour change, and monitoring of client behaviour. The treatment process involved helping clients to realise that they had problems, motivating them to address these problems and then teaching them the skills they needed in order to make and maintain changes in behaviour and lifestyle. Clients were helped to understand the nature of their problems through highlighting the advantages and disadvantages of continuing with present lifestyles or changing to new ones. They were given concrete tasks to complete and targets to achieve, were taught new ways of coping with difficult situations, and encouraged to find new, alcohol-free leisure activities and friends.

Common methods

- Clients are encouraged to identify alcohol misuse as a serious problem and to recognise that it causes other problems
- Staff and clients examine the problems underlying perpetuating alcohol misuse
- Staff use a process model of change (either the Twelve Step process or the Motivational Change model of Miller and Prochaska and DiClemente)
- Staff encourage clients to weigh up the pros and cons of alcohol misuse
- Staff encourage clients to change alcohol misuse behaviour and other aspects of their lifestyle
- Staff use recognised counselling and therapeutic techniques
- Staff have a structured programme involving the setting of a series of concrete goals
- Staff use cognitive behavioural techniques to change attitudes and beliefs and modify behaviours

- Staff offer practical help and support concerning health, housing, welfare rights, child care problems etc.

- Staff teach skills and strategies for coping without alcohol

- Staff encourage clients to develop new leisure interests, occupations, social contacts and support networks

- Staff provide some kind of relapse prevention support.

The only differences in methods which reflect differences between the theories of the centres were the attitude to continued alcohol misuse. The abstinence-orientated programme insisted on abstinence as a pre-condition of treatment whereas the non-abstinence programmes did not. In effect, the differences in theories about the cause and effect relationships between substance misuse and clients' problems resulted in different programmes carrying out methods in different sequences. These sequences of methods either began with abstinence followed by problem solving, or began with problem solving and moved on to controlled use and perhaps abstinence.

Is there, therefore, an alternative interpretation of the lack of differences in treatment outcome between different theoretical models? The study had initially been designed to compare treatment agencies with differing models of intervention in order to determine appropriate protocols for matching. The finding that all agencies were using similar treatment methods despite their different theoretical models suggests that there is no necessary relationship between methods used and treatment theories. The similarity in methods may offer an alternative interpretation of earlier research findings which indicated few differences in effectiveness between agencies adopting different models but larger differences in effectiveness between specific methods. That is that methods used are not necessarily derived from the theoretical understanding of the aetiology of the problem or treatment model.

Discussion

As pointed out earlier, present research demonstrates little or no difference between different treatments and gives few guidelines for matching clients to different methods of intervention. As Lindstrom (1992) demonstrates, variations of outcomes tend to be large within treatments and small between treatments. Although there is some indication that certain methods may be more or less effective (Hodgson 1994), there are few data to indicate that one model is better than another. In contrast, there is some evidence to show that particular methods (common to different models) may be effective. Of the wide range of interventions, those socially based seem most successful. Hodgson (1994) gives an overview of different approaches used in the treatment of alcohol problems.

> There is good evidence to suggest the approaches directed at improving social and marital relationships, self control and stress management are effective. There is at present little evidence to suggest that aversion therapies, confrontational interventions, educational lectures or films and group psychodynamic therapies are effective, nor is there any evidence that use of psychotropic medications is effective. (p.1529)

One of the major recent reviews is that of Holder *et al.* (1991). Hodgson draws the following conclusions about it:

> Approaches which are directed towards improving social and marital relationships are very effective. If we combine the work on social skills training, behavioural marital therapy and community reinforcement there are 21 studies, all of which are positive. Furthermore, investigations of those factors which predict relapse and recovery suggest that family stability, cohesion and social support are among the most important (Billings and Moos 1983; Orford and Edwards 1977). There is good evidence that interventions directed towards self control and stress management training are effective (18 out of 27 studies were effective). (pp.1530–1531)

Lindstrom 1992 also reports favourably on the outcome of social skills training over time, remarking that positive effects were demonstrated at one year follow-up by Erickson, Bjornstad and Gotestam (1986). Work in this area is extremely sparse but Longabaugh and Beattie (1985) have carried out a preliminary study which indicates that the greater a person's social investment, the more influential the social environment will be.

Similarities are evident in the methods of different theoretical models. For example, basic cognitive behavioural techniques are used for brief interventions (Babor, Ritson, and Hodgson 1986; Chick, Lloyd and Crombie 1985), motivational interviewing (Prochaska and DiClemente 1986) and within the Twelve Step model (Lefevre 1988). These can include client monitoring, assessment and feedback, relapse prevention and intervention.

A sequential process model of change is utilised by most clinicians. Client-centred counselling methods and skills of unconditional positive regard, understanding and empathy are used within many models as the initial stage of a sequence, often followed by more structured and directive counselling including cognitive techniques such as awareness raising, information, decisional balances, re-evaluation of life events and drug-related problems. Client-centred and task-orientated counselling techniques, useful for motivating people to change, are also used within most models, including   giving feedback to the client, taking a non-confrontational stance and providing pragmatic alternatives. These methods of interviewing and counselling in the field were developed in the 1980s using notions of individual change processes, apparently in the absence of any coherent theory or testable hypotheses (see *British Journal of Addiction* letters and articles 1992–93), yet they were tremendously popular among practitioners and spread rapidly in the early part of the 1990s.

Similarities in methods used within different theoretical models

Edwards and Orford (1977) highlighted a most significant phenomenon in the alcohol field when he said: 'When two or more interventions are compared with each other the most common result is a tie.' The question is: is this because individual differences cancel each other out?; because non-treatment variables are more important than treatment variables?; or simply because different theoretical models in effect use the same methods (though they may use them in a different sequence and   have different aims)? Despite arguing strongly in favour of a 'matching hypothesis' based on the notion that the 'assumed homogeneity of the target population is illusory', Glaser (1980) concedes that this type of result may also be due to 'unrecognised but common effective factors in all interventions' (p.80).

This chapter has attempted to examine this less popular interpretation of the evidence. Instead of assuming that individual differences may be significant in treatment, it may be equally productive for future research to focus on methods common to a range of successful programmes during and after treatment, rather than explanatory theories of aetiology and treatment outcome—that is, on effective therapeutic components within the treatment process and factors which promote and maintain post-treatment recovery.

This chapter has highlighted the limitations of focusing on individual differences to the exclusion of other potentially influential factors. Factors such as the effective treatment methods or components are seldom considered either in treatment or follow-up studies, often being relegated to the status of 'mediating' variables. In order to introduce a new perspective on unresolved issues of problem definition and outcome measure in the alcohol field, it is clear that the major research needs concern treatment methods and recovery processes, rather than explanatory theories of aetiology. Research in these areas could pinpoint the clinically useful therapeutic methods that all treatment models have in common, rather than theoretical distinctions.

References

Babor, T.F., Dolinsky, Z., Rounsaville, B. and Jaffe, J. (1988) 'Unitary versus multidimensional models of alcoholism treatment outcome: an empirical study.' *Journal of Studies on Alcohol 49,* 167–177

Babor, T.F., Ritson, E. and Hodgson, R. (1986) 'Alcohol related problems in the primary health care setting.' British Journal of Addiction 81, 23–46.

Billings, A.G. and Moos, R.H. (1983) 'Psychosocial processes of recovery among alcoholics and their families: implications for clinicians and programme evaluators.' *Addictive Behaviours 8,* 205–218.

Caddy, G.R. and Block, T. (1985) 'Individual differences in response to treatment.' In M. Galizio and S.A. Maisto (eds) *Determinants of Substance Abuse: Biological, Psychological and Environmental Determinants.* New York: Plenum Press.

Chick, J., Lloyd, G. and Crombie, E. (1985) 'Counselling problem drinkers in medical wards: a controlled study.' *British Medical Journal 290,* 965–967.

Cook, C. (1988a) 'The Minnesota Model in the Management of Drug and Alcohol Dependency.' (Part 1) 'Philosophy and Programme.' (Part 2) 'Guidance and Conclusions.' *British Journal of Addiction 83,* 625–735.

Davidson R., Rollnick S. and MacEwan I. (eds) (1991) *Counselling Problem Drinkers.* London: Routledge.

Edwards, G. and Gross, M.M. (1976) 'Alcohol dependence: provisional description of a clinical syndrome.' *British Medical Journal 1,* 1058–1061.

Edwards, G. and Grant, M. (eds) (1977) *Alcoholism.* Oxford: Oxford University Press.

Edwards, G. and Orford, J. (1977) 'Alcoholism: a controlled trial of treatment and advice.' *Journal of Studies on Alcohol 38,* 1004–31.

Edwards, G. (1986) 'The Alcohol Dependence Syndrome.' *British Journal of Addiction 81,* 2, 171.

Edwards G. (1988) 'Long term outcome for patients with drinking problems: the search for predictors.' *British Journal of Addiction 83,* 917–927.

Erikson, L., Bjornstad, S. and Gotestam, K.G. (1986) 'Social skills training in groups for alcoholics: one year treatment outcome for groups and individuals.' *Addictive Behaviours 11,* 309–329.

Fingarette, H. (1988) *Heavy Drinking: The Myth of Alcoholism as a Disease.* Berkeley: University of California Press.

Frank, J. (1974) *Persuasion and Healing: A Comparative Study of Psychotherapy.* Baltimore: John Hopkins University Press.

Glaser, F. (1980) 'Anybody got a match?: treatment research and the matching hypothesis.' In G. Edwards and M. Grant (eds) *Alcoholism Treatment in Transition.* Baltimore: Baltimore University Press.

Goldfried, S.L. and Bergin, A.E. (eds) (1978) *Handbook of Psychotherapy and Behaviour Change.* New York: John Wiley.

Gorman, D.M. (1989) 'Is the new problem drinking concept of Heather and Robertson more useful in advancing our scientific knowledge than the old disease concept?' *British Journal of Addiction 84,* 843–845.

Heather, N. and Robinson, I. (1981) *Controlled Drinking.* London: Methuen.

Heather, N. and Robinson, I. (1986) *Problem Drinking. The New Approach.* Harmondsworth: Penguin Books.

Hodgson, R. (1994) 'Treatment of alcohol problems; Section 5, Treatment.' *Addiction 89,* 1529–1534.

Holder, H., Longabaugh, R., Miller, W.R. and Rubonis, A.V. (1991) 'The cost effectiveness of treatment for alcohol problems: a first approximation.' *Journal of Alcohol Studies 52,* 517–540.

Jellinek, E.M. and Bowman, G. (1946) 'Alcohol addiction and its Treatment.' *Quarterly Journal of Studies on Alcohol 2,* 98–176.

Keene J. and Trinder, H. (1995) *A Study to Evaluate and Compare Different Treatment Approaches for Alcohol Problems in West Glamorgan.* Cardiff: Welsh Office.

Laundergan, M.A. (1982) *Easy Does It! Alcoholism Treatment Outcomes, Hazelden and the Minnesota Model.* Centre City, Minnesota: Hazelden.

Lefevre, R. (1988) *The Promis Handbook on Alcoholism, Addictions and Recovery.* London: Promis Publishing Ltd.

Lindstrom, L. (1992) *Managing Alcoholism: Matching Treatments to Clients.* Oxford: Oxford University Press.

Longabaugh, R. and Beattie, M. (1985) 'Optimising the cost effectiveness of treatment for alcohol abusers.' In B.S. McCrady, N.E. Noel and T.D. Nirenberg (eds) *Future*

Directions in Alcohol Abuse Treatment Research. pp.104–136, Research Monograph no. 15, Rockville Md.: National Institute on Alcohol Abuse and Alcoholics.

McCrady, B.S. and Sher, K.J. (1983) 'Alcoholism treatment approaches: patient variables, treatment variables.' In B. Tabakoff, P.B. Sutker and C.L. Randell (eds) *Medical and Social Aspects of Alcohol Abuse.* New York: Plenum Press.

Marlatt, G.A. (1988) 'Matching clients to treatment: treatment models and stages of change.' In D.M. Donovan and G.A. Marlatt (eds) *Assessment of Addictive Behaviours.* New York: Guilford Press.

Marlatt, G.A. and Gordon, J. (1985) *Relapse Prevention in Alcoholic Relapse Prevention and Intervention: Models and Methods.* New York: Guilford Press.

Mash, E. and Terdal, L.G. (eds) (1976) *Behaviour Therapy Assessment: Diagnosis, Design and Evaluation.* New York: Springer.

Miller, W.R. and Hester, R.K. (1986) 'Matching problem drinkers with optimal treatments.' In R.W. Miller and N. Heather (eds) *Treating Addictive Behaviours: Processes of Change.* New York: Plenum Press.

Miller, W.R., Sovereign, R.G. and Krege, B. (1987) 'Motivational interviewing with problem drinkers: II. The drinkers check-up as a preventive intervention.' *Behavioural Psychotherapy 16,* 251–268.

Moos, R.H., Finney, J.W. and Cronkite, R.C. (1990) *Alcoholism Treatment: Context, Process and Outcome.* Oxford: Oxford University Press.

Orford, J. and Edwards, G. (1979) *Alcoholism: A Comparison of Treatment and Advice.* Maudsley Monograph, no.26. London: London University Press.

Orford, J., Oppenheimer, E. and Edwards, G. (1979) 'Abstinence or control: the outcome for excessive drinkers two years after consultation.' *Behaviour, Research and Therapy 14,* 409–418.

Pattison, E.M. *et al.* (1977) *Merging Concepts of Alcohol Dependence.* New York: Springer Publishing Company.

Prochaska, J.O. and DiClemente, C.C. (1982) 'Transtheoretical Therapy, towards a more integrative model of change.' *Psychotherapy Theory, Research and Practice 19,* 3, 276–288.

Prochaska J.O. and Diclemente C.C. (1983) 'Stages and processes of self change of smoking: Towards a more integrative model of change.' *Journal of Consulting and Clinical Psychology 51,* 390–395.

Prochaska J.O and DiClemente C.C. (1986) 'Towards a comprehensive model of change.' In W.R. Miller and N. Heather (eds) *Treating Addictive Behaviours: Processes of Change.* New York: Plenum Press.

Prochaska J.O. and DiClemente C.C. (1994) *The Transtheoretical Approach: Crossing Traditional Boundaries of Therapy.* Holmwood, Illinois: Daw-Jones, Irwin.

Project MATCH Research Group (1993) 'Project MATCH: rationale and methods for a multisite clinical trial matching patients to alcoholism treatment.' *Alcoholism: Clinical and Experimental Research 17*, 6, Nov/Dec.

Raistrick D. and Davidson R. (1985) *Alcoholism and Drug Addiction.* Edinburgh: Churchill Livingstone.

Rossi, J., Stach, A. and Bradley N. (1963) 'Effects of treatment of male alcoholics in a mental hospital.' *Quarterly Journal on Alcohol 24*, 91–98.

Schon, D.A. (1990) *Educating the Reflective Practitioner: Towards a New Design for Teaching and Learning.* New York: Jossey Bass.

Schwartz, G.E. (1982) 'Testing the biopsychosocial model: the ultimate challenge facing behavioural medicine.' *Journal of Clinical Psychology 50*, 1040–1053.

Spicer. J. and Barnett, P. (1980) *Hospital Based Chemical Dependency Treatment. A Model for Outcome Evaluation.* City Centre, Minnesota: Hazelden.

Trinder, H. and Keene, J. 'Comparing substance misuse agencies: different substances, clients and models, but are they the same methods?' *International Journal of Substance Misuse 2*, 1,24–30.

Wilson, P. (1992) 'Relapse prevention: conceptual and methodological issues.' In P. Wilson (ed) *Principles and Practice of Relapse Prevention.* New York: Guilford Press.

Further reading

Edwards, G., Brown, D., Duckitt, A., Oppenheimer, E., Sheehan, M. and Taylor, C. (1987) 'Outcome of alcoholism: the structure of patient attributions as to what causes change.' *British Journal of Addiction 82*, 533–545.

Edwards, G. (1989) 'As the years go rolling by: drinking problems in the time dimension.' *British Journal of Psychiatry 154*, January, 18–26.

Miller, W.R. (1983) 'Motivational interviewing with problem drinkers.' *Behavioural Psychotherapy 2*, 147–182.

Miller, W.R. and Kurtz, E. (1994) 'Models of alcoholism used in treatment: contrasting AA and other perspectives with which it is often confused.' *Journal of Studies on Alcohol 55*, 159–166.

Raistrick, D., Bradshaw, J., Tober, G., Weiner, J., Allison, J. and Healey, C. (1994) 'A questionnaire to measure alcohol and opiate dependence in the context of a treatment evaluation package.' *Addiction 89*, 563–572.

Robinson, I. and Heather, N. (1986) *Let's Drink to Your Health: A Self Help Guide to Sensible Drinking.* London: British Psychological Society.

The Contributors

Virginia Berridge is Reader in History at the London School of Hygiene and Tropical Medicine, the major British and international school of public health. At the School she heads a history group which looks at the historical dimensions of science and policy making. She is the author of *Opium and the People: Opiate Use in Nineteenth Century England* (1987, London) and of more general surveys of nineteenth and twentieth century health policy. Her most recent book is *AIDS in the UK: The Making of Policy 1981–1994.* (1996, Oxford: OUP).

Michael Bloor is Professor of Sociology and Director of Research in the School of Social and Administrative Studies, University of Wales, Cardiff. Previously, he worked for more than 20 years for the Medical Research Council's Medical Sociology Unit in the University of Glasgow. He has current or recent research involvement in the prevalence of drug use and of problem drinking in Wales, adolescent smoking behaviour, steroid use among body builders and HIV-related risk behaviour among international travellers. His recent publications include *The Sociology of HIV Transmission* (1995, London: Sage) and *Qualitative Studies in Health Care* (edited with Patricia Taraborelli, 1996, Aldershot: Avebury).

Lawrie Elliott is currently the Director of Health Services Research in the School of Nursing and Midwifery, University of Dundee. He has also held research posts within Glasgow University and the Greater Glasgow Health Board. Lawrie Elliott has published extensively on needle exchange provision within the academic press and has presented papers at a number of international conferences. He also holds a Masters degree in Sociology and is a professionally qualified Registered Nurse.

Jane Frankland is a Research Associate at the University of Wales, Cardiff where she is currently undertaking a school-based evaluation of an intensive peer-led smoking intervention project. Jane has previously worked as a researcher at Health Promotion Wales where she was involved in a range of research including an evaluation of an HIV/AIDS prevention project with female prostitutes in Cardiff and a survey of health sexuality among adolescents in Wales.

Mark Griffiths is a Chartered Psychologist and Senior Lecturer in Psychology at the Nottingham Trent University. After completing his PhD on fruit machine addiction at the University of Exeter (1987–1990) he secured his first lectureshsip at the University of Plymouth (1990–1995). Since then he has established an international reputation for himself in the area of gambling and gaming addictions which culminated in the award of the prestigious Rosecrance Research Prize for 'outstanding scholarly contributions to the field of gambling research' in June 1994.

Gordon Hay is a Research Fellow in the Centre for Drug Misuse Research at the University of Glasgow. He is undertaking research on estimating the prevalence of drug misuse in Scotland and throughout Europe. He has previously studied in the Department of Statistics and Modelling Science at the University of Strathclyde where his research examined the spread of HIV among drug injectors.

Jan Keene is a Chartered Psychologist and Senior Lecturer at the University of East Anglia. She is also a director of the Centre for Substance Abuse Research at the University of Wales Swansea. Her research interests include drug and alcohol misuse, with a specific focus on service provision. This has been supported by the Department of Health, Welsh Office, Home Office and Charitable Foundations. She has written three books and published in national and international journals.

Andrew J. McBride established the Mid Glamorgan Community Drug and Alcohol Team in 1988. A member of the Royal College of Psychiatrists, the Society for the Study of Addiction and the Addictions Forum, he is now Clinical Director of the Community Addiction Unit in Cardiff. His current interests include amphetamine addiction, needle fixation and alcohol detoxification.

Trudi Petersen is a trained psychiatric nurse. She has worked in acute psychiatric settings and in the field of substance misuse. As a CPN with Mid Glamorgan Community Drug and Alcohol Team she was closely involved with running the Well Steriod User Clinic. Her current interests include sports medicine, women's issues and dual diagnosis.

Tim Rhodes is Senior Reserch Fellow at The Centre for Research on Drugs and Health Behaviour, University of London. His current interests include: qualitative sociology; ethnographic research on drug use and sexual behaviour; and rapid situation assessment. He is currently involved in projects with the UK Department of Health, World Health Organisation, UNAIDS, and Council of Europe. Recent publications include: *AIDS, Drugs and Prevention* (1966, London: Routledge), *Outreach Work with Drug Users: Principles and Practice* (1966, Strasbourg: Council of Europe Press); and *Risk, Intervention and Change* (1994, London: Health Education Authority).

Inge Spruit is an anthropologist and social epidemiologist. She is head of the Department of Substance Use and Addiction of the Tribos-Institute, the Netherlands Institute of Mental Health and Addiction. A core programme of the Institute is monitoring the use and abuse of alcohol and illicit drugs. Special attention is given to young people and pupils in school surveys. Another core activity is the production of the Dutch Alcohol and Drugs Report which focuses on societal developments. Applied research and monitoring, policy evaluation, identification of information gaps and dissemination of information are all important aspects of this programme.

Gerry V. Stimson is Director and Professor of the Sociology of Health Behaviour at the Centre for Research on Drugs and Health Behaviour, University of London. His current interests include: drug problems and drug policy; the sociology of public health; and the development of public health interventions for drug users. He is currently involved in WHO cross-national studies of injecting drug use. Recent publications include: *AIDS and Drug Misuse* (1990, London: Routledge) and *Drug Injecting and HIV Infection* (forthcoming, London: Taylor and Francis).

Kathryn Williamson trained as a general practitioner before changing to psychiatry. Co-founder of one of the first British Clinics for Steroid Users when working in Mid Glamorgan, she now works as a consultant in elderly psychiatry at St Cadoc's Hospital, Newport. Her current interest is in developing specialist services for sufferers of pre-senile dementia.

Fiona Wood currently works as a Tutorial Fellow in the School of Social and Administrative Studies at the University of Wales, Cardiff where she undertakes teaching responsibilities and commissioned research projects for the health service. She has been employed on a study to estimate the prevalence of injecting drug use and serious drug use in Wales. Previously she worked as a researcher in the Department of Public Health Medicine, Gwent Health Authority.